'Confessions Of A Seeker' is Richard Sylvester's fifth book. His account of more than thirty years of seeking for "inner truth" through spiritual, psychotherapeutic and philosophical means is sometimes wryly humorous, sometimes deeply serious. During these years, he became involved among other things with hallucinogenic drugs, Transcendental Meditation, gurus, past life regression therapy, personal growth groups, shamanism, channelling and alternative medicine. He came across numerous beliefs including conspiracy theories about shape-shifting lizards and Atlantean crystals. He also covers more philosophical topics including free will, the nature of consciousness, and the essential difference between science and religion. He tackles religious belief head on, with chapters on Catholicism, Buddhism and the Baptist Church.

Richard Sylvester's four previous books include 'The Book Of No One' and 'Non-Duality Questions, Non-Duality Answers'. He holds meetings about non-duality in London and other cities. For further information and contact details visit www.richardsylvester.com.

Confessions of a Seeker

Adventures in Spirituality, Therapy and Belief

Richard Sylvester

ISBN: 978-1987479843
Published by Richard Sylvester
with the kind assistance of Julian Noyce

www.richardsylvester.com
richardsylvester@hotmail.co.uk

To Hitch

Like a gnat attaching itself to a giant, I dedicate this book to Christopher Hitchens.

"About the gods I have no means of knowing ..... Many things prevent my knowing. Among others, the fact that they are never seen."

Protagoras. Fifth Century BCE

"Men dream of what never was nor will be."

Geoffrey Chaucer. Fourteenth Century CE

"It's good to have an open mind but not so open that your brains fall out."

Variously attributed to Bertrand Russell, J. Robert Oppenheimer, Carl Sagan, Richard Dawkins and several others. Twentieth Century CE

CHAPTERS

1. Coffee Bars, Christians And Sceptics 1
2. A Commune 8
3. A Trip 15
4. A Lama In London... 21
5. Transcendental Meditation 26
6. The Guru – Falling In Love 32
7. The Guru – The Lama's Curse................................. 39
8. "Past Life Memories" 43
9. The Guru – Dharmic Partners................................. 51
10. More Of The Guru 55
11. The Guru – The Shit Hits The Fan 59
12. Among The Buddhists 66
13. A Psychic Reading... 84
14. The Lady Of Ladakh... 91
15. Cleaning Toilets For God 96
16. A Psychic Heart Attack..................................... 101
17. Group "Past Lives".. 107
18. Quantum Leap 113
19. Among The Baptists... 123
20. Smokey The Psychoanalytic Goat............................ 128
21. Shadow Night 133
22. The Shaman Of Sheen....................................... 139
23. Synchronicity... 146
24. A Pilgrimage 151
25. Channelling 162
26. Angry Nuns And Lamas 174
27. Gestalt 181
28. How Does Matter Think 186
29. Grimstone.. 192
30. Green And Away 200
31. An Existential Weekend 219
32. Men Who Hate Science 225

33. Stripper On A Train 230
34. In Wales..240
35. Free Will 253
36. Satsang With The Holy One...................................... 258
37. Among The Benedictines 261

38. A Spiritual Potpourri
    Tell Me Who You Are.. 266
    Spiritual Encounter.. 268
    Kriyas.. 269
    A Health Scare...270
    Lizards 271
    Finding Deep Truth 271
    A Problem With Slugs..272
    Jesus in Glastonbury 273
    Traditional Chinese Medicine 273
    Richard's Razor 274
    Another Triumph For Alternative Medicine 275

39. Some Blasts Against Religion
    The Theatre Of Manipulation...................................277
    The King Of The Jews 279
    Scrutinising Sir Roger Scruton 280
    Why Does God Send Hurricanes 281
    The Resurrection Of The Flesh............................... 282
    Trendy Vicar 282

1. Coffee Bars, Christians And Sceptics

This is the book that I was never going to write. Yet writing it has unexpectedly been quite a lot of fun.

When I submitted the first draft of my first book, 'I Hope You Die Soon', to my publisher, he told me that although he liked it he could not publish it because it was too brief. So I was faced with the dilemma of how to make it longer simply to make it publishable. My initial thought was that I might include in it an account of my decades of searching for "inner truth" and "wholeness" through a mixture of Eastern and Western spiritual and therapeutic methods and paths. The book would thus become a kind of autobiography of a seeker. The problem with this plan was that it went entirely against the original spirit of the book, so I abandoned it. Fortunately other material came to me and the book, although still short, was eventually published.

I have a friend who is a second hand book dealer. His stance is that if it is not over one hundred pages, it is not a real book. When I proudly placed a copy of my first book into his hand, he immediately flipped to the last page. It was Page 117 and he simply remarked "Yes, that's a book." High praise indeed. And from an expert. He charitably did not remark on the fact that some of those pages only had about fifteen words printed on them.

I decided that a book about my seeking years was the book that I never wanted to write and I gave it no further thought for about ten years. But life happens, I met new people and one or two of these persuaded me that this material might be of interest to some other people. As I like sitting in comfortable leather armchairs in coffee bars reading and writing and staring out of the windows, I thought "Why not?"

In fact I owe a debt of gratitude to Caffè Nero for the vast amount of hospitality that they have extended to me, just as they owe me a debt of gratitude for the vast amount of money that I have given to them. Caffè Nero and I have a truly symbiotic relationship. I do not hector them about their tax arrangements and they do not hector me about the length of time that I linger over my lattes while writing my books. I try not to develop a sense of entitlement to their armchairs, as otherwise my day could be ruined when all the comfortable ones have alien arses sitting in them.

When this happens, instead of fulminating against the cruel depredations of an uncaring universe, I retreat to the Christian coffee bar which is just across the street. They too have leather armchairs, they make a mean cappuccino and they do not try overtly to evangelise me. I also get a slightly wicked frisson from sitting beneath the well-intentioned quotations from the Gospels adorning their walls while I am writing some particularly virulent anti-religious passage. Childish, I know, but there you are....

The Christian coffee bar does actually put one foot wrong, because of course its staff cannot help hoping that they might be able to save their customers' souls for Christ. The nice young barista gets to know my order and starts to make it as soon as I appear in the doorway. Then one morning he says to me as I come in "As you're a regular, I should know your name."

Oh dear. A tad too familiar. A line has been crossed and once crossed it cannot be uncrossed. In Caffè Nero they know my order *but they never ask me my name.* The next step after that is actual conversation and then I would have to stop going there.

But the nice young barista in the Christian coffee bar already has a friend in Jesus and now he hopes to make a friend of me too. Then, he thinks, he will be able to introduce his two friends to each other so that we can all hang out together.

Does he not recognise that I am an introvert? A well-adjusted one to be sure, but still an introvert.

Reluctantly and because I do not want to appear rude I say "Richard." He smiles at me as though some intimacy has been established between us.

But it has not.

The next time I go in there, he says "I can remember your order but I can't remember your name." He waits expectantly for me to accept this invitation. But I do not. Instead I say "Well, remembering my order is what's important. Remembering my name doesn't matter."

In retrospect I can understand that this probably sounded a lot ruder than I intended it to. But the unwanted intimacy ends and I tend to be served by other members of the staff in there now.

I should add that if anything ever turns me to Christianity, which I truly believe nothing short of torture will, it might be the promise of drinking cappuccino and chewing the fat with Jesus in The Heavenly Coffee Bar In The Sky.

And where torture is concerned, I am of the same frame of mind as Galileo. Merely show me the instruments and I will say whatever you wish me to say.

****

As this is a confession, it relies on memory. Oh dear. That word should always be put in inverted commas. "Memory." That which we think we remember. Now that many of us are more psychologically sophisticated than in previous eras, we are aware that our memories are not the re-playing of a recording which was made at the time that an event occurred, some-how faithfully laid down on the vinyl, tape, disc or hard drive within our skulls. To be accurately recalled whenever we want. Incorruptible until death or dementia strikes us down. Oh no. Rather, each time memories are recalled they are reconstructed and in that way they are somewhat, we might say, like a work of art. A creation. Almost a work of fiction. "Remembering" is in some ways always a creative act.

Nevertheless, the "memories" presented in this book are as faithful as I can make them. Nothing has been consciously invented. Certain names and some other identifying details have been changed for reasons of confidentiality but nothing else has been monkeyed around with. However I would not want anyone to be convicted in a court of law on the basis of anything that I have "remembered" in this book. So if you put me under oath in front of a judge, I will deny everything.

And we should bear in mind that, in spite of the doubts which may surround an event and no matter how unreliable memory may sometimes be, something did actually happen. The following brief anecdote demonstrates that, regardless of what postmodernist relativism may hold, not all versions of reality are equal:-

> *It is said that during the signing of The Treaty Of Versailles in 1919 at the end of The First World War, a German officer remarked to the French Prime Minister, Georges Clemenceau, "I wonder what future historians will say about all this."*
>
> *Clemenceau's terse reply was "Well, they won't say that Belgium invaded Germany."*

****

The reader may feel entitled to ask "What is the point of view in this book?" What is the stance taken, for example, towards such topics as past life memories? Is it being asserted that past life memories are real? Or that they are not real? One clue I can give is that any phrase containing the words "past life" should always be considered to have inverted commas around it. But in fact there is no single point of view presented here, or we could say that there are shifting points of view. After all, the material in this book covers a time period from my early twenties to my late sixties. I would be a very rum fish indeed if my viewpoint had not changed considerably in that time. The one clear thing that I can state now is that on matters of belief and faith and extraordinary claims about reality I am a sceptic.

Scepticism seems to me at this point in my life to be the only intelligent stance to take towards claims about reality and our only real bulwark against superstition. After all, scepticism really only means that we suspend judgement about the truth-reality of some assertion or other until there is enough real evidence for us reasonably to give it our assent. I use the phrase "real evidence" to exclude the so-called evidence brought forward by conspiracy theorists to support their dubious claims.

The opposite of scepticism could be said to be faith.* It seems to me very strange indeed that I was brought up in a culture that considered faith to be a good thing but scepticism to be disreputable, as though the latter were no different to cynicism. Innocent little girls are even named after the supposed virtue of faith by parents who really should know better. But as Mark Twain so simply expressed it "Faith is believing what you know ain't so." Faith is in fact itself so intellectually disreputable that it is difficult to account for its popularity, until we remember that an exhortation to have faith has always been one of the main weapons wielded by popes, priests and princes in order to control the minds of the people. A reasonable translation out of gobbledegook into standard English of the brief sentence "Have faith" might be "Don't think for yourself" or "Don't ask difficult questions."

****

---

*The reader might feel that a more obvious opposite of "scepticism" is "gullibility" rather than "faith". This may be true, but gullibility is not very interesting, whereas faith is endlessly fascinating.

Because this is a confession, and not an autobiography or a memoir, there is an attempt in it to follow only a very rough chronology. You may be more interested in some themes than in others. So if, for example, you particularly want to follow the adventures in religion, "that vast moth-eaten musical brocade" as Philip Larkin called it, you might like to read first the chapters Among The Buddhists, Among The Baptists and Among the Benedictines – the alliteration by the way is accidental – as well as Angry Nuns And Lamas, Men Who Hate Science, Stripper On A Train and the short pieces in the final chapter including The Theatre Of Manipulation, The King Of The Jews and Trendy Vicar. I hope you do not feel that I have been too harsh in dealing with The Holy Roman Catholic Church. After all, as the Oxford don Richard Robinson put it in his book 'An Atheist's Values', The Catholic Church is only "the second most intolerant and active body in the world today." At the time of writing those words more than half a century ago, Robinson was probably awarding the accolade of first place in intolerance to the Soviet regime. Nowadays, since the collapse of the USSR, first place is more likely to go to certain active bodies in the Middle East. But The Catholic Church is surely still up there as a contender for the second prize.

If you are drawn to more philosophical adventures, you might like to start with How Does Matter Think and Free Will. If you are more interested in New Age shenanigans, you could go straight to A Commune, A Trip, the various chapters on The Guru, "Past Life Memories", Group "Past Lives", The Shaman Of Sheen, Channelling and In Wales. Adventures on therapeutic pathways are covered mainly in Quantum Leap, Smokey The Psychoanalytic Goat, Shadow Night and Gestalt as well as in the past lives chapters. And if you want revelations of a personal nature such as might appear on the front page of one of our more scurrilous Sunday newspapers, it is probably best to begin with Synchronicity and Grimstone.

Hopefully you will also find some other delights within these pages. There is material on complementary medicine, Scientologists, macrobiotics, drug trips, existentialists, Glastonbury, Ken Wilber, Andrew Cohen and A H Almaas, Masada, the dangers that lurk in tap water, evolutionary enlightenment, nuns and lamas, detox diets, the joys of smoking, Daniel Dennett, Home Education, Tintagel, Osho, Findhorn, Traditional Chinese Medicine, enlightenment intensives, Sir Roger Scruton, spiritual encounter ..... and much more.

A friend of mine once commented on one of my previous books that it was likely to be of interest "to seekers who are ready to stop." That could equally be a recommendation for this book. In fact I hope that it is suitable both for seekers who are ready to stop and also for ex-seekers who, like me, have already stopped.

Whoever you are, wherever you start and however you read this confession, enjoy.

2. A Commune

My wife and I are driving through the country lanes of Kent, having set off from our home in South London about an hour and a quarter earlier. Eventually we arrive at a large rambling country house in spacious grounds near the village of Biddenden. The house is not exactly derelict but it would be a challenge to the most enthusiastic of do-it-yourself hobbyists.

The house is a commune and the reason for our visit is that my friend Roger and his "wife" Anne live here. I have put the word "wife" in inverted commas because I am never able to work out whether Roger really is married to Anne. Knowing their two personalities, it seems fundamentally unlikely. It could be that in claiming that they are married, Roger is simply giving himself cover to avoid the predations of other women who may want him to legitimise his relationship with them. Roger has already been through one divorce and the loss of his family home so he may feel entitled to be cautious.

His marital status is not the only area of Roger's life where there is ambiguity. Later on he claims, for example, not to know his own age too precisely. He refers mysteriously to "lost papers" as though he were a character in Harold Pinter's play 'The Caretaker'. But Roger drives a car and the fact is that if he wanted to he could simply look at his own driving licence to clear up any uncertainty about his date of birth. His best friend's guess is that he is a couple of years older than me, but he claims to be about ten years younger.

In his twenties Roger had worked in local government but his hippy soul found this too restrictive. He wanted to do something more meaningful, so he trained to be a social worker. However here he discovered that he was expected to suggest some kind of changes to his clients' behaviour. He found this expectation that he would exert social control over other human beings intolerable so he dropped out of his course just before his final exams. Then, searching for freedom, he took a job as a milkman.

The restrictions that this imposed on his life also proved too irksome for him to bear. The story that I have, which I cannot stand up as they say in journalism, is that one morning half way up a driveway with a crate of milk in his hand, he had his final work related crisis. He put down the crate, turned around and walked home, abandoning his milk float where it stood in the road.

As far as I know, Roger never worked again. So it may not surprise you to read that shortly after his milk float crisis, his first wife threw him out and then divorced him.

The house near Biddenden is occupied quite legitimately with the agreement of its owner. There are about twelve members of the commune. Roger and Anne do not live in the house, but in an ancient green caravan at the bottom of the huge kitchen garden. Most of the commune members draw the dole or other benefits. They live on a simple low protein diet and spend a few hours a week each working in the garden growing cabbages, leeks and such like to supplement the huge drums of dried lentils and brown rice stored in the kitchen. Like many seekers of the time, they are macrobiotic.

By this time I myself have been macrobiotic for a while. Later I sometimes describe those macrobiotic years as having been amongst the worst of my life. An enthusiasm for macrobiotics has seized a good number of us spiritual seekers, not just as a way to health and longevity but as a kind of path to enlightenment. The purity which this diet is intended to bring to our physical bodies will be reflected no doubt in our etheric bodies, our chakras and the balance of our yin and our yang. Even in the rather poor area of London where we live, with a population made up of the working class and of low paid professionals employed mostly in the state sector, an amateurish organic food shop has been opened by a friendly hippy couple. Here we can go to ladle vicious smelling honey out of a great vat and buy "brick-bread", loaves so dense that we would not want to drop them on our toes. At home we all sprout aduke beans and alfalfa and make live yoghurt from a culture which every week grows exponentially and threatens to engulf us. This yoghurt is so inedibly tart that most of it has to be thrown down the drain. Our kitchens are filled with the stench of miso soup and wakame.

This macrobiotic religion has come to us from Japan. Each meal seems to conjure up the same inscrutable Zen koan:- "Why are we eating this execrable stuff?" No one is able to provide a clear answer. Like all religions it contains senseless superstitions and it has its own version of the deadly sins. We are not supposed to eat any food unless it has been indigenous to the area where we live for at least five hundred years. Eating dairy products is tantamount to coveting thy neighbour's ox but the deadliest sin of all is consuming refined sugar. One evening I am introduced to a macrobiotic couple, Jenny and Ralph. They are unbearably smug. Ralph, I am told, has purified his senses through macrobiotics to such an extent that if he so much as touches his tongue to a teaspoon of sugar, it will come out in a blister. This is held up to me as confirming his status as a high priest of this dietary path to liberation.

Actually, on the great evils of refined sugar, I still think that macrobiotics got it right. I watched a documentary many years ago about children's teeth, or rather the gaps in their mouths where their teeth used to be. The documentary was filled with furious dentists and smarmy spokespeople for the sugar industry. Mothers were giving their children bottles filled with sugar water to suck on. Naturally their teeth became rotting stumps in short order, so they would probably have been better off chewing the odd strand of wakame. Recent statistics show that the situation has only become markedly worse since then. At about the same time as this documentary, a book came out called 'Pure, White And Deadly'. On the front cover was a picture of a pile of white powder on a saucer. At first sight we were supposed to think that the powder was heroin, but of course when we picked the book up and read the blurb on its cover we realised that the noxious and fatal substance was sugar.

After a while I become vegetarian as well as macrobiotic to achieve even more purity. I am eventually released from this cursed diet by a man who is both a Buddhist and a naturopath and who is therefore twice purified himself.

I have been suffering from various ills, in actuality probably all angst related. But I have been persuaded that they are due to my diet and to various "food intolerances". It has become fashionable recently to be intolerant to all kinds of food. Wheat is a particular taboo. One Sunday I am preparing lunch for some friends, a family of four. After I have taken instructions down the phone about what each of them can and cannot eat, I realise that the only items that I can serve to all four of them may be lettuce leaves and jacket potatoes.

So on a sunny Monday morning I find myself in Battersea in the consulting room of Patrick, the Buddhist naturopath. He declares that I am probably intolerant to wheat. In retrospect I think it is likely that Patrick diagnoses all human ills as being the result of eating wheat. If I were to be knocked down by a bus, as I lay in the gutter Patrick would probably tell me reassuringly that my blood loss was due to wheat intolerance.

Nevertheless I owe Patrick a huge debt of gratitude because he releases me from my macrobiotic and vegetarian curse.

He does this by immediately instructing me to eat only a diet of meat and potatoes for two weeks. He says that I am very unlikely to be intolerant to either of these. Later on we can introduce other foodstuffs and then we will see what they do to my system. But it is my feelings on leaving his office that are revelatory. I almost dance down Battersea Bridge Road with joy. I feel like leaping in the air and shouting with happiness. I have been told to start eating meat again by a naturopath. And a Buddhist. Meat eating has been sanctified.

I stop on the way home at a butcher's shop. I never eat mung beans again.

A little while later, at Swami Muktananda's ashram in Clapham, I meet a woman who is carrying a large shopping bag. It is filled with grapes. She is being treated for some unspecified ills by an alternative healer who has told her to eat nothing but grapes for a month. Pounds of grapes every day. Unsurprisingly she looks utterly miserable.

In Wales I have friends who each summer go on a "detox diet" of such savagery that it is tantamount to self-abuse. It involves the purchase of expensive substances from America and lasts six weeks. It is intimately connected with their spiritual beliefs. Another friend comments to me "I've already got a detox system. It's called my liver."

****

At the commune near Biddenden, Roger and Anne in their caravan have formed a self-contained and semi-detached outpost. They are in rude health, supplementing their diet with copious amounts of weed and alcohol. But when we step into the house and meet the other commune members, it is a different matter. They are all of a piece. They are wan and pasty and drift dully through the corridors and in and out of their rooms like spectres. They seem to be caught between depression and despair. They are bloodless and enervated. None of them seem capable of making a decision as simple as choosing which pair of shoes to put on at the beginning of the day.

We drink herbal tea in the kitchen with four of these spectres and try not to get sucked into the misasma of hopelessness surrounding them.

Then the front door opens and into the kitchen, arms full of bags of dried beans and brown rice, and jars of organic peanut butter, comes Vasu. Vasu is his spiritual name and he enters like a whirlwind. A man in his fifties, Vasu is as ebullient as the others are lifeless. He greets us cheerfully, fixing us with his piercing eyes. He has a firm handshake and a bounce in his step. He bounds around the room issuing instructions to the enervated ghosts. He has them under his complete control. He is the master of the entire domain. The spectres, unable to decide even which side of their beds to get out of in the morning, have handed over control of their lives to him.

Vasu has all the zest that the spectres lack. Vasu is an energy vampire.

****

Much later there are the beginnings of a palace revolution against Vasu. Compliance turns to sulkiness turns to mutterings turns to open dissent. With Roger's help the commune members decide to bring in a paid mediator who will work with them over two or three days to explore and hopefully resolve their differences. He will spend some time with each member in turn, becoming familiar with their individual issues, before facilitating an open group which will not end until some resolution has been achieved. Vasu has agreed to this.

The mediator arrives. The individual interviews begin. Unaccountably, Vasu becomes ill and has to take to his bed. The interviews continue. It becomes clear that all the issues are with Vasu and only with Vasu. Vasu remains in his bed. With the interviews finished, there is nothing to be done except to start the open group meeting in spite of Vasu's absence. It is obvious quite quickly that without Vasu present, there is no point to this meeting.

Vasu fails to recover and eventually the mediator is paid and sent on his way. He has done his best. The next morning Vasu rallies, then rises from his bed fit and healthy. The rest of the commune sink back into their accustomed despondency.

****

A few years later I am introduced to another professional mediator in Wales. His name is Nicholas and he is one half of a New Age couple. Nicholas has decided to commit his life entirely to the peaceful resolution of conflict. To this end he never raises his voice above a compassionate murmur. He has suppressed all traces of shadow material in his psyche. Sitting listening to him, I suddenly understand why he might be very effective in his chosen vocation of bringing discordant members of groups into harmony with each other. Any set of people exposed to Nicholas for more than a few minutes, no matter how violent their previous differences, would surely become utterly united in their desire to throw him in a river.

Later still I am having a conversation with a friend about communes. I ask her whether she would like to live in one. "Sure" she says with a curl of her lip. "Why not? I'd just love to spend five hours every week in a meeting arguing about whose turn it is to do the washing up and asking if I can have permission to fart in the kitchen!"

3. A Trip

It is Thursday evening. About twelve of us have unloaded a van and a couple of cars and unpacked our luggage into two large frame tents in a field in the West Country. Each tent will easily accommodate about ten campers. Five of us, including me, are in a somewhat hippy poetry and music band. The rest are a variety of girlfriends and other pals.

Our band, formed when some of us were at university together, has had some minor success. John Peel has produced a record album of our work. We have an agent and for a brief time he gets us a residency as a support act at the Marquee Club in Soho. We travel up and down the country in uncomfortable Ford Transit vans to perform in front of both enthusiastic and unenthusiastic crowds for ridiculously small sums of money. One evening we perform for fine art students celebrating the end of the final year of their course. The other act booked for that night is Principal Edwards Magic Theatre, a "performance art collective". The students hate us both. They just want to dance. One of them is sick over our feet. Their Student Union entertainments manager, a man of advanced and alternative tastes, will have been lucky not to have been lynched the following day.

Our finest hour is at Watford Town Hall. We have been booked as a support act – I seem to remember that it is to The Edgar Broughton Band but I cannot be sure. During the first of our poems the house lights unexpectedly come on. A furious figure charges down the aisle and leaps onto the stage. He tries to snatch away the microphone. It turns out that this is Henry, the house electrician. He has taken offence at a four-letter word that we have used and he has decided unilaterally to put an end to our act. There is a reporter in the audience and some days later the incident gets written up in The Daily Express under the headline "The Night Henry Blew A Fuse." But the newspaper does not report what Henry actually says because only those of us who are on the stage can hear him.

What Henry actually says is this. "I'm not putting up with this swearing! I've got a fucking sixteen year old daughter in the audience!"

Our spluttering rather than glittering career eventually comes to an end when our agent sells out to a bigger agency which wants to take on all his acts. All his acts, that is, except us.

One of our members is missing from the trip. He is the one who introduced us to John Peel, when he was John's advisor about which poets to book for his Night Ride programme on BBC Radio. Our missing poet has a high stress job in advertising and he has cracked under the strain. He has walked into Broadcasting House and taken all his clothes off. He has announced that he will go home to Liverpool. He will walk all the way "because that's what Jesus would do."

In the field it is the evening before a major music festival is to start. But we are not there as part of the audience. We have been booked, along with other minor groups, to contribute to the entertainment on the first day before the festival proper gets under way. We fit well into the category "minor groups". We are not to be paid but have received free entry to the festival and accommodation in tents as our reward. And special passes giving us early entry to the site. The hoi polloi, paying members of the public, are already turning up but are kept outside the site by high wire mesh fences.

We lay out our sleeping bags, get out our food, beer and weed and sit around outside the tents talking. Guitars are strummed. The night is a fine one.

At some point I notice a figure come by in the darkness. It is a thin man who stops by one of our group and talks earnestly to him. Then he puts something into his hand and flits away.

The "something" is twelve tabs of acid. Free acid. The thin man is attempting to turn on as many people at this festival as he can. Before it has even started. He may be engaged in some insane sociological experiment.

The tabs of acid are passed around. I look at the one in my hand. I have never taken acid before.

Should I take it? I think about it. But not for long.

I take it.

What could possibly go wrong?

As it turns out, quite a lot actually.

****

During the next twelve hours time, space and matter distort immeasurably. And unfortunately for this confession, indescribably. But if you have ever been there, you will know.

Sometime during the night I am lying alone in one of the huge tents. Stretched right across the roof, on the outside but clearly visible, is a gigantic spider. Its legs reach down the sides. Then they start tearing through the fabric. I can see them tearing through the fabric. I can hear them tearing through the fabric. I can clearly see the hairs on each striped leg.

A skull is sitting on the floor near the entrance to the tent. Its jaw starts chattering wildly as it jerkily jumps towards me. It is grinning.

An alligator snickers across the floor.

In the blue fabric of the tent I can see the subatomic particles moving. The fabric is made of pure energy. It is simply pure energy.

One of our group is sitting in the van. He is being sick down the door.

There is some wild dancing in the open air. At least one of us may be naked.

An ambulance is snaking its way through the camp site. I can hear its siren and see its blue flashing light. It is taking an eternity to reach us but I know that it is coming for me. I have been rendered psychotic by the acid and I am to be taken away to a psychiatric hospital. Where I will stay for the rest of my life. I will never recover from this.

It is raining. I hear a strange rhythmic knocking. Like shamans' drums. I look out of the tent. The field in front of me had been empty. Now, instantaneously, another group of tents has sprung up. I look out again a minute or two later. The tents have jumped closer to me. Another minute or two and they have suddenly advanced again. Tents are invading our territory. All the while, that rhythmic knocking. And a strange repeated noise almost like snakes hissing.

But the biggest threat to us is the witch with her coven outside the tent next to ours. She has long black hair and she is wearing a black broad-brimmed witch's hat. Scarlet lipstick. Scarlet nail varnish on her talons. Black cloak. There is a terrible darkness about her. She is the leader of a malevolent group who wish us evil. It is she who has plotted to wreak this havoc on my mind. I can see her glaring at us. I can hear her cackling laughter. She and her minions watch us and whisper behind their hands as they plot to do us more mischief.

****

After about twelve hours, things begin slowly to return to a vague normality. We gradually piece the events of the night together. At some point it had started to pour with rain. The early comers to the festival, wet and cold and stuck outside the barriers, lost patience. They broke through the wire and charged onto the field. Some of them seized the tents that were scattered around waiting to be put up the following day and started to erect them. Others put up their own tents. They hammered tent pegs into the ground with wooden mallets, unzipped and zipped up the fly sheets, unzipped and zipped up the tents, unzipped and zipped up their sleeping bags, trying to make themselves warm and comfortable.

The ambulance was for someone else who was having a bad trip.

And the witch and her coven? They turn out to be a kindly group of hippies who recognised that we were crazily out of control. They kept an eye on us to make sure that we were safe. At one point a security guard, alarmed by our maniac behaviour, wanted to call an ambulance to us. Or maybe the police. The witch talked him out of it, saying that she and her friends would look after us through the night. They would ensure that no harm befell us.

She comes over to us in the morning to make sure that we are ok. She is lovely.

Even years later the sounds of sleeping bag zips and of tent pegs being hammered into the ground produce flashbacks in me.

We never do perform at the festival. We are too mentally dishevelled. Instead, some of us take a trip in one of the cars to Weston-super-Mare. We walk along the front. We eat ice cream. It seems like a nice normal place. Not crazy. Not crazy at all.

****

I take acid a few more times. But it is never like that again. I have mild happy trips after that one. I am glad. One evening I am introduced to someone in a wheelchair. He had jumped out of an upper storey window during an acid trip. Before this meeting, I had thought that such stories were put about simply to frighten us. In spite of the wheelchair, he has founded a very successful health food company. Now he is about to launch onto the market one of the first guarana products to be sold in this country. We try it, then sit around buzzing with energy and thinking up names for the new pills. The one I like best is Gut Glow but he will not use it.

I sometimes describe that first acid trip as like a kick to the head from a mule. While I do not recommend this treatment, it certainly has an effect on me. I realise that the way things "normally" appear is only one possible version of reality. If we mess with the biochemistry of our brain just a tiny bit, a quite different reality is likely to make itself known. Time and space are entirely provisional.

This kick-starts my spiritual search.

Some time after this I start to meditate and I never touch drugs again. Almost never. There are two more occasions.

A few years pass by and I am living in a small town in New Mexico. The use of weed is epidemic here. I am told that the town's supplies are flown in by the Chief of Police using his own private aeroplane, although I cannot stand this story up.

At every social gathering I pass the joint without joining in. I am like a teetotaller in a bar or a eunuch in a brothel. I get fed up with this so one evening I smoke some, inhaling deeply. My clarity of mind disappears almost immediately and a fog descends. It lasts for several days. I never touch weed again, although to this day I occasionally have to put up with mockery about this from my hippy friends.

About a year later I am on an island off the coast of Thailand. I decide to lunch on the local delicacy, a magic mushroom omelette. After that I lie in the sea for about five hours looking at the sky, occasionally saying "Wow!" and "So that's what it's all about!"

I know God. I know the meaning of the universe.

Of course by the next morning I know none of that at all.

4. A Lama In London

I am in London attending an evening course on Buddhist meditation. I find neither the talks nor the meditation practice very inspiring. But the small group is being taught by a genuine Tibetan lama who wears robes and speaks English with an accent which is endearingly difficult to understand. Even though the meetings take place in an uninspiring drab hall, there is something nicely exotic about them and in this way they appeal to me. One of the things that I like is that after each meeting we all hoof it across the road to a pub, the lama included. I seem to remember him sitting there in a comfortable padded window seat in between two of his more attractive female students. In my mind he has an arm draped around one of them and a martini in his other hand. But memory is a fickle friend so although I seem to remember this I certainly would not swear to it in court.

I am not drawn to any of the paths of asceticism as I like food and sex too much. One day I am invited to a meeting with a genuine bearded white-robed Indian guru who is visiting London. I am offered the chance to receive initiation from him and to be endowed with my very own personal mantra. He seems impressive as he sits there gesturing with his graceful hands, speaking heavily accented English laced with spiritual hot words and occasionally breaking off to take up elegant yoga poses. But I baulk at the last minute when I discover that to receive the mantra, I would have to become a vegetarian. Some time before this I had successfully given up vegetarianism, and now I feel that I have no desire to return to it.

One evening, the lama's course is graced by two visiting monks from Dharamsala. If he is the real deal, they are doubly authentic – they cannot speak any English at all. We are invited, if we would like to, to line up to receive a blessing from them. Well, why not?

When it is my turn one of the monks presses his hand down hard on the top of my skull. I do not usually feel any kind of energy at times like this. I have been through several Siddha Yoga shaktipats, one or two from Swami Muktananda himself, some from his swamis or lay deputies, some from the peacock feather, some from the thumb pressed into the forehead. Nothing. Nada. But this lama monk's hand leaves a strange buzzing sensation and a quietness of mind which lasts for some time.

A few years later Terry Dukes, who runs an organisation called Mushindokai which is dedicated to teaching Kempo Karate and a variety of Buddhist arts, tells me this story. He claims that he knew my London lama and was in Cambridge attending a Buddhist meeting with him one evening. Terry says that afterwards they stood on the steps outside the building and chatted while each smoked a cigarette. The lama was in his lama robes, but when they had thrown their stubs away, he bent down, lifted up his robes and pulled them over his head. Underneath he was wearing full evening dress, ready to go straight on to his next engagement, a black tie supper.

I like this story. It appeals to my lack of asceticism. I decide to believe it even though I know that Terry is untrustworthy.* I still have no idea whether it is true or not.

Terry also claims to have been one of the group of people

---

*I knew Terry Dukes, aka Nagaboshi Tomio, aka Shifu Nagaboshi, for a number of years and studied several "Buddhist arts" with him. He had founded his own school, the Mushindokai Buddhist association (MKA), and he was a charismatic and entertaining teacher. He was also, we later discovered, a charlatan. After he was exposed, his organisation more or less fell apart. Nevertheless, I remember spending some fascinating hours with him and other members of who were instrumental in bringing another lama, Chogyam Trungpa, to Scotland to be the first abbot of Samye Ling Monastery. And he claims to have been one of the group of people instrumental in throwing him out later on when his naughtiness became too much for the Buddhists to bear. Chogyam was first well known for his book 'Cutting Through Spiritual Materialism', which impressed many a young seeker, including me. Later he became well known for other things, including driving a car through a shop window in Dumfries while drunk.

Terry tells a story which even he admits is strange. He says that Chogyam's own teacher foretold that he would die by shooting. This seemed a highly unlikely fate for a Buddhist lama living in Scotland. However, after leaving Samye Ling Chogyam moved to the USA, engaged in increasingly bizarre sexual behaviours and was accused of various kinds of extreme bullying and abuse. In the circumstances, Terry feels that the likelihood of him being shot, perhaps by an angry cuckolded husband, increased considerably.

In the event, Chogyam dies of a heart attack, probably induced by alcoholism.

Later on, my London lama becomes well known himself, partly through the success of his book 'The Tibetan Book Of Living And Dying'. By now you may well have recognised him as Sogyal Rinpoche, the founder of Rigpa. After the publication of his book, a Jungian analyst, Ean Begg, receives a commis-

---

MKA chewing the fat in The Golden Egg cafe next to Clapham Common during Saturday lunchtimes. This was after attending his weekly Chinese Yoga classes in a community hall. Chinese Yoga as taught by Terry was a very ancient traditional Oriental system which, it turned out, he had entirely made up himself. It was with Terry that I first discovered that I would rather hang out with charlatans than with saints, as by and large they are more interesting and have more to teach us. In spite of his downfall, I refer to him later on in this book as "my friend and teacher" because that for a time is what he was.

sion to make a series of television programmes about dying and death, in which various thinkers are interviewed in front of members of a live audience who then get an opportunity to ask them questions. One day Sogyal is the guest. At the end of his interview with Ean, a member of the audience asks him "Sogyal Rinpoche, could you tell us what you think about Western attitudes to death?"

Sogyal starts laughing. He is shaking under his robes. While he answers, his giggles continue. "Well, the problem with you Westerners is that you don't think about death until you are dying!" More giggling. "And by then, it's rather too late!"

This answer endears the lama to me even more.

But some years after that there are allegations of sexual misbehaviour concerning Sogyal too. He may have the distinction of being the first Tibetan lama in the West ever to have a lawsuit filed against him by a disaffected female follower claiming that she has been sexually exploited. My friend Christine, who is a psychotherapist and a Tibetan Buddhist herself, and who has a more moralistic outlook than I have, is outraged by this. She expects high standards of behaviour from her Buddhist exemplars. What is more, she expects me to share her reaction. When I fail to do this, we have a minor tiff about it. But to my way of thinking at that time, whatever the truth of the matter, as Sogyal is a lama but not a monk and therefore presumably has not taken vows of celibacy, he cannot be accused of hypocrisy. And as the disaffected follower is an adult, I expect her to take responsibility for her part in whatever may have taken place between them.

All this happened many years ago. Nowadays, if you are interested in finding out more about the allegations made against Sogyal Rinpoche, you will of course be able to read many of the details on the internet. The claims about his shenanigans are both varied and astonishing and they have led to him resigning as the head of Rigpa. After reading some of the available material you may well come to the conclusion that my friend Christine was right and that I was both naïve and unwarrantably generous to him at the time of my conversation with her.

****

I hear another strange story about sexual exploitation later on. After Swami Muktananda's death, there are accusations that he regularly visited the women's quarters of his ashram and gave certain female devotees special initiations involving his penis. Initiations that were not available to all. My informant, who is telling me this story many years later, knows some of these women and has kept in touch with them. She says that some of these initiates took their initiation as a blessing and their lives have been blessed ever since. Others felt that they were exploited and became resentful, and their lives have been bitter ever since.

As with so many stories on the spiritual circuit I have absolutely no idea what to make of this.

5. Transcendental Meditation

It is a sunny afternoon in May. I am standing on the doorstep of an elegant house in Pimlico. I am feeling self-conscious for I have a bunch of flowers and a bag of fruit in my hand. I am about to give these along with a large cheque to someone behind the front door who will receive them on behalf of the giggling guru, Maharishi Mahesh Yogi. Then I will be initiated into Transcendental Meditation, or TM.

I am on the threshold of thirty years of meditation, although I do not know this at the time.

One year earlier I had been standing in the corridor of the London college where I was a lecturer, talking to Pete, an ex-student who had dropped by to say hello. We chewed the fat together and both laughed heartily because Scott, another of his cohort, had taken up TM. We talked about Scott's absurd collapse into superstitious nonsense and congratulated each other that we would never be so foolish as to be taken in by the exotic trappings of an Indian con man.

But then my relationship with my girlfriend ended and I was plunged even more deeply than usual into existential angst.

And I met Johan. I was teaching English literature to a class of foreign language assistants in which Johan was a student. He was Swiss and he seemed to me to be almost preternaturally calm. Nothing seemed to ruffle him. One day after class I asked him how he managed to be so relaxed all the time and he put it down to TM. He had been doing it for some years.

I had read some books on Buddhism and had tried to meditate sitting in the middle of the floor of my tiny sitting room. Abject failure. Pain in the knees. Pain in the spine. Pain in the arse. Alcohol, weed and opium seemed much more effective solutions to life's problems but I was bright enough to realise that they brought with them their own difficulties. As Homer Simpson says enthusiastically of beer "Now there's a temporary solution!"

In Pimlico the door opens and I am led down a hallway and into a quiet room. It is heavily curtained and rather dark. There is the strong sweet scent of incense in the air. Candles are burning. There appears to be an altar of some kind. I hear the recorded sound of Hindu chanting.

I am a rationalist. What have I got myself into, I wonder. But I am too far steeped in blood to turn back. To withdraw now would be embarrassing. I am too much of an Englishman to risk creating even a minor scene. So I grit my teeth and proceed. But I have already decided that I am wasting my money. A lot of money.

I am directed to sit down in a comfortable chair. The person standing next to me seems to be chanting some Hindu prayers. Then he bends down and mutters a word – my mantra – into my ear. He repeats it a few times.

I start to repeat it mentally as I have been instructed to do. I think "This is going to be a long and tedious twenty minutes."

But almost immediately I sink into an incredibly peaceful state. Remarkably, the incessant mental chatter that has been my constant companion for as long as I can remember simply quietens down. The mantra becomes more like a gentle rumble, a vibration rather than a thought. I feel warm and cosy. Trying to describe this later to friends I say "It was like being bathed in warm honey." It seems like an apt metaphor to me. But they do not get it.

It feels like coming home.

The effects are so striking that I have a few moments of paranoia. I wonder whether in some way I have been drugged. Perhaps there is something in the incense?

All too quickly my initiation is over and I am back on the

streets of Pimlico in the bright afternoon sunlight. But much has changed. The unaccustomed quietness of mind stays with me for some time. So does the feeling of cosy warmth. And some colours seem spectacularly bright. The double decker buses passing by are a particularly brilliant red, as if I am seeing them on acid.

Later I discover other effects. The most obvious is that I seem to have become suddenly allergic to alcohol. I meet some friends in a pub that evening and after a pint of bitter I start to nurse a terrible headache. A little experimentation over the next few days tells me that this will happen again and again. I am forced to become a teetotaller. After about six months I find that I can tolerate drinking small amounts of beer again but never the three pints on three or four evenings a week that I have been used to.

Very quickly I lose my liking for weed and opium. I have had a little taste of clarity of mind and I cannot bear any longer to be in a narcotic fog. I remember a line from Joseph Conrad's novel 'Typhoon'. Jukes, the first mate of the steamer Nan-Shan, says as he swelters in the tropics "I feel exactly as if I had my head tied up in a woollen blanket." Now I find that I have as strong an aversion to having my head swathed in a blanket as he does. I do not realise it for a while but my long flirtatious relationship with drugs is over.

I quickly learn that my regular day-to-day experience of meditation is rarely of deep peace and serenity. Often it is of racing thoughts. Sometimes it is of bitter and angry feelings. But occasionally the peace returns. Just often enough to keep me going.

I become a determined and fanatical meditator. I must have my fix twice a day and almost nothing will make me miss it. More than once, when I am invited to friends for dinner, I turn up demanding that before I eat I must first be shown to a spare bedroom to meditate. The other guests will just have to wait for me. Or start without me. I do not care which as long as I get my evening dose.

I become a pain in the arse to my friends in another way. I approach them with missionary zeal. I proselytise. Some of them are infected by my enthusiasm and hand over large cheques to the TM movement just as I have done. It does not take with any of them. They all stop meditating after no longer than a few months, kissing goodbye to their dosh. But I meditate relentlessly on. One of them retaliates by giving me a Tee shirt with the words "Richard medi.....zzzzzz" stencilled on it. I must endure being the butt of their other occasional jokes as well.

Then I sign up for TM's Science Of Creative Intelligence course, handing over another large cheque. This course seems to be Maharishi's attempt to smuggle Yogic philosophy into the West under the guise of science. He has astutely recognised that we young Westerners are not much interested in God, but many of us have read 'The Tao Of Physics' and 'The Dancing Wu Li Masters'. So in some befuddled way we are open to the suggestion that quantum physics and spirituality have something to do with each other. Even though we do not understand quantum physics. Not at all. Not a single mathematics or physics formula.

The way that the SCI course is taught is a shock to someone like me who has been brought up in the vaguely liberal Western education system. We meet once a week in a cramped room in London. Each session starts with a video of Maharishi presenting some aspect of Yogic thought re-envisioned by his team of tame western scientists. Every week, within a minute or two of it starting, I fall deeply asleep. I awake each week to the sound of the tutor switching the video machine off at the end of the tape.

After the video I am expecting some discussion. But no, this is not the TM way. Instead we are asked a series of questions about the video, *which must be answered in the exact words on the tape.* No discussion or deviation is permitted. As I have been asleep throughout each and every tape, I am unable to answer even the simplest of these questions.

But the sleeps are amazing. Well worth the price of admission.

TM's approach to learning seems rather like indoctrination to me. It is one of several cult-like aspects of the movement. But when I compare Maharishi's TM to L Ron Hubbard's Scientology, David Koresh's Branch Davidians or Jim Jones' Peoples Temple, it seems pretty benign. Come to think of it, when I compare TM to the Catholic or the Baptist Church, it still comes out rather well.

I have become a TM addict. As a testament to my addiction I may be the only person who has ever incorporated a TM retreat into their honeymoon. My poor suffering wife. No wonder that I later become divorced.

Before this, on my first TM retreat, I am introduced to "rounding". This is a means whereby the effects of TM are intensified. I am taught to meditate, then perform a series of yoga exercises, then meditate again. Meditate. Yoga. Meditate. Yoga. As much as we like.

Well, no actually. Not as much as we like. We are given severe warnings that we must not exceed the recommended dose or dire things may happen.

But I have always been of the opinion that if two red pills are good for me, then four red pills must be better. So I ignore the warnings and I round and I round and I round and I round.

Pretty soon I become paranoid. When I walk into the retreat canteen for lunch, people look at me strangely. They start talking about me behind their hands. They know what I am up to.

But I am not too far gone to recognise what is happening to me. I ease back on the TM throttle and start following the rules that I have been given. My mental state slowly returns to normal.

Then I hear rumours on the retreat about "TM psychosis", the occasional cases of people wigging out completely. At breakfast one morning I hear that someone has had a serious mental health crisis in the middle of night and has been forcibly removed from the retreat.

I cannot stand this story up. But it is what I am told.

Intensive meditation can make us seriously ungrounded. To be fair to TM, the organisation recognises this and teaches us how to deal with it. Only do intensive meditation in a protective environment. One afternoon I am present as a TM teacher sets up a slide projector in preparation for an evening presentation. He has recently returned from six months of intensive meditation in Switzerland and he is floating six inches above the floor. Not literally. Metaphorically. I watch him with fascination as he again and again puts a slide into the projector and tests it, only to find each time that he has put it in wrongly. He takes approximately a dozen attempts before he gets it right. As there are only two ways to put a slide into a projector wrongly (upside down or back to front), twelve tries qualifies him for an ungrounded gold medal.

I am glad for his sake that he is in a protective environment. I wonder how many attempts he has to make before he can match his shoes to his feet each morning.

6. The Guru - *Falling In Love*

I am on a Transcendental Meditation weekend retreat in Oxford. I have been wildly enthusiastic about TM for about three years. Although I am married, I am even considering giving up my reasonably well paid professional job so that I can go to Switzerland and train as a TM teacher. If I carry out this plan it will be an act of almost inconceivable folly and will probably bring ruination on my life. But I cannot see this at the time as I am blinded by my spiritual fervour.

I am sitting in the retreat house kitchen nursing a cup of tea and earwigging on Tom and Rob, a couple of TM old-timers, who seem to have something important to say to each other. They are talking about a new spiritual teacher who has emerged in the West recently. He is Indian and apparently quite a few TM teachers are abandoning Maharishi Mahesh Yogi to become his followers. He is over here in England at the moment and about to give some talks in London. According to Tom and Rob he is a heretic and a very dangerous fellow. No one who values their spiritual progress should go anywhere near him. If they do, they might deviate from the true path of TM and become lost, incurring bad karma and perhaps many further rebirths.

Although I take no active part in this exchange and in spite of Tom and Rob's dire warnings, I am left on fire with an urgent desire to go and see this man, whose magnificent title is Gururaj Ananda Yogi. There is no rational explanation for this but it feels like a magnetic force is drawing me to him and I have no wish to resist it.

I discover that Gururaj is holding a public meeting in about a week's time at the Porchester Hall in London's Bayswater. I will be able go and listen to the dangerous heretic and make up my own mind. Maybe I can fathom the mystery of what this sudden and strange attraction is.

At this time, the Porchester Hall is not a prestigious venue. It is somewhat down-at-heal and its spiritual aura is zero. Its main attraction is that it is not far from one of the most authentic Indian restaurants in London, a huge chaos of clattering plates and babbling customers called Kahn's. An enthusiastic friend has said to me of Kahn's "You can taste the earth of Mother India there."

But when I arrive at the meeting there is a disappointment. It turns out that Tom and Rob have been misinformed. Guru-raj is not here tonight, he is at his home in the Indian quarter of Cape Town. Instead the meeting is to be about Gururaj, to introduce his teachings to more eager Londoners and to gather in devotees.

The meeting is addressed by Michael, a tall, plausible and impressive German. Michael also has the more exotic name of Shandar, which we are told means "the brilliant one" and is the spiritual name that Gururaj has conferred on him. It is said that Michael had been a bigwig in the TM movement until his defection to Gururaj's camp. The story of his defection is almost tailor-made to appeal to a spiritual romantic like me and it deserves to be told right now.

Apparently Michael had been at a TM convention held for those who were in the upper echelons of Maharishi's move-ment. But he had felt bored so he decided to cut one of the meetings. Hanging out in the kitchen (kitchens seem to have some karmic importance in this chapter), he met a woman from New Zealand named Theresa. She was also on the run from the tedium of a presentation about the coming Age Of Enlightenment, which was to be ushered in when sufficient punters were practising TM. Theresa was one of Maharishi's head honchos at the time.

Something about Michael made her share a secret with him. She had come across another Indian teacher who had impressed her even more than Maharishi. He was the real deal. She had already in her heart committed herself to him and would be announcing her defection from TM soon. She was to commit her life henceforward to spreading his teachings to as wide a public as possible. She had a photograph of this guru and if Michael would like her to, she would show it to him.

By the way, it turns out much later that Theresa may have given more than her heart to her new guru. But that is a story for another chapter.

Theresa produced the photograph and showed it to Michael. It was at this point, by his own account, that he uttered the wonderfully dramatic line "This is the master that I was born to serve."

The photograph was of course of Gururaj.

To a seeker of my fervour and commitment this story is irresistible. I am irretrievably hooked as I sit in the drab Porchester Hall and listen to tales of the power of Gururaj's meditation techniques. On my way out at the end of the meeting and in spite of the unknown people crowding around me and hemming me in, I chance upon an acquaintance from a TM group that I had studied with. Oliver has already defected to Gururaj and is full of enthusiasm. "You won't regret it" he says. The "synchronicity" of this meeting is not lost on me.

I am now as eager to abandon TM as I had two weeks earlier been eager to leave my job in order to train as a member of Maharishi's spiritual hit squad. And so it is that I find myself a few evenings later in an elegant Georgian house in Blackheath to discover more. A friend of mine, Gail, has decided to come with me.

The deal that I have been offered contains within it a story which is highly seductive to a spiritually inclined young man like myself. I must provide a passport style photograph which will be posted to Gururaj in South Africa. Having received it, he will go into a profound state of meditation and tune in to "the deepest spiritual level" of my being. Once there, he will attune himself to my "most subtle vibration" and emerge with a mantra chosen specifically and precisely for me. In return for this service, I have only to make a donation, an amount of money chosen specifically and precisely by me. This will contrast strikingly with the sum that I had to give to the TM organisation in order to receive their mantra, for that payment consisted of an arm and a leg and a part of another leg.

Gail and I each hand over our photograph. In the meantime we are to be taught what is called Gururaj's "preliminary technique". This will tide us over and begin to create a connection with the guru so that his energies can start to flow to us and transform our spiritual being.

For the preliminary technique we have to lie on the floor in the yoga corpse position and repeat Gururaj's name like a mantra, preferably twice a day for twenty minutes each time, the same dose as prescribed for TM. For myself it works like a charm and I am able to ignore the slightly spooky and cultish aspect of this practice. I happily return to Blackheath a couple of weeks later to be given my "full technique", a mantra which also sometimes leads me into deep meditation. In fact at the second "checking session" in Blackheath something quite transpersonal takes place. As I meditate I feel myself becoming evanescent, almost like a cloud, and expanding until my being fills the entire room. I am enjoying this translucent space enormously when suddenly Gail coughs and instantly I am back contained once more in my too too solid flesh. I spend the next few moments thinking evil thoughts about Gail, who has so cruelly interrupted my transcendence.

While these shenanigans with Gururaj's movement have been going on, my wife, who works for a foreign airline, has been out of the country on a training course in an exotic capital city. When she comes back to London, I badger her into joining Gururaj's brigade, just as I had earlier badgered her into practising TM. Once more the poor woman is dragged into a transpersonal adventure by her spiritually incontinent husband.

A few weeks later we have to go to a different centre in London to be taught another technique, tratak. This is a candle meditation which, we are told, will work specifically on our ajna chakra, or "third eye". It will increase our powers of concentration, our memory and our ability to focus. If we have latent psychic abilities, it may also cause these to blossom.

There are three of us in my little Morris Minor convertible as we drive up to town. I park and we find the centre, wait our turn, and are then taught the technique in a small group by a nice young man called Tim, one of Gururaj's senior teachers in England. Once again I go into deep meditation and experience profound transcendence. But I am beginning to notice a quite serious side effect of these deeply relaxed states. They seem sometimes to have the unfortunate result of bringing up their opposite. The deeper the peace I feel in meditation, the more likely I am to feel a nearly explosive rage sometime afterwards. In Blackheath, this had focussed on Gail after she had coughed. Here there is no such obvious focus, but nevertheless, when I am pointing my Morris Minor towards home after the initiation and I am held up while an old lady dodders slowly across the road, the red mist descends and I feel quite alarmingly strongly that I would like to run her over.

Later on I discover that this is quite a common phenomenon, and not just with meditation. I take part in personal growth groups where we reach extraordinary heights of loving ecstasy together. Afterwards there is a tendency for chaos to erupt in our lives. One day I am discussing this with a young woman from New Zealand who has been a participant in many personal development groups. "Yes", she says drily, "You go on these courses, you feel wonderful, you're in love with everybody. Then you go home and for the next six months your life falls apart!"

I suspect that this has something to do with Jung's wise saying "The brighter the light, the darker the shadow." Another quotation that may be relevant here is Sondra Ray's "Love brings up anything unlike itself." In the "psycho-philosophy" of meditation, this is explained as the process by which transcendence stirs up unconscious material so that it can come to the surface and be released from the psychophysical system.

In TM this process is called "de-stressing" and it can often be "distressing". However, the dark feelings involved usually do not last for very long. It is for this reason, when later on I teach meditation myself, that I give my students the following advice:- if immediately after meditating they feel like phoning their boss and telling him to "Fuck off!", it is probably wise to wait for twenty four hours before actually dialling his number. If after that delay it still seems like a good idea, well hell, why not make the call, enjoy the moment and then start looking for a new job.

All these years later, I still think from a psychotherapeutic point of view that these feelings are better out than in. That is because I feel that brief anger is preferable to long-lasting irritation. But if you are really committed to a lifetime of feeling interminably annoyed, then it is probably best to avoid any effective meditation technique like the plague. Woody Allen has a good line about this approach to life:- "I don't get angry. I prefer to grow a tumour."

Of course if you subscribe to a religion, then you may be suffering from an enormous handicap when it comes to dealing with your anger or any other aspect of your shadow. Having committed yourself to a life of virtue and morality, it is possible that you are only ever able to express your persona. In that case, instead of Woody Allen's line, you could contemplate the following:-

"That there is a devil, there is no doubt
But is he trying to get in, or is he trying to get out?"

As a virtuous and moral person, you might also consider C S Lewis's well known lines:- "She has devoted her life to caring for others. You can recognise the others by the haunted looks on their faces."

But then again, if you are religious you should ask yourself the question "Why on earth am I reading this book anyway?"

7. The Guru – The Lama's Curse

I am sitting in an office in a large elegant terraced house in Notting Hill. This is the London headquarters of the British Meditation Society, which is a branch of Gururaj's new International Foundation For Spiritual Unfoldment. Thanks to the defection to his organisation of several TM teachers, Gururaj's movement has grown with astonishing speed. Many young seekers like myself, who are put off Osho (too much sex) and Swami Muktananda (not enough sex), are flocking to him. So IFSU has opened branches in several countries, including America, Australia and Britain.

Gururaj by the way calls himself a tantric guru and will have nothing to do with asceticism, although unlike Osho he does not encourage rampant sex and the consequent spread of venereal disease. He could be said to be the guru of choice for the respectable bourgeoisie. He likes to tell the following story:-

"A young married couple came to see me. They were followers of a guru who insisted that they be celibate. They hadn't had sex for months, so naturally their marriage was in serious trouble.

"I listened to them and then I said 'You go home right now and you go to bed!'"

He pauses here for dramatic effect before almost shouting "'With each other!'"

He laughs uproariously, pulls his elegant embroidered guru's shawl tightly around himself and subsides into giggles.

In the office I am in a state of anxiety. I am trying to earn browny points with the Society by helping out, but it is not going well. Charlotte, who is in charge, has briefly shown me how to operate the complicated telephone system but I have not really taken in what she has said. I am filing papers but every time the phone rings I flick the wrong switch and lose the call or I have to run in to Charlotte's room and interrupt her work in order to ask her for further instructions. She has a sweet nature but even her patience is slowly being eroded.

Suddenly there is a loud rap on the brass knocker of the front door. I walk down the impressive corridor and pull the door open, trying to look both welcoming and efficient.

Standing on the steps is a wild looking young man. He is rather dishevelled and he seems to be in a state of some shock. He is holding out his right hand. There is an object in it which appears to be related to the story which he starts incoherently to try to gibber out.

I look down at the object. It is a human skull. Or rather it is a cranium. He is holding it upended like a macabre cup and in the centre of its hollow is a large gemstone in a silver setting. He is jabbing it towards me and he seems to be hoping that I will take it from him.

Which I will not.

Out of the gibberish I piece together this story:- the skull is Tibetan, and trapped within the jewel is the soul of a long dead lama who has been cursed by black magic. The lama is to spend as much of eternity imprisoned in the gem as his unknown tormentor has the power to conjure. The wild young man seems to have made it his mission to release the lama.

Now he wants me to help him.

It seems that somebody has told him that if anybody can lift the curse, it is Gururaj. This is what has brought him to Notting Hill to knock on our door.

I explain to him that Gururaj is not here, then ask him to wait while I seek advice from within – from within the building, not from within my soul. Perhaps Charlotte knows how to lift black magic spells. She listens with as much patience as she can muster while I stammer out the story almost as incoherently as the wild young man. I am sure she will come up with a solution which is both wise and compassionate.

She sighs. "Tell him to chuck it in a rubbish bin!" she says.

I am genuinely shocked. I had not known what to expect, but it was something a little more spiritual than this.

I start to protest. She looks at me, sighs again and says "Well, that's what Gururaj would say! He wouldn't have any time for such nonsense!"

I walk back to the front door. I do not have the heart to pass the unedited reply on to the wild young man so I just tell him "I'm sorry. Gururaj can't help. You'll have to try somewhere else."

He looks quite miserable as he turns away and walks down the steps.

I go back to the office. I have to admit that it is one of the things that I quite like about Gururaj's gang. They are nothing if not pragmatic.

****

About a year later I am at a retreat which Gururaj is holding at the University of Keele during the summer vacation. It is evening and about two hundred of us are in the student union bar. Through the crowd and at the other end of the large room I see coming through the door the wild young man. He is wearing a sheepskin motorcycle jacket and to my mind he seems to have a dense black aura around him. With a slight sense of panic I realise that he has seen me and has started to weave his way through the throng to reach me.

There is nothing that I can do except wait to be accosted. He greets me like I am his brother. I am after all the only person that he knows in this crowded room.

At least he does not seem to be carrying a skull.

He explains that he is now living in Germany but he is

visiting England for two weeks. He has heard that Gururaj is in Keele and, desperate to see him, he has motorcycled from London without stopping. He has to be back in London by the morning.

He seems to be expecting me to arrange an immediate private audience.

But Gururaj is of course in his private quarters drinking whiskey with his most favoured devotees. So I simply do not have that power.

Somehow I extricate myself from the situation by pointing him vaguely in the direction of someone who I suggest may be able to help. Yet I suspect cannot. Then I make myself scarce.

I never see him again. But there is apparently a sad denouement to this story.

Some time after this at the Oktoberfest in Munich a bomb goes off. Thirteen people are killed including one who is English. The one who is English is the wild young man. Or so I am later told.

8. "Past Life Memories"

A preliminary note on the notion of past lives:- During the development of Hinduism, some scriptures accepted the doctrine of reincarnation, whilst others condemned it as heresy. Some scholars assert that a belief in rebirth was not a part of Hindu teachings before the relatively late era of the Upanishads, and was not widely accepted before the Buddha's time. It may even be that Hinduism in general took its belief in rebirth from Buddhism and not vica versa.

The philosopher Julian Baggini has some sceptical words on rebirth. Writing about the "evidence" for past life memories that some Buddhists offer, he reminds us that "the plural of anecdote is not data." But if you are nevertheless interested in some of the anecdotes, or data, or evidence, you might like to read Francis Storey's book 'Rebirth As Doctrine And Experience'.

I am lying on a mattress on the floor in a basement flat in Blackheath, London. There is a woman sitting on the floor by my side. The flat belongs to my sister, and the woman is her American lodger. My sister met her in the Siddha Yoga movement and like many of Swami Muktananda's followers she goes by her spiritual name, which is Madhura.

Among other things, Madhura is a past life regression therapist. Past life regression has become popular amongst the faintly hippy spiritually inclined seekers of whom I am one. The theory on which it is based is this:- some present problems and miseries are based on traumas which occurred in previous lifetimes. By accessing memories of these traumatic events, we can free ourself from their subconscious power over us and live happier lives. Dealing with our karma in this way will also materially hasten our spiritual progress. Because it is traumatic events in past lives with which we are concerned, the memories accessed in past life regression are often of violent deaths.

Another therapy which has become popular amongst the spiritually inclined is rebirthing. This sometimes focusses on traumas incurred at the other end of life, during birth rather than death. It claims among other things to release memories of breach births, umbilical cords wrapped round necks, being unwanted by our mother and intrauterine "experiences" during pregnancy.

This is my first session with Madhura and I am feeling sceptical. It is a very practical issue which has brought me to lie on the mattress in her therapy room. Since the age of fifteen I have been scared of flying. This has so far not been much of a problem for me as I have simply been able to avoid my fear by not getting on aeroplanes. However I am now married to a member of an airline's staff and so I have been given access to virtually free travel almost anywhere in the world. It seems absurd to keep saying "No" to this fabulous opportunity so I am now determined to deal with the problem. If I succeed, my wife will also be immensely pleased.

After some preliminary relaxation techniques, Madhura asks me what if anything I can see. My honest answer is "Nothing." Nada. Just undifferentiated blackness. Madhura tries again. Eventually, desperate to find something to please her, I manage to detect a faint beam of light within the blackness.

Madhura asks me what kind of light it is. I struggle with this but eventually, because I have to say something, mutter "It's like a searchlight." I feel completely stuck and a bit hopeless because I am not coming up with the therapeutic goods. There is a long pause during which nothing happens and then Madhura asks me "What do searchlights do?"

This is possibly the single most effective question that any therapist has ever asked me.

I reply "They search."

"Go on then" says Madhura. "Search."

I follow her instruction and the beam of light begins to sweeps around. At first there is nothing but the light and the surrounding blackness. Then suddenly high up I see a little shape picked up by the beam. It is a small biplane, the kind that has fabric covered wings. Clearly on those wings I can see its insignia, two black swastikas.

Now I am inside it, piloting it.

"Oh God!" I think. "I was in the Luftwaffe!"

The plane begins to fall from the sky. It comes down clumsily on an airstrip, races bumpily along and crashes, tipping on to its nose. The joystick plunges messily through my belly. This seems as good a reason as any to be frightened of flying.

Looked at from inside the enclosed world of transpersonal beliefs which I am awash with at that time, there seems to be something karmically ironic that I, born of lapsed Jewish parents the year the Second World War ended, might have been a Nazi in a previous life. But my sense is of a young man simply and rather innocently entranced by the experience of flying and dying as the result of a training flight going wrong, rather than a convinced and passionate follower of National Socialist ideology.

I do not know whether it is this experience which now allows me to board an aeroplane less nervously. I have also shared my fears with my guru. He tells me to meditate on his photograph while I am flying and at that time I am happy to buy into his totemic ritual. So my wife and I take our first flights together, a two week trip to India, mostly spent staying on a houseboat on Dal Lake in Kashmir. The flights cost us only about £20, thanks to her status as airline staff. Of course we are very low priority passengers and we nearly get stuck in Delhi when we are trying to fly home. Delhi has been flooded while we were in Kashmir, flights are cancelled, crowds mill around the airport in chaos, whole families squat on the floor. Nevertheless, after a few hours delay, dear old Air India manages to squeeze us on board a circuitous flight to London via Moscow.

Some years later, after my wife has left the airline industry, we are flying from Los Angeles to Hong Kong. There are almost no cheap flights from America to Asia, but a Chinese student of mine has given me a little-known telephone number which connects to an obscure desk at an American airline. It has one old rusting jumbo jet which has been converted to bring Vietnamese refugees to America. To make a bit of extra cash, the airline then sells cheap tickets to Hong Kong rather than fly back empty. This is not a luxury operation. The Vietnamese are much smaller than Americans so the airline has taken out all the seats and reinstalled them with far less leg room, squeezing in many more rows. Someone has scribbled the Vietnamese characters for "Toilet" in ballpoint pen on pieces of paper torn from a child's school exercise book and has stuck them to the toilet doors with sticky tape. It is the only flight that I have ever boarded where at check-in I am asked our body weight. I have the presence of mind to add a few pounds to each of us. My thinking is that if all the passengers do this, we will probably clear the end of the runway at LAX, which we do. We make a bizarre stop in Anchorage where we have to disembark for a while. In my memory there is a stuffed polar bear in the airport waiting area. Or maybe it is a model. There is a display of leaping salmon too. The descent into Hong Kong at that time takes us so close to high rise apartment buildings at each wing tip that it seems, if only we could open the windows, as if we could shake hands with the residents hanging out washing on their balconies. But to compensate for the nerve-racking nature of the flight, we are each allowed, in groups of about ten, to spend a little time upstairs in the first class lounge, where we can relax and still our anxious hearts.

On the first flights that I take after my regression therapy, the ones to and from Delhi and Srinagar, I do not die. In that sense my therapy has clearly worked. But although I seem to have dealt with my fear of flying, I keep going back to Madhura to see if we can dig up more past life memories. Perhaps we will find other traumas that I can be released from. Much later I realise that it is in the nature of many types of therapeutic intervention that they are likely to go on for ever unless we actively make a decision to bring them to an end. As long as we go on digging, we will always find more bones. Unless we decide at some point "I've got a lovely pile of shiny white bones now. I think that's enough", the mountain will grow ever higher as our savings grow ever smaller. A friend tells me that her mother is thinking of terminating therapy after fourteen years. I say to her "That's not therapy. That's a lifestyle." Then I am introduced to a man who has had twelve years of psychoanalysis, two complete analyses lasting seven years and five years respectively. In spite of these lengthy interventions, he has remained chronically depressed. He has developed some wonderfully intricate stories to explain why he is so unhappy, but absolutely no ability at all to deal with his misery.

Nevertheless he tells me one of the funniest jokes that I have ever heard, depression being no bar to a wicked sense of humour. It involves reincarnation as a rabbit.

With Madhura, I "remember" several more past lives. In one I am a spy in Oliver Cromwell's England, betrayed by my friend and by my lover and hanged. They have been having a secret affair. In another I am hacked to death in a tribal African society. In a third I am both victim and murderer in fogbound Victorian London.

In the most emotionally charged of these scenarios, I am an aristocrat in France at the beginning of the revolutionary period. I am standing in an elegant drawing room. My young wife is sitting on an ornate couch, with another gentleman standing behind her. I am not supposed to see what happens next, but I do as he rests his arm on her shoulder and surreptitiously strokes the back of her neck. She almost swoons with pleasure and an unbearable fever of jealousy erupts in my body. This memory also ends in death as we are taken to the guillotine in a tumbril and then executed. Somehow this incident seems to free me from some of my current tendencies to jealousy. Maybe this is just the power of suggestion.

As well as past life regression, Madhura guides me through various other visualisations to lay bare further issues which I have. At that time I am a witty little beggar, always ready with a joke or bon mot – sometimes tiresomely so. In one session I find myself on top of a huge block of ice in a polar landscape. I am dancing frenetically. Madhura asks me why. I reply "I'm dancing to keep warm." The irony of this strikes me immediately, even before Madhura says "Wouldn't it be easier to come down off the ice?" In another session she guides me into summoning up my subpersonalities. She tells me to visualise a house with many rooms. In each room there is one of my subpersonalities. I am to stand outside the house and call to them all to come out. A great crowd appears at the front door, but then there is a commotion and pushing through them, shouting and joking and demanding attention, is a small character who looks like a cartoon version of Toulouse-Lautrec. He shoves everyone else aside and fires quips off to left and right. No one else can make themselves heard. He is a fitting image for the two-dimensional character that I have sometimes become.

These two images strike home and I begin to reign in Quick-witted Richard so that other subpersonalities can begin to get a hearing. It is a simple matter. I just do not give voice to every quip that races into my mind.

Madhura also gives me the best description of the ego that I have ever come across. "The ego" she says "is a loop tape right at the front of the brain, embedded in our forehead. It has only one message recorded on it and it plays all day long. The message is 'See, I'm right! See, I'm right! See, I'm right!'" Later on I add to her account the sophistication that it also has a device attached to it that filters out all evidence to the contrary. I call this The Cognitive Bias Machine.

One of Madhura's therapeutic techniques involves constructing affirmations at the end of the sessions to help overcome whatever negative issues have come up. I am to repeat each affirmation in my head ten times in the morning on waking and ten times in the evening on going to bed. But there is a problem with this procedure. As more and more issues reveal themselves, the list of affirmations grows longer and longer. At one point I have ten of them. That is ten affirmations to be said ten times each. I make that one hundred repetitions! Twice a day!

I am getting thoroughly fed up with this morning and evening ritual, but I fear that if I give it up I will not be getting my money's worth from this very expensive therapy. I am therefore extremely relieved when, while Madhura is away on a trip to her home in America, my guru, Gururaj, tells me to stop having past life therapy. He says that we each have so many past lives that there will never be an end to exploring them and that there is no point to this anyway. He explains that meditation and the grace of the guru will quite naturally take care of our samskaras, the seeds of our karma, from our past lives. I am happy to believe him, although he may just be protecting his own turf. I have noticed a pattern among gurus at this time – they do not seem to be too eager for their devotees to see therapists. Or indeed for them to see anyone but themselves.

When Madhura returns from America, I let her know that my days of regression therapy have come to an end.

Later I am visiting some friends, Grace and Ted, a married couple. They are showing me an antique Georgian dining table that they have recently purchased. It is beautiful – such a wonderful patina – and I am envious. I say rather pathetically "I wish I could afford a Georgian dining table." Grace looks at me witheringly and says "You could, Richard. But you choose to spend all your money on therapy, retreats and travel!" After only a moment's thought I have to acknowledge that this is true.

Up to this point I have lived by Socrates' dictum "The unexamined life is not worth living." Now I am beginning to wonder whether the too-much examined life may not be worth living either.

9. *The Guru – Dharmic partners*

On retreat with Gururaj, excitement is sweeping through some of the devotees. We have discovered that we each have a "dharmic partner", a special person who will be our perfect lover. Finding them and being with them will greatly accelerate our spiritual progress.

Those of us without an actual partner become obsessed with finding our dharmic lover. Those of us already with a partner look at them surreptitiously throughout the day and wonder "Is this already the one? Or should I be looking for another?"

Gururaj's community of followers already contains some particularly blessed couples. First and foremost are Shandar and Sudevi.

Shandar and Sudevi are Gururaj's premier devotees, the President and First Lady of his movement. They travel around the world with him as he holds retreats in various countries. Their parents gave them ordinary Western names, Michael and Theresa respectively. Shandar and Sudevi are the names that Gururaj has given them, names which sum up their particular spiritual qualities.

Sudevi is fond of telling us that "Sudevi" was the name of one of Krishna's gopi, or cowgirls. According to Sudevi, she was not the most intellectual cowgirl in the herd, but nevertheless became enlightened because of her fierce devotion to Krishna. Sudevi is really telling us that although she is not too bright, her great loyalty to Gururaj trumps all.

Actually Sudevi is doing herself a disservice. It is true that she has almost none of the usual social skills, but she is highly intelligent. However she has a weakness for both incarnate and disincarnate spiritual masters. She has already deserted Maha-

rishi Mahesh Yogi and later on will desert Gururaj. Then, after
a spell as a personal growth workshop leader at which she turns
out to be unexpectedly brilliant, she will take up the cause of
another spiritual being. He will be a disincarnate channelled
entity of unusual provenance, seemingly the love child of an
attractive charismatic woman who may have had an affair with
her own ego.

It is Shandar and Sudevi who have created Gururaj's movement with astonishing speed, by defecting to him from their
positions high up in the Transcendental Meditation hierarchy,
bringing with them some of Maharishi's other teachers.

Their defection to Gururaj comes at an opportune time,
when many of Maharishi's teachers are already becoming disaffected. Throughout the development of the TM movement,
Maharishi had always warned his followers not to become side-
tracked in their spiritual search by siddhis. Siddhis are special
powers which are said sometimes to develop in seekers en route
to enlightenment. They may include teleportation, levitation,
the ability to walk through walls or to be in more than one
place at the same time and a variety of other physical and psychic powers. Maharishi's warning had been that although such
powers might develop naturally as we meditate, we should not
deliberately seek them out because that would interrupt our
path to enlightenment. He said that enlightenment was like
a diamond mine. On the way to it we would inevitably come
across the occasional diamond lying by the side of the road.
But if we sat down and became entranced by these solitary dia-
monds, we would never reach the mine itself.

I loved this metaphor for the importance of sincerity and
dedication in our spiritual search, this warning not to be side-
tracked by jimcrack gewgaws offered by spiritual mountebanks
like Sai Baba with their magically produced vibhuti and "Rolex"
watches. It appealed to my self-image as a serious seeker.

Then Maharishi suddenly and completely changed his policy

and contradicted everything he had previously taught on this matter. He set up a "siddhi course" in which meditators could learn to fly, levitate or hop, depending on whom you listened to. Naturally this course was long, demanding and very expensive.

No one seems to know quite what brought about this change of heart in Maharishi. One guess is that TM had simply reached the limits of its rapid expansion and was no longer pulling in the dollars, so some new cash cow had to be found. An unintended consequence of the changed policy was that many people left TM, including some of the teachers.

So Shandar and Sudevi are our premier dharmic couple. In fact they have married each other because Gururaj has instructed them to do so. This will ensure their even more rapid spiritual growth.

Or maybe it is simply that Gururaj has a wicked and a very dark sense of humour. For it would be difficult to imagine a more unsuited pair.

As time goes by we begin to notice the trouble that other dharmic couples are in. We suspect that our dharmic lover is not after all the person who will make us perfectly happy, but the one who will make us perfectly unhappy, who will jiggle into life all of our samskaras and make us face all of the deepest issues that we have not yet dealt with. With our dharmic partner life may become a super-pressurised growth group with only two participants in it and painful in the extreme.

Nietzsche's dictum comes to mind: "What does not kill me makes me stronger."

As we contemplate Shandar and Sudevi and the other dharmic couples, some of us simply go off the idea.

Where one of our couples is concerned, it appears that Gururaj may be just a little bit racist. Tim is a good looking blond English man. Lakshmi is an attractive dark Indian woman. It is said that Gururaj has taken Lakshmi aside and tried to persuade her to abandon Tim. "Why do you want to marry an English man? English men are not intelligent! And they're unhygienic! Why not marry a nice Indian man instead?"

Tim and Lakshmi ignore Gururaj and get married anyway. They are perfectly happy for a while. And then they are not. Which proves Gururaj neither right nor wrong. Which proves nothing at all.

Much later, Shandar abandons Sudevi and runs off with a cute Austrian blonde. So our premier dharmic relationship has also bitten the dust. This too proves nothing, but by now those of us who have not already found our dharmic partner have to be honest lost interest in the whole project.

10. More Of The Guru

On retreat a girl goes to Gururaj and tells him that she intends to travel to India to attend the Kumbh Mela, the huge gathering of ascetics, swamis and Hindu followers. Perhaps she thinks this pilgrimage will be propitious. Gururaj says that she should not go, that it would be dangerous to her health.

She ignores his advice and goes anyway.

Later on we hear that she has died there.

****

One evening at satsang I stand up and ask Gururaj a question. He asks me to repeat it, saying "Let us hear that again. You have such a beautiful voice." I cannot help glowing under this accolade.

But by the next morning I have lost my voice completely. I cannot speak at all for three days. I interpret this as some kind of karmic comeuppance, as punishment for my lack of humility.

On another occasion, while on a retreat with Gururaj, he promotes me to a more senior position within his organisation. Once more I glow. Two hours later I trip and fall heavily in the grounds of the university complex where we are staying and severely injure my ankle. For weeks I have to limp around clumsily and painfully with a walking stick. Once again, I think, my spiritual arrogance has brought me low.

****

Shandar introduces us to the notion of "old souls" and "young souls". Old souls have spent many lifetimes learning the lessons that they need to learn, working through their karma and seeking enlightenment. They have grown not just old but also deep and wise. They have developed a powerful yearning for enlightenment. They write books with titles like 'The Wisdom Of An Old Soul' and 'Words From An Old Soul'.

Young souls have not had many incarnations yet. So they have not had the time to accumulate wisdom and are still enmeshed in maya, or illusion. They may be overly fond of doughnuts, beer and television and by and large they are to be pitied. They have not yet realised that life is a serious business.

We, of course, are old souls.

****

We are told that the higher we climb on the spiritual path, the greater becomes the danger that we might fall from it. And the closer we approach to enlightenment, the more precipitous will be the fall if we stray from spiritual righteousness. I even have a memory that we are told that in those circumstances we could be reborn as a slug.

Can that memory possibly be accurate? I do not know but it seems so. Later on I read a Tibetan Buddhist sutra which goes into salacious and lip-smacking detail about some of the many Buddhist hells. Buddhists face the possibility of far worse than existence as a slug.

****

Gururaj is more than a guru to us. He is the Avatar of the New Age, an incarnate Godman. Somehow it is difficult to write these words now without a shudder at our gullibility, our desperate desire to believe in his and our specialness.

The more special and different the guru, the more special and different the chela.

Gururaj subtly and not so subtly encourages this belief. He speaks about "standing outside the universe", of experiencing the whole of creation from that perspective. He talks about the joy of complete enlightenment as being "greater than a thousand orgasms."

Occasionally he overplays his hand. One morning before satsang, Shandar and Sudevi have to come on stage to make an apology on his behalf. The previous evening Gururaj had got a little carried away. He had stated that he was the reincarnation of Krishna, Buddha and Jesus. No one raises the least objection to the claim that he is both Lord Krishna and Lord Buddha. But some Christians in the audience have gone to Shandar and Sudevi and complained that he cannot be Lord Jesus. For Lord Jesus, as the son of God, is unique and cannot be placed in the same ball park as these other avatars. Shandar explains that Gururaj had misspoken, had expressed himself carelessly. What he had meant was that he carried within him the Christ energy, not that he had literally been the Galilean son of a carpenter. This satisfies the Christians and peace is restored.

Sometimes Gururaj is let down by his not quite perfect English. One morning he is talking about spiritual laziness and he quite good-humouredly berates the women for "sitting there on your fannies" He has learnt this word in America. In American English it means "asses", or what are known in British English as "arses". He does not realise that in British English the word "fanny" has a different meaning. Once again Shandar and Sudevi have to offer an explanation. And an apology.

One morning as we wait for satsang, Gururaj appears from the side of the stage with Shandar on one side of him and Sudevi on the other, each clasping him by an arm. They form a perfect picture of our very own holy trinity, our loving guru and his two most devoted followers, as they help him into his seat. We adore this picture of spiritual unity.

It is only much later that we discover that Shandar and

Sudevi are supporting Gururaj in this way because at 10.00 o'clock in the morning he is too drunk to walk without help. Nevertheless he gives his usual brilliant performance, weaving a variety of spiritual ideas together with great aplomb. There is something magnificent about this. He is so drunk that his legs will not obey him properly, yet his mind is still as sharp as a razor.

Once, carried away perhaps by his own brilliance, Gururaj at satsang asks for a question, then for a second, then for a third. He proceeds to expatiate on all three at once, creating out of the answers a tapestry that makes perfect sense.

****

One evening Shandar expounds an extraordinary theory to us. Homosexuality, he explains, may be the result of a soul taking its first incarnation as a man after many incarnations as a woman, or its first incarnation as a woman after many incarnations as a man. Thus its "soul mind" may still be imprinted with its old pattern of attraction. So even though it now has the body of a man, it continues to feel the attraction that a woman would normally feel. Or vica versa.

Why Shandar tells us this is a total mystery.

11. The Guru – The Shit Hits The Fan

It is seven o'clock in the evening. I have been running a meditation centre in the spare bedroom of our house in South East London for about two years and I am waiting for my students to arrive. They have received their mantras from Gururaj, my guru and the Avatar of the New Age, and tonight I will be checking them to see how they have been getting along with them.

So far my teaching of meditation for Gururaj and the British Meditation Society has been going well in a small way. Every so often I manage to attract a group of up to a dozen new students. I invite them to an introductory evening where I talk to them about Gururaj and his techniques. After a while I become bored with doing this, so I tape my talk and they listen to it while I drink tea downstairs. Then I answer their questions. Those who want to learn to meditate supply me with a small photograph of themselves and a donation which I send to Gururaj in South Africa. Eventually I receive a list of individual mantras back from him along with any special instructions which he wishes them to be given. Because I am one of about forty senior teachers, I am allowed to initiate my students into these mantras myself.

One evening I initiate a young woman. Afterwards I ask her how her meditation went. She replies "I once did something like this before. Only that time I had to take all my clothes off." Apart from that, the initiations are largely uneventful. But I find it best to ground myself afterwards, usually by drinking a bottle of beer and watching some television.

At seven o'clock on this particular evening the phone rings. It is Tim, the nice young man who is currently the head of Gururaj's British operation. He sounds anxious.

Tim tells me that in a few days time there is to be an important meeting in London for all of Gururaj's senior teachers. I must be there. If I have a previous engagement I should cancel it. There is some very serious news that has to be imparted to us all.

I ask Tim if he can give me any more details but he is clearly reluctant to do so. I push him, explaining that I have got about half an hour before I see my group of meditation students. I do not want some amorphous concern hanging over me during their class.

Tim reluctantly gives me some clues. Certain worrying facts about Gururaj have recently come to light. Some of these are to do with his relationships with women. But there are other concerns. They cast doubt on his claims to be an all-seeing satguru and the Avatar of the New Age. All is to be revealed on Friday. I must be there.

After this phone call, I am in a state of shock. For the first time since I became a follower of Gururaj, a scintilla of doubt has arisen in my mind. More than one scintilla. Several scintillas.

So that Friday evening finds me sitting with the other senior teachers in a large room in London. Important members of the hierarchy of the organisation are also there. Some of these, it turns out, are the men who have been procuring vast quantities of whiskey for Gururaj during his retreats and the women who have been fucking him.

Hell hath no fury like a woman scorned. It is because of Gururaj's sexual shenanigans that the shit is now hitting the fan.

Apparently, some time ago Gururaj had approached one of his more senior female teachers and propositioned her with the following story. He claimed to be the reincarnate Jesus Christ. She, he said, had been Mary Magdalene. Two thousand years ago they had been lovers. Now it was time for them to rekindle their affair.

To a certain kind of ego, both spiritually inclined and credulous, this story was irresistible. It worked. In fact it worked so brilliantly that he tried it on two more women. It worked with them as well.   Perhaps he was taking his cue from Krishna and the gopi. Or from Joseph Smith and the Mormons.

So now there were three Mary Magdalenes. What could possibly go wrong?

Inevitably somebody blabbed. Or boasted. I do not know which Mary Magdalene first let out a little hint of her special relationship with the satguru, but the other two were not long in catching on. Notes were exchanged. Details were compared. Fury was unleashed as each Mary realised that she was not unique. Quite naturally, all three felt traduced.

It appears that Gururaj's other multiple sins would have gone unreported if it had not been for the Mary Magdalene scandal. Many other transgressions were already known to the hierarchy but they were prepared to keep silent for the higher good. As Kurt Vonnegut writes "So it goes." So it usually goes. The Catholic Church. Tibetan Buddhism. The Church Of England. I could go on. And on. And sadly on. All those terrible secrets, hidden "for the higher good".

There are few phrases in the English language so baleful and leading to so much mischief as "for the higher good."

The rage of the three Marys would not be brooked. Consequently there is now hell to pay. At this meeting in London all the skeletons come rattling and tumbling out of the cupboard. We sit there dumbfounded as Gururaj's litany of other sins is also laid before us.

Item:- Gururaj has on multiple occasions lied about the origination of his mantras. To whit, he claims to obtain each one while meditating deeply on the handwritten application form and photograph of each individual devotee. Every mantra is said to be uniquely created to match the highest spiritual vibration of the devotee concerned.

This claim has been tested by the suspicious hierarchy. They have tricked Gururaj by putting the application form and photograph of the same individual through his system more than once. Each time he has originated a different mantra for that person. They have tested him with other individuals. Same result.

Item:- Gururaj has on multiple occasions lied about the origination of the spiritual names that he confers on special persons in his organisation. To whit, he claims to obtain each one while meditating deeply on the unique qualities of that person and tuning in to their most subtle spiritual essence.

But a sharp-eyed follower of Gururaj, who lives in the same area of Cape Town as he does, claims that the names he gives are actually the names of the houses that he passes as he drives from his home in the Indian quarter to his office. It appears that when Gururaj decides to confer a spiritual name on another devotee, he simply selects the next house in the road. Is he having a laugh? Or is he simply lazy?

Item:- Gururaj is an alcoholic. Members of the hierarchy are kept busy on retreats bringing in supplies of whiskey for him and smuggling empty bottles off the premises. On occasion he is so drunk that he has to be helped into his seat at satsang by two of his closest followers.

Noted on behalf of the defence:- in spite of this, Gururaj never fails to give a coherent and interesting talk.

Item:- There are accusations of shenanigans involving money. No further details of these are forthcoming.

Item:- Gururaj is accused of losing his temper and hitting his wife and her daughter. On more than one occasion.

All that seems to be missing is cocaine, which is not so fashionable at this time as it later becomes.

If a guru had set out deliberately to alienate all of his followers no matter what their values were, he could not have done better than Gururaj. If we are prepared to ignore one of his apparent sins, we come up against another. For myself, I do not give a damn about the sex or the alcohol. I am after all at this time a little louche myself. However I am a touch concerned about the origin of his mantras and spiritual names, more so about his lying in general and looseness over money. But none of these are hanging offences as far as I am concerned and I would probably have forgiven him for them. My sticking point is the allegation of violence against a woman and a child.

The meeting ends. We stumble away into the night. We each have to decide what to do.

Do we stay or do we go?

Gururaj himself is coming to England in a couple of weeks time. He will address a meeting of all his teachers who wish to be there.

I have never practised Zen and I have never struggled with a Zen koan for more than a minute before losing patience with it. But what seems to happen is that the koan "What is the sound of one guru lying?" entirely occupies my internal space. I am a man obsessed and possessed. It feels as if I can think of nothing else. "What is the meaning of this catastrophe?" "Does it have any meaning?" "Is it in fact a catastrophe?"

I wonder whether this is some kind of test of our loyalty to our guru. In this way infamy has been justified throughout the ages.

Do we stay or do we go?

We have each invested energy, love, time and money into the grand project of bringing this Avatar of the New Age to the world. Is it all to be for nothing? Have we been fools? Have we been fooled? This project has obsessed us and provided us with meaning and purpose, not to mention a number of amiable companions and in some cases lovers. In a world in which many of us want to be special and different, we have been special and different with brass knobs on. We have basked in the reflected glory of our guru. Not for us the lesser magic of Swami Muktananda, Osho or Maharaji. Not for us Bubba Free John, Sri Chinmoy or Sri Aurobindo and The Mother. For we, most blessed amongst the blessed, have the real deal.

Except that we do not.

Do we stay or do we go?

In the event, our meeting with Gururaj is an anticlimax. He plays it very low-key. We sit around a large table with him at the head. In my memory he does not even try to justify or excuse his behaviour. I can remember very little of what he says except that at a certain point he looks at each of us in turn and asks us individually "Will you stay or will you go?" One or two say that they will stay. One or two see that if they stay they will have the chance of becoming much bigger fish in a much smaller pool. Most of us prevaricate. I am one of these. When Gururaj turns his deep limpid eyes onto me and in his sonorous voice says "And what about you, Richard?" I say "I haven't decided yet."

But really I have.

I will go.

After this I never follow a guru again. Gururaj has given me the finest inoculation against gurus that anyone could ever have. That projection or transference or whatever we want to call it is gone. Busted. Over.

Years later my Buddhist friend Christine becomes very concerned about my spiritual welfare. She has detected my failure to commit myself ever again to any spiritual teacher. She wonders whether the "betrayal" by my guru all those years ago has wounded my heart so much that I am no longer capable of trust. She hopes that I can get over my broken heart so that I might follow her own guru, an aged Tibetan lama who throughout all his waking hours constantly revolves a prayer wheel in his hand.

Christine is a spiritual romantic. Even more so than I am.

But the inoculation, unlike the flu vaccine, is for life. And I am grateful to Gururaj for that.

****

After the near total collapse of his organisation, Gururaj carries on in the guru business but in a much smaller way. An acquaintance of mine who stays in contact with him tells me that at one point he sends out envelopes to his remaining followers in Britain with the message "Put In A Pound For Pops."

One of the stories that Gururaj entrances us with in the early days of his movement is about his heart operation. He claims to have had heart surgery from Christian Barnard, the famous South African surgeon who pioneered the first heart transplant. He says that during the operation he remained conscious, or perhaps superconscious. He was able to hear everything that the surgeons said and to amaze them afterwards by repeating some of it back to them. We take this as more evidence of his exalted spiritual status.

I guess that at least some of this story is true. Because not many years after these events, Gururaj dies of heart failure. At the time that this happens he is still quite young.

And in spite of everything, if you go on the internet today you will find that there is even now an organisation dedicated to him and that there are still teachers who are offering his techniques.

But to be honest, I do not know how he transmits his mantras from beyond the grave.

12. *Among The Buddhists*

I am sitting uncomfortably on the floor in a decommissioned fire station in Bethnal Green. In front of me is a large and impressive golden Buddha statue. I am a student on an introductory course to Buddhism run by The Friends Of The Western Buddhist Order. The fire station is their London headquarters.

The FWBO was founded by an Englishman, Dennis Lingwood, aka Sangharakshita. Sangharakshita seems to be a bit of a renegade. He does not appear to have been given the authority to teach by any established Buddhist tradition but has set up his own school. In the world of Buddhism, this is considered to be bad form. The FWBO is to become mired in a considerable amount of scandal, but as I sit on the floor in their centre in London's Roman Road with aching knees I do not know this yet.

I do not particularly take to The FWBO. They teach me "metta bhavana", or "loving-kindness" meditation. It turns out that I am not very good at this. Perhaps this is because for years I have been doing a very lazy meditation practice and frankly that suits me. I am realising that I do not like any meditation in which I have to do anything much. Or maybe it is because at that time I am not very loving or kind. Nevertheless I grit my teeth and persevere because I am a seeker and seekers have to seek. It might after all do me some good.

As well as the meditation practice, there are lectures, which I find dry and uninspiring. But I am a seeker and seekers have to seek, so I sign up for an FWBO weekend retreat near Oxford. There are more lectures, which I find just as dry and uninspiring as the London ones, and walking meditations around the garden. By now you will be able to guess how I find these. But I am a seeker and .....

In spite of my lacklustre experiences with The FWBO, I do not give up on Buddhism. I am still feeling flirtatious where the Buddha is concerned so I am prepared to venture out on another date. The FWBO itself figures again in my story, so I will be returning to it later.

****

A few years later I join another Buddhist group, this time a Tibetan one. It is low-key and local and I meet some interesting people there. I still cannot get along with Buddhist meditation techniques, which seem dull compared to dear old Transcendental Meditation or the techniques of my now disgraced guru. But I like the woman who runs the group. After a few months, she offers some of us regulars the opportunity to go to Oxford, which is turning out to be quite a vortex of Buddhist activity, so that we can "take refuge in the Buddha, the Dharma and the Sangha." This seems to be the Buddhist equivalent of "confirmation" and "first communion" in The Church, though without the wine and with less hocus-pocus. Our kind leader tells us that she will drive us there in her car.

I am the only person among the chosen ones who declines this invitation. She lets it be known, subtly, that she is disappointed in me. I am not sure why I do not want to take refuge, but it may have something to do with the following tiny incident which happens a couple of weeks earlier.

After our meditation, as we sit on the floor, our leader passes round to each of us a handout with some extracts from Buddhist scripture printed on it. She wants to use these in the discussion that is about to take place. We read the passages and then a few of us casually put the handout on the floor next to us. We are firmly told that this is not respectful to the Buddha. We must not allow his hallowed words to touch the ground. But it is ok to put them on the leather pouffe in the centre of the room.

By this stage in my life I have an adverse reaction to this holy-holy stuff. This is one of the nails in the coffin of my slightly half-hearted attempts to have an affair with Buddhism.

****

A previous nail goes in about fifteen years earlier. While living in America I accept an invitation from an attractive Texan girl to accompany her to a meeting of her Nichiren Shoshu Buddhist group in Albuquerque. As she drives me in brilliant sunshine along the desert highway, I am enjoying listening to the country music coming from her car radio and to her homespun Texan wisdom. At random unexpected moments she likes to exclaim "My daddy didn't raise no fools! Oh yes he did! He raised my sister!"

I am not expecting the craziness of the group members when I meet them.

They chant in the hope of manifesting world peace and a luxury car. I think of Janis Joplin. "Oh Lord, won't you buy me a Mercedes Benz." This could be the anthem of the group.

It turns out that one of its members, Bernie, had actually died in a car crash two weeks earlier. The group leader explains that this had happened because on some higher spiritual level Bernie had chosen to die. Apparently this was the best way he could fulfil his dharma. The evidence for this is the somewhat circular argument that Bernie's death had taken place.

****

I come across Nichiren Shoshu, aka Soka Gakkai, aka Nichiren Buddhism, again some years later. In my endless search for truth I am a student on a Workers Educational Association course in comparative religion. It turns out to be the worst educational experience I have ever had. The tutor is well-intentioned but self-confessedly knows nothing about world religions. He is himself mildly Church of England and he thinks that teaching a course on this subject will enable him to learn about it himself. It has apparently not occurred to him that his complete ignorance of the subject might be an impediment to him teaching it to others.

His strategy is simple. Each week he will invite in to the classroom a representative of a different religion to talk to us as a guest speaker. Lazy teaching taken to the ultimate degree. Unfortunately his ignorance is so profound that for some of the weekly classes, without realising it, he invites someone from a tiny and unusual minority sect as a representative of a major world faith. Thus the exponent of Islam that he brings in to address us is a member of a fanatical and extreme group.

The intention of the course is to make each of us more tolerant towards world religions. But on me it is having precisely the opposite effect.

Knowing nothing about Buddhism, he invites two members of Nichiren Shoshu to talk to us about it. He has no idea that Nichiren Shoshu is in fact a bizarre and late offshoot of Buddhism. It was founded about eighteen hundred years after the Buddha's death by an extremist nationalist Japanese monk, Nichiren Daishonin. Like many a demagogue before and since, he believed that only he understood the true path to wisdom. Few other Buddhist schools, if indeed any, accept this strange sect with its bizarre teachings and practice as even being Buddhist.

I walk into the classroom in a cheerful mood and looking forward to the session on Buddhism very much. I wonder who the tutor has invited in to address us. Then I catch sight of the two clean-cut Sokka Gakkai representatives with their shining smiley faces and their neatly ironed white shirts and respectable dark ties. I recognise the little altar that they have set up and my heart drops. I have seen an altar just like this one before in Albuquerque. The pair turn out to be every bit as vacuous as I expect them to be. They are the Buddhist equivalents of Jehovah's Witnesses, Scientologists or Mormons. Or any fundamentalist missionary anywhere in the world.

Nevertheless, being a lecturer myself and therefore knowing intimately the demands and stresses of the profession, I am quite generous in my assessment of our tutor during the course, even on the tiresome feedback forms that we have to fill in to keep the bureaucrats satisfied. But I am brought up short after the last session when I give one of the other students, an elderly and rather haughty lady, a lift home. She interrupts me abruptly as I am trying to excuse the many shortcomings of the tutor.

"Well!" she expostulates, "I think he was awful! And" she continues, "I think he is having a nervous breakdown!"

****

The next nail that goes into the coffin of my flirtation with Buddhism is hammered in by a book. It is a very handsome book too. It has sat on my bookshelves unread since I bought it many years earlier in a second hand bookshop. It is a hardback edition of an ancient sacred Tibetan Buddhist text called 'The Jewel Ornament Of Liberation'. Unopened, it leaks a kind of spiritual and intellectual effluvia into my living room.

Unopened and unread is how it should have remained.

An acquaintance once visited me and seeing my shelves of books for the first time said "Gosh! You've read a lot of books!"

I replied "Never confuse books owned with books read. They are not necessarily the same thing at all."

My brother collected postage stamps. But he did not write many letters.

Once I heard someone on the radio recalling his first meeting with his tutor when he was a student at Oxford. It was in the tutor's study, a room lined wall to wall and floor to ceiling with shelves of impressive looking books.

"Young man" said the tutor, "I will give you a piece of advice. Never lend books to anyone. Only a fool lends books. You see these books?" The tutor waved his hand airily at the volumes. "They were all lent to me by fools."

If only I had been fool enough to let someone borrow my copy of 'The Jewel Ornament Of Liberation' instead of deciding to pick it up and dip into it, I might be a Buddhist today.

I take it down from the shelf. It has an impressive looking "Om" symbol on its faded and torn dust jacket. I prepare myself for a spiritual experience. I let it fall open at a random page.

Let serendipity be my guide.

Unfortunately it happens to open at a description of some particularly nasty Buddhist hells. It turns out that there are quite a number of these, with some of them being reserved for specific kinds of sinners. One hell, for example, is inhabited by those "whose mouth is the size of the eye of a needle but whose belly is the size of a mountain." Presumably this is reserved for the greedy guts among us, the doughnut eaters and the latte guzzlers. I could very easily end up there myself. I am partial to both.

I read on. It emerges that this is one of the milder hells described in the book. There are other, triple X-rated hells, descriptions of which might make the proprietor of an S & M club blush. Some involve red-hot lances being inserted into sensitive parts of the body. There seem to be at least as many hells as there are levels of enlightenment. Perhaps this is intended to preserve the harmonious balance of opposing forces in the universe.

Clearly some salacious medieval Tibetan lamas expended a great deal of exultant and imaginative energy dreaming up these hells, or elaborating on ones that had been dreamt up earlier in India. Perhaps the lamas got their rocks off in this way, but certainly they also intended to frighten the people into obeying their injunctions in an intensely hierarchical and patriarchal society. They demonstrated that they could give the Christian Churches a good run for their money in their imaginings of the torments awaiting us in the afterlife.

To terrify its audiences further, 'The Jewel Ornament Of Liberation' also makes it clear that they have an almost inconceivably small chance of taking incarnation as human beings in any case. Most of their numerous lifetimes will be spent as hungry ghosts, or as denizens of one or other of the hells, or as slugs or dung beetles. These lifetimes will involve eons of terrible suffering.

My long flirtation with Buddhism nose dives as I read some of the pages of this toxic scripture. Like nearly all religions, I think to myself, Tibetan Buddhism seeks to control the people by terrifying them into submission with threats of dire punishments and torture. It is true that, while the torments of Anglican, Baptist, Calvinist, Catholic, Lutheran and Methodist hells are eternal, the torments of Buddhist hells only last for a very long time. But it is made clear that "a very long time" is an unimaginably vast number of years spent in writhing agony. Perhaps our skins will be flailed off by demons during the day, and will grow back overnight so that they can be flailed off again the next day.

It takes a sick mind to think up a vision like that.

Priests, popes and princes have always colluded with each other in order to control the minds of the people. Buddhists, it seems, are disappointingly no exception.

****

In spite of 'The Jewel Ornament Of Liberation' I decide, ever the seeker, to give Buddhism another try. A Tibetan Buddhist organisation, The New Kadampa Tradition, holds weekly meetings in the Quaker Friends Meeting House in the town where

I live. With a friend of mine, Sabine, I decide to go along and check them out.

I am aware that The NKT have changed their name from Manjushri after adverse publicity and a bizarre Buddhist power struggle. I also know that they have had a serious spat with the Dalai Lama. He claims that they follow an entity which is at least partly demonic. I have even attended a public meeting held by the Dalai Lama where he has said that their practices threaten his life. But I want to see for myself how I feel about them. Perhaps after all they will turn out for me to be the way, the truth and the light.

In going to the meeting, I am ignoring an earlier brush that I have with this organisation when they are still known as Manjushri. Driving across the north of England after two weeks of solitary retreat in a cottage on a remote Scottish island, I find myself within twenty miles of their northern headquarters, an impressive and rambling priory. I decide that I may as well check them out so I make the detour. My main objective is to discover whether they welcome individuals who are not affiliated with them but who nevertheless want to go on retreat there. Some spiritual organisations will do this.

When I get to the priory, I wander around the empty corridors of the huge country house looking for someone to talk to. Eventually I see a door marked "Office". I knock and go in. Perhaps I am in a slightly paranoid state after my hermit's retreat, but it appears to me that I am met by five hostile stares from the five pairs of eyes in the room. I put my enquiry to them. They seem to me to react as though I have asked if I could dine that evening on their pet dachshund. Oh no! Of course not! That would be impossible!

I would have to attend some of their courses before that could possibly happen!

Indoctrination first. Then retreat.

I have received a great deal more openness and kindness

at a Christian retreat centre in Dorset where I once stayed for a week.

Manjushri has in fact grown in popularity with astonishing speed. To my mind, this is in itself cause enough for some suspicion. One of the main ways that a movement, whether it is spiritual, religious or political, can become popular very quickly is to make a plausible but fraudulent offer to the public.

All demagogues know this.

In my home town, Sabine and I arrive for the meeting and are welcomed warmly enough. We are the only newcomers there. We sit through a talk about Buddhist doctrine which is notable only for its patronising tone. We find out later that in his daily life the speaker is a primary school teacher. It shows. After being addressed like not very bright ten year olds for half an hour, we meditate for another half hour. It is a simple technique. Just pay attention to your breathing. Watch whatever comes. Etcetera, etcetera.

Then there will be tea and biscuits.

I cannot explain my reaction. I can only report it. During the meditation I feel a great weight of oppression settle on me. I feel stultified. I feel imprisoned. I feel almost as if I am suffocating. I cannot wait for the session to be over.

When finally it actually does come to an end, I glance at Sabine. She glances at me. As far as I know neither of us is telepathic but I fancy that at this moment we can each tell exactly what the other is thinking.

The regulars, who to be fair seem to have enjoyed their meditation, turn to us in a friendly enough way and ask us if we are staying for tea. Simultaneously Sabine and I both mutter our apologies, insist that we have another appointment somewhere else quite soon and lie our way out of the building as quickly as we can.

Out in the evening air I feel that I can breathe again at last. We decide to go to a local bar and swap impressions.

Sabine's experience has been pretty much identical to mine. Neither of us can explain it but we both feel repelled by New Kadampa Buddhism. We sink a beer or two and vow never to return.

****

Then I read an extract from another Buddhist text. It is in a book titled 'Rebirth and the Western Buddhist' by Martin Willson, an English Tibetan Buddhist monk. This extract seems to me to be every bit as poisonous as the one that I came across in 'The Jewel Ornament Of Liberation'.

The passage is taken from a text called the 'pravrajyantaraya-sutra'. First it describes certain negative acts which, if you commit them, will result in disastrously bad karma. These negative acts are called "four modes of behaviour" and the passage goes on to state what the awful karmic consequences will be. You will have terrible rebirths. Lest there be any doubt about this, it lists what these rebirths may be.

The passage is worth quoting, so it appears below. If you would like to have a bit of fun, before you read on after the dotted lines, stop and see if you can guess what word I have omitted from the brackets:-

"If, Mahanama, a householder is given to four modes of behaviour, he will have to endure adverse conditions: he will be born again and again, born either blind, dull-witted, dumb, or as an outcaste, always living in misery, always a victim of abuse. He will become a hermaphrodite or a eunuch, or be born into lifelong slavery. He may also become a (--------------), a dog, a pig, an ass, a camel or a poisonous snake, and thus be unable to put the Buddha's teachings into practice."

....

....
....
....

The word I have missed out is "woman".

Perhaps you are recovering from a sharp intake of breath right now.

The astonishing last sentence is worth reiterating to be clear. The sutra states unequivocally that the results of negative karma may include being born as a poisonous snake, a pig or a woman. And like a poisonous snake and a pig, a woman is unable to benefit from Buddhist teachings. The best she can hope for is to be reborn as a man in a future lifetime.

The idea that a woman is a kind of inferior man, who will have to wait for enlightenment until she has accumulated enough merit to be reborn as an actual man, is quite a common one among Buddhists. My friend and teacher Terry Dukes told me many years ago that the Buddha strongly resisted the suggestion that women should be allowed to join his sangha. When he was finally persuaded reluctantly to accept women, he apparently declared that because of their influence the purity of the dharma teachings would only last for five hundred years. Without women in the sangha, it would, he said, have lasted for a thousand years.

Of course I do not know if this is really what the Buddha said. Neither does anybody else. We are talking of events which are supposed to have happened about two and a half thousand years ago.

The fundamental and appalling misogyny expressed in the sutra that Willson quotes has obvious parallels in Western thought. In fact Judeo-Christianity displays a level of misogyny which is surely worse than anything that we could find in the Buddhist sutras. In the foundational myth of the Abrahamic religions, proto-woman in the form of Eve brings sin itself into the world by listening to the seductive hiss of the serpent. Thus she sets off the causal chain that leads to all subsequent evil and suffering. It is worth repeating that word "all". According to some major strands of Christian belief, it is Eve's flawed nature that is solely responsible for our loss of Edenic bliss. Poor old Adam, like all subsequent men, can only really be blamed for a certain understandable weakness, or as it is sometimes known "thinking with his dick". Ah, the sublime joy of scapegoating!

Freud's fantastical notion that a woman is a castrated man continues the myth of women's inferiority into the twentieth and even the twenty-first century. Yet any reasonable person might be able to suggest a simple answer to Freud's agonised question after his "thirty years research into the feminine soul," "What does a woman want?" Perhaps she wants to live in a world where she is not disempowered by patriarchal and patronising men, including Buddhist monks, Christian priests and Freudian psychoanalysts. That at least might be a start.

And we could in any case remember, with reference to both Buddhism and Judeo-Christianity, Wendy Doniger's definition of a myth:- "A myth [is] a story that a group of people believe for a long time despite massive evidence that it is not actually true." We might remember this in the case of Freudian psychoanalysis too.

To be fair, the passage that Willson quotes about snakes, pigs and women is from an ancient text. Nowadays it is common for apologists for religious superstitions to offer a historical and cultural justification for the most unpalatable passages of their sacred works. They may tend to say something like "Times and attitudes have changed. We must understand that it was once quite acceptable for Buddhist monks to compare women to poisonous snakes and pigs, or in other societies for priests to demand that a girl be stoned to death at the door of her father's house if she was found not to be virgo intacta on her wedding night" ('Deuteronomy' Chapter 22). They might add "We must see such statements in the context of their times. Of course attitudes have changed since then."

But the astonishing thing about Willson, a Westerner born in the middle of the twentieth century, is that it does not seem to occur to him that there is a need to gloss this toxic and misogynistic passage in any way. Having chosen to quote it, he then appears to accept it absolutely at face value and to regard its repulsive sentiments as unexceptional. He does not bother to offer any comment on it. As far as we can tell, he takes its repellent teaching as read and then sweeps blithely on, presumably expecting us to accept it too.

****

By now my disillusion with Buddhism is more or less complete. But there is one more episode to report. I promised that I would return to The FWBO and I do so now.

I publish on the internet a couple of short articles about Buddhism. I am not sure why I do this – perhaps I am feeling dyspeptic, perhaps I just like stirring things up. One of the articles is about the terrible threats of Buddhist hells, the other is about the foul little misogynistic passage that Martin Willson quotes.

Then I receive an invitation. Will I go to a seaside town not far from my home to give an afternoon talk about non-duality? I accept with alacrity. I like talking about non-duality, there will be tea and cake and afterwards there will be plenty of time for a walk along the beach to take in some sea air. Perhaps there will even be a fish and chip supper.

The only problem is that this invitation has been communicated to me via a go-between. I do not know the lady who has actually issued it. In fact I know nothing about her at all except that she goes by a lovely spiritual name. In my experience, this does not necessarily bode well.

Everything goes quiet for a while. I contact my go-between to see what is happening. He tells me that the lady with the lovely spiritual name wants to check out what I have written about Buddhism before confirming her invitation.

I think, prophetically as it turns out, "I don't expect I'll be going to the seaside any time soon." After all, what I have written is neither spiritual nor respectful.

I never hear directly from the lady and the talk does not take place. But I do discover that she is a member of an organisation called The Triratna Buddhist Order.

The Triratna Buddhist Order is actually The FWBO under a new name. There has been a rebranding of Dennis Lingwood's organisation and the reason why it has changed its name, or rather has had to change its name, is both interesting and instructive.

The FWBO has become embroiled in a scandal. It has been exposed in the mainstream press, which is unusual as national newspapers like The Guardian do not usually concern themselves with the goings-on of obscure Buddhist sects.

This briefly is what happened. Some of the senior teachers in The FWBO were pressurising reluctant young men to have sex with them. They were using some cultish persuasions to achieve this. These included the bizarre argument that the young men would be hindering their own spiritual progress if they refused. This progress, according to their teachers, depended on the young men acknowledging their latent homosexuality and thus overcoming their dependency on women.

Some of the young men, who actually did not have any latent homosexuality to acknowledge, were persuaded out of a naive respect for their teachers to go along with practices that they found repulsive. Later, unsurprisingly, they felt angry, hurt and disgusted.

There are more graphic descriptions of what happened on the internet if you want to read them. I do not intend to go into the details here. It is not my intention to be prurient.

A certain amount of time passed by before some of the young men involved found the courage to blow the gaffe on The FWBO and the shit hit the fan. After the unwanted publicity, The FWBO found it expedient to change its name and also to refocus much of its energy away from England and towards India, where presumably back copies of The Guardian are not readily available.

It is ironic that the lady with the spiritual name probably thought better of her invitation to me because of my comments about Buddhism and misogyny, as The Triratna Buddhist Order of which she is a member could itself be thought of as astonishingly misogynistic. Sangharakshita's right-hand man, Alex Kennedy, under his spiritual name Subhuti, has written what must rank as one of the most bizarre spiritual works of the twentieth century. Its title is 'Men, Women and Angels' and it seeks to demonstrate why women are spiritually inferior to men. Published in the nineteen nineties, this lamentable book with its hideous views continues to embarrass The Triratna Order to this day. If you would like to know more about it, there is a wonderfully scathing review of it by Anita Doyle on the blog page of www.tricycle.com. I highly recommend reading this review.*

Meanwhile an invitation for me to give a weekend of talks in Italy from another woman with a lovely spiritual name also evaporates into thin air. I strongly suspect that it is for the same reason.

I described at the start of this chapter how many years ago I attended a meditation course at The FWBO's lovely converted

---

*I should add in fairness that Alex Kennedy/Subhuti has now written an apology in which he withdraws the views that he expressed in his book. The book itself is apparently no longer available, all remaining copies of it having been pulped. His apology can be found on the internet.

fire station and also how I went on one of their weekend retreats. This was long before the scandal became public and long before I knew anything about it. But when he heard that I was going on the retreat, Terry Dukes, who knew a great deal about the Buddhist scene in Britain at the time, said to me with a mischievous grin as he rolled himself a cigarette "Watch yourself, Richard! They're a homosexual mafia!"

Although it was a dull retreat, at least I emerged with my virtue intact.

More recently my daughter attended a Triratna meditation course at the fire station. In view of their sexual preferences, I felt that she would be safe.

She was.

****

Postscript:- It is only after rereading this chapter in order to edit it that I recognise that there is a pattern to all of these Buddhist shenanigans. Over a period of many years I have made several attempts to connect with Buddhism, to embrace it and to make it my "spiritual path". But each time something about Buddhism has thrown me back and thwarted my ardour. Nowadays I give talks about non-duality, and when I become aware that a newcomer who has come into the room to be in the audience is a Buddhist, I tend to think "It's quite possible that you're going to be trouble." Sometimes I am right about this. I ask myself why that is and I come up with a couple of possible answers.

A clue to one answer lies in Freud's insightful phrase "the narcissism of small differences". The fact is that the closer someone else is to us in their beliefs, the more fiercely they may fight with us in order to defend their tiny differences. This helps to explain why the most vicious crusade launched by The Catholic Church was not against Islam but against other Christians sects which somewhat dissented from The Church's view. My talks on non-duality are in some ways quite close to Buddhism. Non-duality could be said, like Buddhism, to be "a philosophy of no-self". But in other ways it is different, and these differences sometimes seem to get the Buddhist goat*. An Evangelical Christian or an Orthodox Jew on the other hand, whose views on the nature of existence will probably be much further away from my own, may be more likely simply to ignore what I have to say, regarding it as being beyond the pale of sensible discourse altogether. Perhaps they might even pity me for my obviously mistaken views. They are less likely to perceive what I have to say as a threat to their own entrenched beliefs.

Another answer may be that in the West, some difficult and unhappy people might find it easier to join a Buddhist group than to do the really tough work of dealing with their own psychological issues, including their shadow material (there will be more on this in another chapter). By changing their name, clothing, hairstyle and diet, or simply by assuming a holy-holy attitude, they may be able to disown and distance themselves from the aspects of their psyche that they are uncomfortable with, rather than integrate them. Any of this may also give them some cachet among their new Buddhist chums and a feeling of superiority over non-Buddhists in general. But the shadow material and other issues may still be there, lurking beneath the surface waiting to be jiggled into irritable life, perhaps by the

---

*This note might throw some more light on the meaning of the phrase "the narcissism of small differences" as it manifests itself within Buddhism. "I always suspected that looking into this matter of doctrine in Buddhism would be opening a can of worms. Not least because there are enough scriptures to sink the Titanic, and enough technical terms in Pali, Sanskrit, Chinese and Tibetan to make Derrida's stuff seem like a Ladybird book. But how wrong I was. Not a can of worms at all – more like a veritable hornets nest. Nothing has sewn more confusion, debate, schisms and rifts between Buddhists of various schools than the real meaning of 'no-self'." Phil Davies, in a personal communication with the author.

provocation of some slight challenge to their dearly held beliefs.

Whatever the truth of this, the worst drubbing that I have ever had at the hands of one of my audience members was from a Buddhist – a practitioner of Dzogchen Buddhism to be precise. Lionel, a dapper little man from Finchley, having argued with me rudely throughout much of one Saturday afternoon, finally simply told me to "Fuck off" from my own meeting.

13. A Psychic Reading

One Saturday morning, hot and sunny just like almost every other morning in New Mexico, I am driving up Interstate 25 from Socorro to Albuquerque. Socorro is a one cow town in southern New Mexico which figures briefly in the film 'Alice Doesn't Live Here Anymore'. In an early scene a young boy, about to leave the town for ever, gives his judgement on it. "Socorro sucks", he says pithily. But strangely, because Socorro has on its outskirts a major technological university, it is said to have a higher percentage of Ph.D's amongst its population than New York City. And for me, teaching English 101 to freshmen at the university, it certainly does not suck. It is a welcome haven of high desert under clear blue skies, an escape from the damp cold gloom of South East London during the depredations of the early Thatcher years. By accepting a posting to Socorro I have even escaped the ridiculous flummery of the wedding of Prince Charles to Diana.

And Socorro's inhabitants, in the manner of Americans, have taken me to their hearts in acts of generous integration. As well as being accepted as a member of the organic food co-op, and of Dr. John's bizarre meditation group which centres on a stout Mother Earth figure in Albuquerque who channels a great cosmic being, I have been given a place on the University's academic ten-pin bowling team. It is because of this that I win the only sporting trophy of my life, a tiny cheap piece of metal awarded by the American Bowling Congress and engraved with my name and the words "Most Improved Average". Our team at Ed's Bowling Alley is of course the only one with even a single Ph.D to its name. We have no chance of winning the league, but if a philosophical debate comes up with the teams in the lanes next to ours, we will cream their players.

Ed, by the way, is a huge man who keeps a handgun always in reach under his cash register. When it is his turn to bowl, he takes it out and sticks it in the back of his trousers. He has fat stubby fingers with which surprisingly he also makes beautiful gold jewellery. Ed, in spite of his size and his gun, is a gentle man, who is under the control of his diminutive but ferocious Irish-American wife. One day I come across them in the Kentucky Fried Chicken Restaurant together. He turns away from the counter with a family bucket, which I assume is to be shared between the two of them. But no, he tucks into it all on his own, while she pecks like a sparrow at her own tiny meal.

In spite of the welcoming warmth of the Americans on the faculty and in the town, I have been suffering from enormous culture shock. Americans are just so ….. well, different. I have had conversations with Nepalese tailors in Kathmandu and Kashmiri boatmen in Srinagar who have seemed less alien. One evening at a faculty party I talk for about twenty minutes to a Hungarian astrophysicist. We have almost nothing in common except that we are both European, yet this conversation feels somehow wonderfully comforting. In fact I have never previously in my life been so aware that I am a European. I feel that if we could only marry the best qualities of Americans, boundless enthusiasm and openness to new experience, with the best qualities of Europeans, wisdom and some sensible scepticism about the world, we could have a wonderful culture. But George Bernard Shaw's riposte to a beautiful actress who proposed that they combine his intelligence with her beauty by having a child together is well know. What if we instead ended up with some grotesque bastardisation of American gullibility combined with European cynicism. What a monster we would have bred.

However there is one American member of the faculty with whom I do feel very much at home. Andy is thoughtful, deep and ironic. Conversation with him comes close to what it is like to talk to my cosmopolitan friends back in London. One day I tell a colleague how much I enjoy Andy's company. I add that he seems almost English to me.

"Yeah" she drawls laconically, "you know why that is?"

"No." I say "Why is it?"

She looks at me as if she cannot believe how I could so easily have missed the obvious, before saying sharply "It's because he's depressed!"

And I have to admit that she is right. This seems so often to mark out the English from the Americans.

But then you know what they say. "If you're not depressed, you're not paying attention."

So I am driving up I-25 under a clear blue sky on a Saturday morning. My wife is sitting by my side. We have been arguing so the atmosphere is tense. Nevertheless we have a plan for the day. On the southern outskirts of Albuquerque there is a New Age bookstore that has flotation tanks out the back. Also known as sensory deprivation tanks, an hour or so spent floating in the dark warm silence of one of these offers the possibility of a transcendental experience without either hallucinatory drugs or long hours of meditation. I have booked myself a session and my wife is content to while away the time browsing the bookstore, with its shelves of esoteric and metaphysical volumes and its glass cases filled with crystals, Buddha statuettes and dream catchers. Later we will wander round the shops of the city and be able to eat a rare foreign meal. A "foreign meal" in New Mexico means anything that is not American or Mexican and it is generally hard to come by. But Albuquerque has French, Italian and Japanese cuisine. It also has a Greek restaurant, although this is only able to sell its doner kebabs by calling them "The Greek Burrito". There is a rumour that about another hundred miles to the north on the road to Taos there is an actual Indian restaurant – that is Asian Indian, not Native

American. This later proves to be true, although it is pretty bad and would probably not survive three months in that centre of Indian cuisine, Brick Lane in London's East End.

Flotation tanks are quite the rage at the moment in Albuquerque, but then New Age enthusiasms come and go with breathtaking speed in America. Almost every week a friend rushes up to me to tell me excitedly about the latest fashionable technique in personal and spiritual development. If I sign up for a weekend workshop I will become an expert in it. A second weekend will make me a teacher. By the third weekend everyone will have forgotten about it and moved on to the next transpersonal fad. Most of these new fashions are in any case an endless revolving reworking of the same old basic techniques. In Marin County, California, there are said to be five hundred therapists all recycling the same twelve processes and therapy-ing each other with them. As the American ambassador to England recently said of our new service based Thatcherite economy "But surely you can't all earn a living opening doors for one another?"

The session in the flotation tank proves a disappointment. The water is tepid and I spend the hour feeling physically uncomfortable and faintly bored. No transcendental reality reveals itself to me. I have no cosmic visions nor insights into the deeper meaning of the universe. I do not even have a revelation about my own unconscious. I get out of the tank, dry myself off, put my clothes back on and return through the door into the bookshop to collect my wife so that we can go on our way.

It turns out that while I have been floating in the tank, a local psychic has been offering her services in the bookshop. Rather than browsing metaphysical books, my wife has had a psychic reading.

The atmosphere in the car as we drive the last few miles into the centre of Albuquerque is now even more frosty than it was before. The psychic seems to have said something to my wife which she both does and does not want to pass on to me. Without telling me directly what it is, she hints that it is something quite dark about me, something that might even threaten my health and wellbeing if I do not mend my ways and start to conform more closely to how a well-behaved husband should be conducting himself.

Back in Socorro the next day, I find myself chewing on the ambiguous hints that my wife has tossed my way. I hatch a plan. I have long theorised that psychics may pick up somehow on the conscious and unconscious material that their clients are harbouring, only to feed it back to them. "Right", I decide, "I'm going to phone this psychic and make an appointment for a reading myself." I will not, of course, let her know that I am the husband that she apparently bad-mouthed on the previous Saturday. I am genuinely interested in finding out whether the reading that she gives me might contain any of the darkness that my wife has hinted at.

On Monday morning I make the phone call. It is easy to arrange an appointment. On the following Saturday, we will drive to Albuquerque again and I will drop my wife in the centre of the city to do some clothes shopping at a mall and then meet up with some friends of ours. I will join her at their apartment later. The psychic lives on a ranch in the hills a little way out of town, but she will drive to her office in the city where she sees her clients and meet me there for my appointment.

Saturday arrives, another hot day with clear blue skies of course. After leaving my wife at the mall, I drive to an undistinguished area of low-rise ugly buildings and wait outside the anonymous looking locked office for the psychic to arrive. I am slightly early. Time passes. Now the psychic is late. More time passes. Now the psychic is very late. I check the address carefully, and yes, it is the right office. I spot a payphone on the corner of the street, find some change in my pocket and go to give her a call. She picks up almost immediately. She is hugely apologetic. She had got into her car to drive to the office but it would not start. She has phoned a friend who lives nearby. He is at this moment driving over to her house with his truck to give her a lift to the office. If I do not mind waiting she should be there in less than half an hour.

I do not mind. I go back to the office. I wait. And wait. And wait some more. Eventually I return to the payphone and call her number again. She picks up. She is now almost beside herself with apology. "I'm so sorry! You'll never believe what's happened! My friend can't get his truck to start either. I'm stuck here. We'll have to put your appointment off to another time." I tell her "That's ok" and add that I will phone her on Monday morning when I am at home with my diary. Then I hang up.

I drive into the centre of the city to join my wife at our friends' apartment. At this time I do not know whether or not I believe in psychic powers but I sure as hell believe in good old Jungian synchronicity. Two broken-down vehicles. I can take a hint from the universe. I already know that I probably will not phone her on Monday.

And on Monday I do not phone her. Whatever forces of darkness or light may be at work in the universe, I am not meant to know what the psychic lady told my wife about me.

Unless my wife decides to tell me herself.

Which she does not.

****

These are some of the things that psychics have told me:-
  Soon the sun is going to disappear from the sky. Within a few days, two new suns will replace it. The psychic knows that this will happen because she has seen it in a vision.
  My seven foot tall spirit guide is standing behind me, dressed in a white robe. He is a handsome and imposing man with a dark complexion.

My blond friend Tim and I were in the Luftwaffe together in our last lifetime.

My wife and I will probably have a third child. (Shortly after being told this, my wife and I divorce, leaving our family of two children without another sibling.)

I should take up gardening.

As a wizard in a past life in China many centuries ago, I conjured up a storm to destroy a village just for the fun of it.

If I do not end my relationship with my married Oriental lover, I will become an old man before I have finished being a young man.

Many lifetimes ago in Atlantis, crystals were placed in my chakras to control my thoughts and emotions. My informant can remove them. At a price.

One day I will travel to foreign cities to give talks.

I must sit with my hand held out of an open window in a flat in the Finchley Road in London, my other hand stretched out with its palm towards a plump Indian lady in a sari. In this way, her shakti energy will be able to drive my demons down my arm and out of me into the passing traffic. Then I must sit at home each evening with my feet in a bowl of warm salty water – presumably to drive out more demons.

14. The Lady Of Ladakh

I am in Ladakh. I have travelled from the tiny capital, Leh, to a monastery in the countryside. There is an important lama dancing ceremony going on here. It will last all week but I am only here for the day.

I watch the lamas, from young boys to old men, dressed in extravagant brightly coloured robes and headdresses, as they move slowly and hypnotically to the sound of drums and deep brass horns. The chanting of the older monks seems impossibly guttural.

I am sitting on an uncomfortable bench next to an attractive Western girl so my thoughts are not entirely on holy matters. She is wearing a traditional tall Ladakhi hat. Because Ladakhis are smaller than Westerners it is perched precariously on the top of her head, making her look even more unbearably cute.

We start chatting to each other. She is American and she has been travelling on the Indian subcontinent for about three years. Occasionally she gets in touch with her parents back home in Oregon to reassure them that she is ok. She makes me a proposition. Alas, it is of an entirely innocent kind.

She has noticed the camera slung round my neck and she suggests a trade. If I will take some photographs of her and post them to her parents, she will give me one of her rings of power. She takes a cloth bundle out of her bag and undoes the ribbon that fastens it. She rolls it out to reveal several dozen rings. She has made these herself and she sells them to help finance her hippy travels.

To be honest, they are not wildly attractive. They each consist of a few small dull stones strung on an equally dull piece of wire. The stones are not even semi-precious. But she explains to me that each ring is imbued with a special power and she will choose the one which exactly matches my spiritual energy, the ring which will help me on my journey to enlightenment.

At this time I am a sucker for such stories. My credulity seems to know no end. So I readily agree and I take a few head shots of her. Though I say it myself, these later turn out to be rather good. As soon as I can, I get them developed and send them to the address in America that she has scribbled for me on a little piece of paper.

She chooses a ring from the bundle. It is not the one that I would have chosen for myself but I am in her hands. She puts it on one of my fingers and assures me that I will soon start to notice changes in my energy.

A few days later I leave Ladakh. I had arrived by plane but I leave by bus. There is little to do on the slow tortuous journey except count the buses and lorries that did not make it, the ones that lie smashed at the bottom of the mountains. I remember the public safety notices along the mountainous road to Srinagar. "Death Waits With Icy Hand On Beacon Highway." At the halfway point in Kargil, I and the other passengers spend the night on straw mattresses in a guest house. Here we each pick up several tiny travelling companions to keep us company on the rest of our journey.

I eventually arrive in Delhi and after a night or two in a more comfortable guest house to recover from the journey, I take a train to Bombay. From there it is another train and then a bus ride to Swami Muktananda's ashram in Ganeshpuri, where I am to stay for a few weeks. Occasionally I touch the ring of power and move it around on my finger.

At the ashram I try to monitor the effects of the ring on my chakric system. But this proves to be impossible because so much else is going on. There is the shakti energy of the guru, the purifying effects of meditation and chanting, the numerous alternative health treatments that I sample, the soothing hours spent in the hot spring public baths in the village and the unfamiliar diet of rice, dahl and vegetable curry eaten off banana leaf plates with my fingers. And as it is the monsoon season, there is also the horrible fascination of watching the green mould as it gradually spreads over my rucksack, camera case and other possessions.

But I do have strange and vibrant dreams, the kind of dreams that seem to have a special reality. So perhaps the ring of power is working its magic after all.

Or perhaps not. Of course I will never know.

The time comes for me to leave Ganeshpuri. It is early in the morning and I am waiting with a group of other departing ashramites at the village bus stop. At last the bus comes slowly down the rutted road and lurches to a halt. We crowd round it to squeeze on board. Just as it is about to set off I manage to grab the handrail and swing myself onto the platform. As I do so, I feel a little snap and the ring of power is gone. The wire has broken and the not even semi-precious stones lie scattered in the mud. For a brief moment I consider jumping off and rescuing them, but the bus moves on and soon it is too late.

A trivial and meaningless accident maybe. But I am inclined in those days to take synchronicity seriously. So the credulous part of myself says "Ah, it has done its work!"

****

Postscript:- I catch that bus away from the ashram in September. Not much more than a month later Swami Muktananda dies of a heart attack. Before his death he shows that he has about as much political acumen as King Lear, when he leaves his kingdom jointly to his attractive young secretary and her brother. They are to rule over it as the sibling gurus Gurumayi and Nityananda.

Naturally civil war breaks out almost immediately as it had

done between Lear's daughters, Goneril and Regan. Nityananda allegedly – and I do really want to stress the word "allegedly", for it is a story put about by the enemy faction – gets a young ashramite pregnant. She is – once more allegedly – spirited away to Bombay where she undergoes an abortion. After some more shenanigans, Nityananda disappears from the ashram. It is said by some that he has been marched off the premises in the middle of the night at gunpoint. He never returns. After this his name is more or less expunged from the records like Trotsky's from Stalinist Russia. Then Siddha Yoga becomes Gurumayi's exclusive domain.

I do not know whether the story of what happens to Siddha Yoga after that will ever fully be known. Rumours abound, as they always do. Nityananda sets himself up as a guru in a small way but the animosity of the ashram continues to follow him around. Occasionally he travels to the West to hold meetings, but if this becomes known in advance then angry Siddha yogis turn up to hurl abuse at him like enraged Scientologists. Because of this, his satsangs have to become private affairs which can be attended "by invitation only". One day I am invited to one of these in London. Nityananda seems a nice enough chap but all that I can remember about the satsang is that it is very dull.

After some time, Gurumayi disappears from public view. The rumour factory starts working overtime and some bizarre stories get about. One of these is that she has a playboy lover and she has been seen with him sunning herself on the beaches of the south of France and skiing on the snowy slopes of Switzerland. Another is that she is being held prisoner by Mafia gangsters who have taken over Siddha Yoga and are milking it as a cash cow.

Some people simply shake their heads, look wise and say of Gurumayi "Beware of what you wish for."

****

Update:- since writing the above, I have been told that Guru-mayi is back on the scene and is still running Siddha Yoga, though whether as a cash cow or not I do not know. Some assert that the devotees are milked for all they are worth, some say that the organisation is pure and holy.

15. Cleaning Toilets For God

I have cleaned toilets and swept floors on three continents.

I am not boasting. This is simply a statement of fact. I have stayed in ashrams in India, the U.S.A. and France, and part of the deal is that we have to do seva for the guru. This is not only so that the toilets are cleaned, the floors are swept, the kitchen pots and pans are scrubbed and the gardens are weeded and kept in good order. It is also good for working off past karma, accumulating merit, grounding the shakti energy from our last darshan with the guru, clearing chakric blocks and heaven knows what other spiritual what-not.

There is a great deal of social differentiation in seva. Seva for one ashramite may mean spending hours painstakingly sorting through huge sacks of rice to remove tiny stones, while for another it may involve drinking tea or sipping whiskey or smoking ganga with the guru as part of his personal retinue. As a toilet cleaner and floor sweeper my status is a little above a hobo sleeping in a doorway but definitely beneath the rice sifters. In an ashram, the seva manager has immense power as she or he can allot you a miserable job or elevate you to a position close to the guru.

I experience a little sociological revelation as I scrub the sinks and toilet pans and sweep the floors. In these roles I become invisible, but only for the few hours a day that seva lasts. People who have swapped stories and laughed with me at breakfast step over me as they enter the loos or pass by me as I sweep the steps without seeing me. I become almost literally invisible to them. I cease to exist as a person until seva is over for the day. Then the cloak of invisibility falls off me and I reappear as Richard, someone they can tell jokes to and share confidences with.

Only on one continent, however, is there a fight for my body and soul between two of the ashram's queen bees. At Swami Muktananda's ashram in India, the home of Siddha Yoga, the seva manager is an attractive young American princess whose power has clearly gone to her crown chakra. At my first meeting with her she gives me my role as a toilet cleaner with evident relish and makes it clear that as I am only intending to stay in the ashram for a few weeks, I have no chance of promotion. Past experience has led me to expect this so I resign myself to my fate with as much good grace as I can muster, which is not a lot.

The next morning I get down on my knees and start scrubbing, accumulating merit with each sweep of my cloth and brush.

A day later I am having breakfast in the ashram canteen. It is a bizarre concoction which includes "scrambled eggs" made from tofu. This is the closest thing to an American breakfast that the Western cooks can create in the ashram culture where eggs are forbidden in case, heavens forfend, eating an egg should interfere with our spiritual development. In two of the Abrahamic religions God seems to abhor the pig. But in the many Hindu religions the Gods seem to abhor the egg as well. And the onion. Apparently it is all to do with tamas. Or rajas. Or something. A couple of days after this I discover that it is much better to leave the ashram in the early morning and wander over to the village tea house a little way down the street. Here for a few rupees I can have a magnificent artery clogging breakfast of banana pancakes and chai.

Chewing the fat with a few people over breakfast in the ashram, I happen to mention that among the skills that I have accumulated in life so far is the ability to read hands. The organisation which trained me, Mushindokai, is the creation of a lovable rogue named Terry Dukes, although he prefers to be known by the Japanese titles of either Sensei or Shifu. He insists that the system he teaches be called "hand analysis", or even better "cheirology". This sounds much more intellectually respectable than "hand reading" or even worse "palmistry". It is also, he tells us, a Chinese system. To our minds this gives it a cachet far in excess of any superstitious Western practice, and the fact that we are "Chinese Cheirologists" flatters our egos.

A woman sitting next to me at the breakfast table, an old hand at the ashram game who knows the ropes much better than I do, pricks up her ears.

"Does the ashram clinic know about this?" she asks.

"No" I reply, "I didn't know there was an ashram clinic."

"What seva are you doing at the moment?"

"Toilet cleaning." I grimace.

"That's a complete waste of your time! You could be offering your hand analysis in the clinic. You need to go and see the clinic manager as soon as possible and get yourself transferred there from the toilets."

It turns out that the ashram clinic is not there just to treat the occasional insect bite, twisted ankle or case of diarrhoea. Its long white single-storey building is full of little self-contained consulting rooms where any ashramite with a relevant skill is put to work to earn money for the ashram funds. The deal is that the practitioner gives their services for free but is released from toilet cleaning jankers and any other unpleasant labouring tasks. If I am transferred there, this will immediately move me many rungs up the ashram social ladder, rather like a peasant girl marrying the squire's son in an English village. The aristocracy of the ashram, Europeans, Americans and Australians who have been out here for two or three years or more, will start treating me with some respect instead of with curt disdain.

The "clinicians" consist of anyone who is regarded as having a relevant and marketable skill, ranging from the respectable to the flakey. Apart from conventional medicine, the treatments on offer include Alexander Technique, Rolfing, nutrition, psychic reading, homeopathy, Shiatsu, herbalism, channelling, reflexology, naturopathy, iridology – the exact mix depends on who happens to be staying at the ashram at the time. Soon, thanks to me, Chinese Hand Analysis will also be on the menu.

At the earliest opportunity I wander over to the clinic and knock on the manager's door. She is an Indian woman who is somewhat older and a great deal more pleasant than the seva princess. I explain to her as clearly as I can why I have come to see her.

"You must start here as soon as possible" she says. "Go and tell the seva manager that I need you in the clinic and that she must release you from any other work immediately. You are to be transferred from today."

I leave her office feeling elated at my promotion in one leap from disregarded and lowly toilet wallah to respected health care professional. But I am feeling slightly nervous about facing the princess.

I knock on the seva manager's office door and go in. She does not seem to be pleased to see me. She turns a supercilious look on me. I appear to have interrupted something important. Perhaps she was painting one of her delicate toe nails.

I explain the situation to her.

She seems outraged, either because I have gone over her head, or because I have taken matters into my own hands, or perhaps simply because I have shown any kind of initiative at all. She clearly has no intention of allowing me to get out of scrubbing the latrines.

She tells me in no uncertain terms that she is the one who has been put in charge of seva – by the grace of the guru, she implies. It is she and not the clinic manager that decides who does what, where and when. I am to go back to the clinic manager and tell her this, then report for toilet duties as usual that afternoon. The conversation, she intimates, is over, as is my career as the ashram hand analyst. I am to close the door behind me as I leave.

I walk slowly back to the clinic, pondering what she has said. I am wise enough in the ways of politics not to have given up all hope. I know that the outcome of this situation will depend on which of these bees really is queen and I simply do not have enough information to make that judgement for now. However, if it turns out that the sting of the American princess is more powerful, then my hopes of social elevation will be dashed. I will remain a harijan and I will continue to be stepped over, unnoticed, by the ashram's nobility.

In the clinic manager's office, after I have told her what has happened, one expostulated word immediately makes the situation clear. "Ridiculous!" she explodes. "You start here tomorrow morning! Go back to that young madam and tell her! If she has a problem with that, she can deal directly with me! I'm not having you wasting your time cleaning toilets when you could be earning money for the ashram!"

I return to the princess's office. I relay the message to her. I make it quite clear that I will be cleaning no more toilets, for now I am made brave because I have a protectress.

Checkmate.

While my hand is on her office door as I am leaving, the princess delivers her parting shot. It is magnificent. Swami Muktananda's injunction to us, repeated in many of his discourses, sometimes several times over, is that we should "love one another." She glares at me and utters the sacred words that I have remembered ever since. "Just because Swamiji tell me to love you, it doesn't mean I have to like you! And I don't!"

I slam the door as I leave. A petty act, but a satisfying one.

16. A Psychic Heart Attack

We have been trekking in Nepal, my wife and I, taking the newly opened route from Dumre to Manang. Because it is new, after the first two days there are no guest houses. We stay in villagers' huts, sleep on straw mattresses acquiring fleas as travelling companions, and eat villagers' food. I leave Dumre weighing more than I have ever done before in my adult life after a period of good living in America in the state of New Mexico. I return to Dumre some weeks later weighing less than I have ever done before in my adult life, after an unremitting diet of rice, dhal and "spinach". I have put the word "spinach" in inverted commas because this is not spinach as we know it. It is an unholy bastard alliance of cabbage and something else that has most definitely not evolved to be pleasing to European tastes. But I have met two American Peace Corps workers on leave in Kathmandu who tell me that in the village where they work they have had only potatoes to eat for weeks on end. So I should be grateful and stop complaining like the wingeing pampered Westerner that I am.

It has been a tiring trek, made more strenuous than it might have been because we have been caught by the early arrival of the monsoon. Paths that existed on the way up have been washed away on the way down, in one case stranding a jeep which should have had more sense than to follow a feeble track so close to the rainy season. With no way of going forward or back, it now sits temporarily abandoned on the mountainside. It looks as if it is posing for an advertisement in a glossy magazine, the kind that is full of pornography for the middle classes – pictures of naked Aga cookers, provocative Range Rovers and seductive marble kitchen worktops. A stream that we had easily forded on our ascent is now a dangerous rush of water and small hurtling rocks. We stand with a little group of Westerners on the bank, waiting our turn to be carried across one by one on the shoulders of a wiry Gurkha with a stout stick.

My one great mistake is at the highest point, at the village of Manang, where I take a glass of the local home-made beer. Then I hang my sleeping sheet on a line to dry, stand back and recognise in the evening light that my ineffectual washing of it has had no effect on my flea companions which are still lurking in its seams. Suddenly the mother of all headaches hits me. My skull feels as if it is going to explode as I realise that the sour local brew does not mix with newly arriving at this altitude.

Back in Kathmandu we are doing what many backpackers like to do most. We are mixing with other backpackers, exchanging news of where the best places are to eat and terrifying the bejesus out of each other with horror stories that we have heard on our travels. In Thailand, for example, it turns out that it is impossible to travel by bus (certain death by bandits), train (certain death by Communist insurgents) or boat (certain death by pirates). Nevertheless most of the Westerners going anywhere, including us, seem to arrive at their destinations safely.

One Western couple at our guest house in Kathmandu tells us some news which is bound to lodge in our vaguely New Age, faintly hippy brains. Not far from the city there is an Ayurvedic medicine clinic where a couple of simply wonderful doctors work. However good the state of our health, they will make it even finer. We do not need an appointment. We can just turn up there, wait and eventually we will be seen.

Of course we have to take time off from our busy schedule of bicycling to Buddhist temples and eating at cafes in Pie Alley in order to get ourselves checked out at this clinic. Perhaps if there are no subtle physical diseases going on, the doctors can unblock a chakra or two or clear some samskaras from our sushumna nerves and so hasten our spiritual evolution.

So one fine morning we take a tuk tuk out to the clinic, a simple one-storey building on the edge of a village, and join a group of other Westerners and locals gathered on the steps outside. After a wait of half an hour or so it is my turn to be called in to see a pleasant doctor in a spotless white cotton smock, matching trousers and a Nehru hat. He takes my pulse, or more probably the numerous pulses that he is able to detect, prods my stomach, looks into my eyes and at my tongue and asks me various questions about my diet and habits.

Then he tells me that I have a heart problem. It could have become serious if I had not come to see him. However I must not worry. He is able to give me medicine which will see me alright.

He reaches into a large jar on a shelf and gives me a small packet made of folded white paper. In it, he tells me, there is a powder which I must take in water before I go to bed that night. In this way I will have a long and healthy life instead of an early death. Some rupees change hands.

That night in our guest house, just before I go to bed, I stir the powder into a glass of water and drink it. It tastes very nasty. It tastes very much of pepper. But I drink it down. Then I climb onto our mattress under our double mosquito net, the one that always seems to have one hole in it and one mosquito inside it.

I settle down to sleep. Within a few minutes something very disturbing starts to happen. A ferocious pain begins to burn in my chest. I sit up in bed to try to alleviate it but it only gets worse. A pressure and a heat builds up and I begin to wonder whether the medicine is actually inducing a heart attack in me rather than preventing one. But what can I do other than bear it? It becomes even more painful as I sit propped up in bed and the seconds of the night tick by.

At some point I must have drifted off to sleep, still sitting up, in spite of the pain. And in the morning I discover that I am alive and that the pain has gone. I can only hope that some karmic load has been lifted from my heart chakra, for I certainly do not feel physically any different.

****

A few days later we fly to Delhi and then, as previously arranged, my wife boards a plane bound for London while I travel north to Leh Ladakh and then south to Swami Muktananda's ashram at Ganeshpuri. I hardly give my brush with Ayurvedic medicine another thought. About eight weeks after my meeting with the good Nepalese doctor, I arrive back in London to be greeted at Heathrow's arrival gate by my wife and two gently mocking friends. My wife is holding a large dish of my favourite pudding. My friends are holding a home-made banner with the words "Welcome Home Guruji" written on it in brightly coloured primary school crayons. One of these friends, Luke, is Anglo-Indian. For as long as I have known Luke, he has felt that his parentage gives him the right to take the piss out of what he sees as my spiritual pretensions and my attempts to appropriate his cultural heritage.

I settle back into the gloom of an early London autumn. The culture shock on returning to England is enormous – far greater than on going to America, as I had been warned would be the case. Life in New Mexico is so easy. Things simply work. When I drive to the mall, I just park, without any danger of a near life-and-death struggle over the last parking space. When the boiler breaks down, I just phone the boiler man and, miracle of miracles, he turns up when he says he will. And he fixes it. And he does not charge me an arm and a leg. Almost every day is sunny, bright and glorious. New Mexico, a state larger than the United Kingdom, has a population at this time of just over a million people. If I go to sleep while driving, lulled by the constant country and western music from the numerous local radio stations, there is almost nothing to hit except the odd cow or a cactus.

And without being troubled by any signs of deep thought among my American friends, my mind has gone gently to sleep. This has happened so gradually that I neither notice the process nor miss my mind until it slowly begins to wake up again on reacquaintance with the intellects of London friends and colleagues. How strange it seems to spend time once again with people who actually know something about the world. To my American friends, national politics is what happens in their state, and international politics is what happens in the states that neighbour theirs.

Then a month later news reaches us from India. Swami Muktananda, who is over seventy and who has already taken at least one heart attack, has had another one, this time fatal.

As part of the funeral and memorial ceremonies, there is to be a continuous chant over several days and nights at the London "ashram", actually a large Vicky and Eddy house in a suburban street in south west London. We are all invited to come and participate for as long or as short a period as we like.

So the next evening I dutifully turn up to do a stint of a few hours or so. I am sitting with about two dozen other devotees in the large meeting room, cross-legged on the hard floor, uncomfortable as I always am when I force myself into the half lotus position, my back, knees and hips all taking their turn to complain. We are chanting "Om Namah Shivayah" or "Om Guru, Jaya Guru" or "Shri Ram, Jai Ram" while someone plays the harmonium. Time passes slowly.

I want to stress that what I am going to describe in the next paragraph does not actually happen. And yet it does actually happen. There is no way to justify or explain these contradictory statements except to suggest that there are two alternate realities. In my experience of it, the event has none of the qualities of a vision, an imagining or even a night-time dream. It is simply what really happens next. And yet if it was that simple, I would not be here writing about it now.

For no reason at all, I suddenly roll backwards until my spine is pressed upon the floor. Then I raise my legs in the air so that I am in sarvangasana, the yoga shoulder stand. I support my back with my hands and stay in this position for a time while the chanting continues. No one around me seems the least surprised. Then suddenly there is an explosion in my chest and I crash full tilt to the floor, blood spurting from my mouth and covering my shirt. Consternation! Ashramites rush to me, shocked, horrified, desperate to help.

Then there is a momentary quiver in reality. I like to think of it as a ripple in the fabric of space-time, but to be honest this seems a little fanciful. Suddenly I am back sitting cross-legged on the floor once more, chanting along with the other ashramites, my knees and hips still aching. No one around me has moved or noticed anything untoward. I have to work out with a mental effort that as no one is the least concerned, what just happened definitely did not happen. Even though it did.

So far since that time, and touching wood, I have escaped any other kind of heart attack, either psychic or physical. Do I owe the pleasant doctor in the Nehru hat a debt of gratitude? I have absolutely no idea.

17. Group "Past Lives"

There is an inner circle of people standing facing outwards and an outer circle of people standing facing inwards. I am in the outer circle looking into the eyes of my partner who is in the inner circle. We are participating in a past life exercise. It is the Sunday afternoon of a Self-Unfoldment workshop. Self-Unfoldment is an organisation which runs highly challenging personal and spiritual development courses, and this workshop is part of an intensive six month course designed to turn us into trainers and assistants who will be able to work for the organisation.

Self-Unfoldment is wholeheartedly committed to a belief in past lives and to the therapeutic benefit of exploring them to release ourselves from current misery and disfunction.

I am already in an exhausted and heightened state after two and a half days of exercises and lectures punctuated by nights of only three or four hours sleep. The rule on these workshops is that the work always goes on until it is finished, no matter how late into the night we have to stay. The next morning's session always starts on time, regardless of when the previous session ended. Anyone who is not punctual knows that they will be "processed" mercilessly by the trainer until they cough up whatever issue with authority they have that is causing them to be late. No excuses – no late trains or broken down cars – will be tolerated. The degree of commitment required to be on this course is phenomenal. One weekend a participant, an elderly lady, is brought into the room on a stretcher. She completes the weekend lying on the floor rather than miss it. She is said to be suffering from pleurisy, although I cannot verify this.

The session before this current one ends at about two-thirty in the morning. I then climb into my little Morris convertible, drive home to get four hours sleep, and return exhausted to the course. On my way home, at about three o'clock in the morning in the Old Brompton Road, I am immensely irritated because a huge Rolls Royce holds me up while it laboriously makes a five or seven point turn in the middle of the road, before lumbering slowly off in front of me. The Roller stops at the next traffic lights and I draw up along side it. I turn my head towards the driver, intending to give him a filthy look, for he is no doubt a bloated plutocrat. In fact I find myself staring at an elderly man in rolled up shirt sleeves and braces. He is unshaven and he looks incongruously shabby in the luxurious leather seat. Nevertheless, as he is at the wheel of this opulent symbol of class oppression and inequality, I prepare my most uncharitable face for him. But suddenly he turns to me and flashes me a smile of unparalleled delight. He seems to be saying "Look at me, isn't this just the most fun machine in the whole world!" He is like a child with a much-loved toy. My irritability immediately dissolves, my heart melts and for a moment I feel uncomplicated love and share in his joy.

In the past life circles, my partner and I continue to gaze into each other's eyes and follow the instructions given by the trainer. Suddenly I am no longer in twentieth century London but in a medieval city. What is more, I am a hunchback. Dressed in rags, I am in a hovel with straw on the floor. My partner's features and clothes have also changed. She has become a nun of rather unappetising appearance. But she is kind to me. I have the sense in fact that she is the only person who has ever been kind to me.

Before long, the trainer instructs us to change partners. The inner circle rotates one way, the outer circle the other, and I find myself facing a new partner. This is Jeremy. I have already taken an irrational dislike to Jeremy. We look into each other's eyes and in short order we are on the fields of Waterloo, foot soldiers in Napoleon's army. Jeremy is thrusting a knife into me, but this, he explains later during our "debrief", is a mercy killing because I have been wounded. It is not an attack. Whatever my mind does or does not make of this, my hostile feelings towards Jeremy disappear at that moment and I never feel irritated by him again.

Once again we change partners. This time I am facing Karen, a woman whom, although she is quite attractive, I have hardly noticed on the course so far. We hold each other's gaze and this time find ourselves on a green outside a castle in the medieval age of knights in armour. What is more we are deeply, deeply in love. But this does not have a happy outcome, as she is snatched away from me by the lord of the manor and his henchmen, leaving us both bereft.

This is the last change of partners and the end of the afternoon session. It leaves Karen and I with an interesting social problem. How do we behave now, when we barely know each other but have just shared the intense experience of being in love. For about four minutes.

Karen and I engage in some desultory conversation, quickly realise that we have very little in common and wordlessly agree to put our transpersonal experience behind us.

Several people on the course have this intense experience of "in loveness" with each other. Some of them decide to act on their feelings, with almost inevitable catastrophic consequences. Three couples break up, as in each of them one party abandons their partner and embarks on a relationship with their new transpersonal lover. Within a few months all of these new relationships, which involve at least seven children, dissolve. Of the four couples who start the course together, only one survives at the end.

On another occasion I am partnering a Scottish girl in a transpersonal exercise. She is the friend of a friend of mine. We are to sit opposite each other cross-legged on the ground, hold each other's gaze and repeat some phrases over and over in unison. I do not remember the exact words but this is close enough:-

"You are my father and my mother,
My brother and my sister,
My husband and my wife,
My friend and companion,
My lover and beloved,
My soul and my life."

I do not even like this girl. A group of us had eaten lunch together earlier that day and she had seemed to me to be both sharp-tongued and immature. Nevertheless we emerge from the exercise gazing at each other like soul mates. At that moment we could probably have eloped with each other. It is a little while before reality kicks back in.

Ram Dass gives a good account of the havoc that can be created when the transpersonal leaks into the social like this. He describes coming down from the mountain – in other words returning to everyday life after he has spent a long period in seclusion with his guru. He seems to fall rapidly in love with several women and from his description may before long have collected a small harem, had he not realised that this might be a problematic way to enact divine love on the streets of America.

****

In the febrile atmosphere of our course, spontaneous remembrances of past lives involving the whole group also break out, perhaps demonstrating the power of mass hypnosis or mass hysteria or a little of each. On one occasion Tony, a handsome blond man, starts speaking like a Roman emperor. He has the charisma to carry this off. Within moments most of us have assumed positions in his court and are enacting some highly melodramatic Imperial crisis. Disappointingly, within this scene I seem to be some kind of minion.

But the apotheosis of our group past lives is undoubtedly when we all discover that once upon a time we were the last Jewish rebels holding out against the Romans at Masada.

I cannot remember who initiates this drama, but suddenly we are all atop the rocky Judean plateau in the first century CE. It is the final moments of our hopeless revolt against foreign rule. We have agreed to kill each other and for the last of us to commit suicide to avoid falling into the hands of the Roman troops. As we act out this slaughter, we know that we have also agreed to take incarnation as a group again and again in order to help each other's spiritual development. We feel exceptionally noble, heroic and blessed by the divine.

Unfortunately I find out later that history does not really support this version of reality. The group of Jewish rebels at Masada, the Sicarii, seem to have been a particularly violent and obnoxious sect. They had actually been thrown out of Jerusalem by the general Jewish population because they were so very quarrelsome and unpleasant. That is why they had ended up living at Masada. They were extremists even amongst extremists, fanatics even amongst fanatics, and probably thieves and murderers to boot. They hated other Jews just as much as they detested the Romans. They may themselves have slaughtered several hundred Jews in a nearby settlement, thus giving the Romans a run for their money in this activity. They are considered by some historians to have been proto-terrorists.

****

During the course we also do exercises which are designed to take us back to "memories" of our very early years, in order to discover and release traumatic incidents that may have occurred then. Half of us lie on the floor in the darkened course room while our partners sit by us and lead us through a practice designed to relax us and then regress us. I had a difficult relationship with my father, who died when I was fifteen. In short order, I find myself standing up in my cot hanging on to its bars. I seem to be about eighteen months old. It is night-time and I am howling. Suddenly the bedroom door flies open and my father appears in the doorway. He is furious at having his sleep interrupted and he shouts angrily at me. Something seems to die in me at this moment. What my father cannot see is that I am screaming because there is a spider in my cot. At my young age, it appears to be huge.

I come out of this exercise seeming to understand why I had difficulties with my father yet feeling no better about him. But in a later exercise, as I lie on the floor while my partner practises her skills on me, I become overwhelmed with sadness at what he missed because he was not close to his children. I have two young children myself at this time and they are more important to me than anything else in my life. Any resentment I may have been harbouring towards my father dissolves instantly and I never feel any negativity towards him again.

18. Quantum Leap

I am sitting in a crowded room in London. Like most of the people here I have given up possession of my bank card, cheque book, cash, watch, car keys, house keys, books and pens, along with any cigarettes, chocolate, chewing gum or sweets that I know that I had about my person. We do not have mobile phones at this time, but if we had, they too would be confiscated. All these possessions have been collected into bags by stern looking helpers who are behaving like prison guards. This is strange because we know them and until this evening they have been warm and friendly to us. Now they are cold and unforthcoming. They refuse to answer any of the questions that we ask them.

Theresa, one of the facilitators who is running this group, is standing at the front of the room. It is she who has induced us to give up every symbol of security and comfort that we had brought with us. But she is not yet satisfied. She suspects that knowingly or accidentally we are still harbouring "contraband", items that we are not allowed to take on the journey which we have all signed up for and which we are about to undertake. Perhaps a stick of chewing gum is nestling in the bottom of a rucksack. Maybe there is a cough sweet in the pocket of a coat. Possibly a cigarette lies forgotten in a handbag.

She seems to sniff, then quiver. Her eyes move about the room. She fixes her gaze on someone and approaches them. They declare their innocence of either intentional or unintentional smuggling but she insists that she senses something forbidden in their jacket. They search through their pockets, and mortified come up with half a packet of chewy sweets that they had forgotten they were carrying. They protest that it was an innocent mistake. Theresa looks at them balefully and the sweets are confiscated.

She goes on to the next unlucky suspect. And the next. Almost every one is a hit. The last cigarettes, bits of chocolate and fruit pastilles are ruefully given up.

How does she do this? Perhaps she has the olfactory sense of a bloodhound.

Theresa declares herself satisfied and we move on. We are each induced to sign a form agreeing that our organs can be donated to a lucky recipient in the event of our untimely death. It becomes clear that the organisation running this show has no material resources – if anything goes wrong it will be pointless to sue. Our personal insurance policies will probably not cover us for some of the activities that we will be involved in. If the worst comes to the worst, my widow and semi-orphans may be sent to the poorhouse.

Everything, from the unfriendly guards around the room to the removal of our comforting treats, is calculated to make us as nervous as possible. In my case at least it works.

We are led out of the building and onto a coach. It is late afternoon. We are driven who knows where for some hours until we arrive in darkness at a large country mansion in extensive grounds.

Once we have disembarked from the coach and collected our bags, people are allocated to their rooms. Eight of us, including myself, are shown to a large frame tent which has been erected on the lawn. Here, for a reduced fee, we have agreed to stay. We eight have uncomfortable camp beds, but this hardly matters as over each of the next seven nights we will only get between two and a half to four hours sleep. There is just enough space to squeeze in our bags. We have been asked to bring one set of smart clothes with us – a nice suit for each man and an elegant dress for each woman. I hang my suit up on the frame of the tent next to my bed.

We gather in the large meeting room and the mindfuck continues. For those staying in the house, every room has an en suite bathroom. But no one is allowed to use the bathroom attached to their room. Instead, each person is allocated a specific bathroom attached to a different room in another part of the house. They are only permitted to use that one. It may even be on a different floor to their room. We in the tent are also each allocated a bathroom off someone's room. We must not use any other. It appears that privacy is another comfort that has been removed from us.

We sit down to supper. Small quantities of bland food. Cooked without seasoning. Served without seasoning. Flavourless without seasoning. Of course no alcohol or stimulants of any kind. More comforts gone.

Back in the meeting room we are introduced to Quantum Leap applause. At certain times, especially when someone has shared some particularly sensitive secret of their inner life, we must recognise their courage by standing up and clapping and cheering. Two helpers stand at the front of the room with a home-made "applause-o-meter". They watch us carefully and by hand move an arrow up or down the meter. Only when it has reached 100% are we allowed to stop applauding and sit down. But there seems to be no rhyme or reason to this process. It does not appear to have to do with either the overall volume of the sound we make or with our degree of enthusiasm.

It is some time before I work out that what is being judged here is unanimity, or confluence. We are not allowed to stop until everyone has joined in wholeheartedly. As long as one individual holds back, all the others must continue.

We have to stay alert and pay attention at all times during the meetings. On an average of three hours sleep a night, this proves difficult. If our attention wanders or our heads nod, we must stand at the back of the room holding a log of wood above our head. We may only sit down when we are deemed to be fully alert again.

We must never leave the room unless there is an authorised break. It does not matter how burstingly full our bladders are.

****

The next morning we gather outside on the lawn where, under the watchful eyes of Michael and Theresa, we are to be introduced to Quantum Leap running. Michael and Theresa, who were the head honchos in the guru movement that I once followed, have reinvented themselves as personal growth facilitators since our guru's disgrace and the subsequent near-collapse of his movement. They have developed Quantum Leap after the model of Werner Erhard's est, but have added meditation to the programme, a practice which est did not offer. In fact they sometimes call Quantum Leap "est with heart." The two of them are in control of this show, but the preliminaries this morning are introduced by Theresa. She leads us through a series of warm up exercises involving star jumps and a series of yoga exercises including "Salute To The Sun". Before she starts, she turns to the fields beyond the fences where animals are grazing and says "Good morning sheep-people. Good morning cow-people." I do not know whether I find this endearing or cloying.

The concept of Quantum Leap running is simple. There is a cross country course. We must run flat out until we can go no further and then stop. Across fields and ditches, over styles and fences. As soon as we have recovered sufficiently we must continue. And so on until we finish the course. We must not pace ourselves. Pacing ourselves is absolutely forbidden.

We are divided into two groups. One group will run. The other group will scatter around the course and cheer and shout encouragement. Then the groups will swap. This will happen every morning.

Although I disliked sport at school, I enjoyed cross country running. Our course was through the parkland of a stately home and up and down steep inclines, some of them heavily pockmarked with mole hills. Unlike in football, rugby and cricket, there was no team to let down by fumbling the ball. So I find Quantum Leap running quite exhilarating, whether running or cheering.

Michael and Theresa have ingenious ways of dealing with the inevitable conflicts which arise between different members of the group. We have biffing bats, light bats covered in foam. We can hit each other with these with little danger of harm. We have stout cushions which we are encouraged to pummel with our fists or to hit with tennis racquets. I have taken an irrational dislike to one member of the group, Jack. Jack and I are instructed to wrestle in front of everyone, but the wrestling must be done kneeling down so there is little chance that we can damage each other. This proves to be quickly exhausting and in a very short time I find that my animosity towards Jack has dissolved.

The overarching rule is "Get it out into the open." Do not sit on it. Do not harbour a grudge. Do not feed on resentment. Cough it up. I have immense respect for this approach to conflict, as I do for this dictum that Quantum Leap has borrowed:- "We cause just as much hurt to ourselves and others when we take offence as when we give offence."

Although much of their approach has been taken from the encounter group movement via est, in creating Quantum Leap Michael and Theresa have added some very important transpersonal elements. One of these is that our goal should never simply be to express what has been repressed, but where possible to reach a genuine feeling of resolution with the other person. Quite often, though not always, this happens.

****

The days pass and lack of sleep takes its toll. We are waiting for the centre piece of the course, a twenty-four hour outward bound element. We have no idea when this will happen. It may be sprung on us at any moment, day or night. A bell will be rung and with a maximum of twenty minutes notice we will be loaded into a coach again and driven who knows where to do who knows what.

In the middle of one night, sleep deprivation psychosis hits me. I wake up in my uncomfortable camp bed to discover that while I have been asleep, terrible tricks have been played on me by the course helpers. My smart suit, hanging by my bed, has been removed and in its place they have left a diver's wetsuit. This can only be the preliminary to some terrible physical test that we are to be subjected to in the morning. But worse has happened. I look out of the opening of the tent and realise that the whole structure, with all eight of us in it, has been lifted up in the night and put down in a strange place far from where we went to sleep. This has been done, it seems clear to me, to disorientate us as a further test. I think "I should sound the alarm and wake everyone up so we can start dealing with this terrible situation right now." But I am exhausted so I decide that I simply cannot be arsed. I sink back into bed and fall asleep once more. Someone else can take charge in the morning.

But when the morning comes, it turns out that while I have been asleep the course helpers have visited us again. They have taken away the diving suit and brought back my smart set of clothes. What is more, they have returned the tent with all its sleepers to its original location.

I am very relieved that I did not sound the alarm in the middle of the night. I could have become the most unpopular of all the campers.

One evening the bell is rung for the outward bound trip. We dash to collect our sleeping bags and backpacks, put on our boots and assemble in the yard. Then we are told to disperse again. False alarm. Just another mindfuck.

Eventually the trip does take place. We set out by coach late in the evening and arrive in the middle of nowhere. We are led into a large cave where we are to spend the night. I unroll my sleeping bag on a slab of rock and sleep as best as I can. In the morning we are divided into smaller groups of six and sent in different directions. Each group has a set of instructions.

Our first instruction is to elect a leader. Over the course of the day, the group that I am in elects four leaders and deposes three. We are, it turns out, a highly dysfunctional set of six people. The most dysfunctional set of six people that the course leaders have ever come across.

In between our squabbling we find our way, with maps provided for us, to meeting points where we are met by professional outward bound personnel. They put us in canoes. They make us abseil down cliffs. They blindfold us and instruct us to crawl on our bellies through muddy obstacle courses. During this test our leader freezes in front of me and I spend fifteen minutes lying motionless in the mud with her boots a few inches from my nose.

She is the last of our leaders to be deposed.

****

The course participants have worked with each other before. We are well-versed in past life regression and quite used to people spontaneously re-enacting earlier lives. If there is such a thing as "past life psychosis", I experience it. At times my whole body seems physically inhabited by the forces of other lives. I seem to grow immensely tall and strong, or twisted and deformed. From powerful Roman centurion to hunchback dwarf in the Middle Ages, the lifetimes flow. In the febrile atmosphere of the course, this seems to be not much more unusual than drinking my morning mug of stimulant free Barley Cup.

One morning we are shown a film on a projector. It is a collection of highly graphic sex scenes. The film has been smuggled into the country in the luggage of the organisers to be used on the course. It includes scenes of copulation, sadomasochism and possibly – I cannot quite remember – even bestiality. This is intended to help us overcome our remaining sexual hang-ups.

Our outer selves are not ignored. Towards the end of the course we are introduced to three stylists who have been brought along for the day to give anyone who wishes it a makeover. In small groups various women disappear behind the scenes, to reappear transformed in expertly applied makeup and with newly styled hair. They look gorgeous. At this time I have long hair and a bushy beard. As I also wear glasses, there is actually very little of my face visible. Theresa challenges me over this, suggesting that it is part of my defences and that it prevents me from being open with people. She wants me to go off with the makeover elves. I resist this fiercely but she keeps prodding away at me until suddenly I think "What the hell!" I jump up and disappear behind the scenes where I am shorn of hair and beard. By an effort of will I manage to hold on to my moustache.

I like the transformation. I notice later, when I am back in the real world, that people do react to me differently, more openly. Perhaps they had found that mass of almost impenetrable dark brown hair and beard intimidating.

On the last evening there is a formal celebration supper. This is what the smart suits and dresses are for. A diver's wetsuit would have been thoroughly inappropriate.

****

Afterwards, when we have returned to normal life, most of us do feel more empowered, more assertive, as if we have really broken through certain personal barriers and blocks. Of course it is a moot point how long this lasts for each of us, how real any transformation is.

The course no longer exists, but if it did, I would recommend it. If nothing else, it would be a great deal more interesting than the average week's holiday in Malaga.

A year later I am invited to be one of the helpers in London at the beginning and end of the next course. I am instructed to dress rather formally and to wear at the opening meeting a pair of intimidating sunglasses. I am to play one of the stern unyielding guards.

I really enjoy playing this part. As it happens, the other guards rather let the side down by allowing their friendly feelings to overcome them, so I am fingered as the only real bastard in the room. Eight days later, when the group return to London after their ordeal, I can let the act drop and there is much joyful hugging and laughter.

Many people know of Philip Zimbardo's Stanford Prison Experiment, in which ordinary students apparently quickly became sociopathic when put in positions of power over others. This is supposed to occur through a process known as "deindividuation". The experiment has been held to show that within each of us an inner sociopath lurks just below the surface, waiting to emerge as soon as opportunity allows.

But doubt has been cast on Zimbardo's findings. According to the journalist Jon Ronson, all of the sociopathic behaviour in the "prison" was exhibited by only one of the student participants. Moreover, that participant has stated that he was play-acting throughout because he believed that this was what Zimbardo expected and wanted. The student reported that he had seen 'Cool Hand Luke' and had deliberately based his character on the Captain, the sadistic prison warden in that film.

So it seems just as likely that when given the opportunity to play a part, almost any part, some of us find that it is our inner thespian that has been liberated rather than our inner sociopath. This at least is what I like to think about my one delightful afternoon spent as a bully.

19. Among The Baptists

For some time I have a loose association with a group of Baptists. This is a somewhat uneasy alliance. On the one hand they value my psychological know-how and invite me occasionally to hold workshops on Transactional Analysis, Stress Management and Assertiveness. On the other hand, they know that I do not share their superstitious beliefs. Nevertheless, for a while we manage to rub along together.

One weekend I am staying at a retreat house with members of the group. Their leader Frank and I are in the kitchen doing the washing up together. He takes it as an opportunity to proselytise me. Eventually I lose patience, turn to him and say "Frank, can you really look me in the eye and tell me that I am going to burn in hell for all eternity because my beliefs are different to yours?"

He shuffles uncomfortably, looks at the floor and mutters "Well, of course none of us really know what will happen when we die."

I think but I am too polite to say "Ok, but that's not what your Church says."

One member of the Baptist group is an attractive raven haired woman, Tricia, the wife of a local minister. She is initially friendly to me, sharing many of my psychological interests. She has even done some training in psychotherapy herself. But she soon begins to suspect that I am of the devil's party as she senses the stench of the fiery pit about me.

Tricia arranges a talk on Anger Management for the Baptists, which I attend. The speaker is a depressed nervous looking woman with a dull washed-out energy. She seems to be trying to ward off despair. Everything she says encourages the unhealthy repression of angry feelings. None of it is about honesty and openness, or handling confrontation in a healthy and responsible way.

I ask her several questions. Each one irritates Tricia more than the last. Eventually I ask the depressed woman "What do you do with your own anger?"

She replies "I talk to God about it."

I say to her "And does that work for you?"

"Yes" she says. But she sounds utterly unconvincing.

Tricia glares malevolently at me and snaps that I have taken up too much time and that I should now give other people a chance to ask their questions. I shut up for a while but as no one else seems to have any questions I eventually continue. Tricia's look tells me that I have now made a permanent and probably dangerous enemy. For Tricia is a witch burner.

It is some time before I find out through talking to another member of the group, Jacqueline, that Tricia has been spreading the worst rumour about me that she has been able to concoct. But it is not that I roast and eat babies on the Sabbath, nor that I dance naked with the devil and consort with his minions. It is that I am that most dangerous of all people .....

..... a Buddhist!

I tell Jacqueline that this is a terrible slander and that I am most definitely not a Buddhist, although I consider myself at that time to be a bit Buddh-ish.

Shortly after this, the invitations to run workshops end.

****

One evening I am at a party with some of the Baptists. Donald, a man in his thirties whom I know slightly, decides to confide his heart's sorrow to me. Three years earlier his wife left him and now she has divorced him. He is beginning to get over his grief. In fact he has recently met a young woman whom he would like to ask out on a date. But there is a problem. According to his Baptist faith, once married is always married. Married unto death. And presumably beyond. He fears that if he starts a new relationship, this will anger God mightily, whereas what he desires is to be a delight unto God.

What a dilemma! Nestle in the warm arms of a fresh young lover, or please God.

Perhaps the phrase "false dichotomy" drifts through my mind. I cannot remember.

I ask Donald why he thinks that God would want him to be miserably alone and celibate for the rest of his life. I suggest that perhaps God might be pleased to see him in a loving relationship once more. This might even strengthen his faith.

My feeling is that as he does not really know whether he will displease or please God by taking a new lover, he may as well gamble on the second. This is my own version of Blaise Pascal's famous wager*, and to my mind it is a lot healthier than Pascal's original.

Donald brightens noticeably as I talk to him. I seem to be winning him over to a less toxic point of view. But then I notice Frank's baleful presence. He has been earwigging on our conversation and he has drawn close to join in. He fears that I may be seducing Donald to Satan's viewpoint.

Frank tells us that the minister of their own church has written a book about marriage and divorce. This book expresses

---

*Blaise Pascal suggests that it is safer for us to bet on the assumption that God does exist than that he does not, and to live our lives accordingly. If we do this and we turn out to be right, we gain paradise and avoid eternity in the fiery pit. If on the other hand we turn out to be wrong, we will merely have forgone a few trivial earthly pleasures such as coveting our neighbour's ox or his wife.

An intelligent teenager should be able to spot the numerous flaws in Pascal's argument so I will not trouble you with them here. But you can find them on the internet if you want to.

exactly what Donald fears. God wants us to stay faithful to our partner, no matter how faithless they may be to us. One wife or husband is enough for any good Baptist. If they happen to run off with the milkman or the milkmaid, we must accept this as part of God's plan and remain steadfastly alone till death. Our traitorous partner may have divorced us, but in God's eyes we are still married to them.

Donald's shoulders droop as Frank's poisonous theology falls around him like an ugly fog.

Ironically, Frank has himself been divorced and has remarried. But he patiently explains to us that he wedded his first wife before he became a Christian. So conveniently, in God's eyes and in his own, that initial marriage did not count. This seems to me to be an ingenious point of view and for a Baptist a somewhat Jesuitical position to take.

I give up and leave Donald to his self-imposed torture, slumped in a prison cell with the door wide open but unable to walk out of it into the clear light of day.

****

Some months later a friend of mine, a freethinker like myself, begins a relationship with a member of the group. One evening she and her new partner are invited to a dinner party. She finds herself sitting with seven other people, all of whom are Baptists.

Around the dinner table they start to discuss an absent friend of theirs who is also a Baptist. They are very worried about him. He appears to be straying from the path of Baptist rectitude. His attendance at church has become intermittent and he has started to voice doubts about his faith. There are other signs too that Satan might have him in his sulphurous grasp.

Finally one of the guests looks around the group and pronounces solemnly "You all know what the real problem is, don't you?"

The others look at him and wait. My friend too waits for the portentous revelation. When it comes it is this.

"He's started reading books, you know!"

But what most alarms my friend is that the other guests immediately nod and murmur their assent. They all know what is meant by this, that the devil lurks, waiting to seize the soul of anyone who opens up their mind to new ideas and to fresh thoughts that might threaten the old superstitions.

20. Smokey The Psychoanalytic Goat

I start smoking cigarettes at the age of eleven. Not regularly. Just when I can get my hands on them. When eventually I buy my first pack in Woolworths, I am terrified that I will be apprehended for being under age. But the ciggies are handed over without demur. No adult cares that I may be setting out on the road to emphysema or lung cancer.

I find the whole business of smoking fascinating and sensuously delightful. As it is designed to be. Oh, that lovely object of desire, the flip-top cigarette pack wrapped in cellophane, with its inner lining of silver foil. Almost as good as opening a Christmas present. Slender silver cigarette cases. Zippo lighters. Oval Passing Clouds. Black Balkan Sobranie with gold tips. Soft pack Gauloises that immediately confer on the smoker an aura of existentialism. The unique smell of the Paris Metro, a sublime mixture of Gitanes, underarm sweat and garlic, now alas lost forever. The everyday brands – Senior Service, Capstan Full Strength, Craven A. When times are hard, Players Number 6. "You're never alone with a Strand."

At various times I try pipes, even a clay pipe and a Kapp and Peterson Meerschaum, cigars and roll-ups. Making roll-ups is a serious and time-consuming business. Sometimes I use a machine consisting of two little rollers and a red belt on a metal frame, sometimes I roll by hand. Sometimes I use a strange tin box with rollers inside and a slit in the lid for the finished cigarette to pop up through. It looks more like a device for doing a magic trick than for bringing death closer in tiny increments.

I have a colleague, Pierre, an alcoholic Frenchman who claims to have been an officer in the Foreign Legion. His tales are so spectacular that this might just be true. He sits in the staff room at lunchtime endlessly making cigarettes using one of these tin boxes. He inspects each cigarette for faults before almost always disassembling it, putting the tobacco back in the tin and starting again. Only about one in ten of his cigarettes passes the Quality Control Department in his brain. This neurotic habit may have the virtue of considerably improving his health, for it leaves him little time in which to actually smoke.

I spend years more or less constantly in a state of "giving up smoking", "wanting to give up smoking", or "just having failed to give up smoking". One of my strategies is to "give up smoking" but cadge cigarettes off my friends. Every so often I suffer an attack of guilt and present them with multiple packs as payback. This actually seems to suit everybody concerned. Twice I give up smoking for over a year but, whatever I try, I inevitably drift back to my twenty a day.

A friend decides to train as a hypnotherapist. To complete her training she needs guinea pigs. She offers to give me two free sessions of anti-smoking therapy. What have I got to lose? Nothing, it turns out, but I have nothing to gain either. I lie on her floor in a light trance, listening to her suggestions that I no longer want to smoke. The sessions have no discernible effect on me. I leave her house and light up immediately, inhaling deeply. Ah, the satisfaction.

Then I hear about Vicky. Vicky is an American. She is from Kentucky but living with her English husband in a small town near to me. She offers an unusual anti-smoking therapy. It sounds bizarre but it will, she claims, have me off ciggies in two sessions. It seems to be vaguely transpersonal so I am immediately attracted to it. Once more I think "What have I got to lose?" apart, this time, from the cost.

Vicky's technique depends on discovering what my deepest psychological motive is for smoking. The theory that lies behind this is sometimes known as The Payoff Technique and it goes like this:- no matter how much we might declare that we want to give up some negative piece of behaviour, if we nevertheless continue to act in that way, we must be getting something out of it that we want. This is the payoff. So if we can somehow recognise what our ultimate reason is for engaging in this particular piece of destructive behaviour, we should be able either to give it up or to find a non-destructive way of achieving the same goal. This theory appeals to the therapist in me. Indeed, I have taught The Payoff Technique to many of my students.

I lie on Vicky's massage table in her darkened therapy room. She talks me through a relaxation process which involves me visualising myself walking down a stone staircase into a cellar. Once there, I relax onto what looks like a psychoanalytic couch and wait for my "spirit guide" to arrive. This will be the helper who will assist me in plumbing the depths of my own psychological cellar, or subconscious.

After a few moments I have the distinct impression that my guide has entered the cellar. He sits down in an old fashioned leather armchair immediately behind me, just as a traditional psychoanalyst might do. I turn my head to look at him.

I am surprised.

For my spirit guide turns out to be a huge goat. He is about the same size as a tall man. He has long off-white shaggy fur and a long shaggy beard. He has long curved horns. He looks remarkably like the devil when he is represented as a goat in traditional Christian illustrations, except that he is sitting with one furry leg crossed over the other in the armchair and he is somehow holding a note pad and a pencil ready to write down my psychoanalytic ramblings.

I shall call him Smokey The Goat. One of the most surprising things about Smokey is that from his fur smoke is actually rising. It curls around and drifts across the cellar like the smoke wafting from a score of cigarettes.

Smokey turns out to be a most empathic listener. For a goat. He pays me close attention and makes the occasional suggestion.

I am well-practised in passive-aggressive behaviour at this time and it becomes clear that my deepest reason for smoking is that it is my indirect way of telling virtuous, good and moralistic people to fuck off. This is my payoff. Like so many other people, I am smoking as a covert act of rebellion against "niceness".

Smokey asks me if I am prepared to give up this payoff. I tell him without hesitation that I am not. So he suggests that I ponder whether there might be a less self-destructive way of achieving the same end. I am stumped by this.

But then suddenly I have a brainwave.

"I know", I tell Smokey, "I can just tell them to fuck off directly!"

Smokey seems very pleased with this suggestion and indicates that the session is over. He gets up and leaves, smoke still rising from his furry coat.

I pay Vicky for the session and say goodbye. I walk to my car and clamber into the driving seat. Before I start the engine, I take out a pack of Embassy, withdraw a cigarette, admire its immaculate beauty, and light it with my Zippo. Then I inhale deeply.

I think "Well, that was a bloody waste of time and money!"

****

That evening my wife and I happen to be hosting a dinner party in our huge attic flat, part of a rambling country house in Kent. There are about eight of us sitting round the old pine kitchen table, eating and drinking and chewing the fat. Most are smoking. At the end of the evening, when the guests have all gone, I clear the table and pick up the two ashtrays, each of which has a pyramid of cigarette butts in it. It is only as I empty these into the waste bin that I realise that throughout the evening I have not smoked. What is more, I had not even realised that I was not smoking.

It is like a mini miracle. I do not feel that I have given up smoking, I feel that I am a non-smoker. That I have never smoked. That it has never been an issue. Thank you, Smokey.

I am so confident in my new status that I do not bother to go back to Vicky for my second session.

****

A year later I once again take up smoking. At the time I am a member of a student group which is doing a postgraduate training in Humanistic Psychology. The group is awash with niceness, virtue and good intentions. As usually happens in such cases, the few rebels act out their rebellious nature in a number of ways, one of which is smoking. In the tea breaks. Outside on the pavement. If need be, in the rain or snow. Smoking in the course room is naturally forbidden, for it would not be nice. Rebel groups usually contain the most interesting people, so I cannot bear to be excluded. Once more I reach for the John Player Specials.

Perhaps Smokey comes to me in a dream or whispers to me while I lie one evening in a hot bath. I cannot remember. But after a few weeks I do have the sense to go back to Vicky for my long-delayed follow-up session. I have never smoked again.

****

Postscript:- I have sometimes been asked since that time for Vicky's contact details by friends and acquaintances who want to give up smoking. Alas, shortly after my second visit her husband was promoted to a new job in America and she returned to Kentucky. I have lost contact with her. So if you want to give up smoking do not phone me or write to me about her. I cannot help. I can only suggest that perhaps you try making some kind of sacrifice to Smokey The Goat.

21. Shadow Night

*"She who bears her own shadow liberates
the collective."* Sylvia Brinton Perera

It is Tuesday evening and my co-tutor and I are sitting with our fifteen students in a circle. We are all wearing fancy dress.

Stephanie is wearing wellington boots, dungarees and a shapeless farmer's hat. She is holding a spade. Stephanie is extremely nice. She has an excess of middle class politeness but underneath this we sense a critical and disapproving energy. She has received a lot of feedback about this, which up to now she has been very resistant to. But this evening, as we go around the group and each person is given a chance to explain why they are dressed as they are, she says "I've come as a farmer so that I can shovel my shit."

Stephanie has "got it". For this is shadow night on the counselling training course that we run, the session where each of our students is invited to come dressed as a part of themselves that they normally reject. It is an opportunity for them to recognise and "own" a "disowned" part of themselves and hopefully to integrate it, so becoming more comfortable in their own skins.

Hilary, a winsome slender girl who trades on her sweetness, is wearing a bomber jacket and leather skirt, net stockings and stilettos. She has put on scarlet lipstick and vivid purple nail varnish. She is ostentatiously chewing gum with her mouth open. Johnny, our streetwise ex-heroin addict, is dressed like a city financier in suit and white shirt. He has on a tie, possibly for the first time in his life. Bob, a police sergeant, is wearing classic cartoon burglar's costume of striped shirt and eye mask. Jane, our socialist social worker, has on a rubber Margaret Thatcher mask.

133

One of the rules that my co-tutor and I impose on ourselves when we are running our counselling courses is that we never ask our students to do anything that we are not prepared to do ourselves. So every year on shadow night, we always dress up too. I am wearing a pair of old trousers held up with braces and a grubby shirt. I have a packet of fags in my rolled up shirt sleeve and a copy of 'The Sun' newspaper under my arm. I am "owning" the obnoxious bloke inside, the geezer who wolf-whistles at pretty girls as they pass by on the street. This is about as far from my public persona as I can get. My co-tutor, in leopard print skirt, bright red lipstick and equally bright red nail varnish, is "owning" her inner tart.

I am known by the students to be a bit of a political lefty myself. Later in the evening they challenge me good-humouredly to acknowledge my own inner Margaret Thatcher. Somewhat reluctantly I put on the Iron Lady's mask. I am then both intrigued and a little appalled at how easy it is for me to slip into her bombastic and patronising tones. I start bossing everyone around with great aplomb. I am even a bit reluctant to give up the mask when someone else wants to take their turn with it.

Only Edward has entirely missed the point. He has come dressed in Arabian costume, apparently simply because he likes it. He seems to have got the idea that the dressing up is an entirely random idea, just a bit of fun. Even by the end of the evening and after a lot of frustrated feedback from the group and the tutors, he shows little grasp if any of the concept of the shadow.

To my mind our greatest success with shadow night is Stephen. Stephen is a serious-minded, pleasant young man who is somewhat afflicted by belief in Christianity. He has a need to be virtuous and to behave responsibly and with maturity at all times. This gives him an over-solemn demeanour and a rather deadened energy. Spontaneity seems to be entirely unknown to him. He possesses some genuine wisdom, but this is contaminated by his self-conscious need to be nice. He has something of the air of an Edwardian curate about him. He never swears and he cannot quite hide his disapproval when others do, especially when it is we, the tutors, who are doing the swearing. He does not really "get" shadow night at the time, appearing in saintly robes which emphasise his persona – the part of himself which he wishes to project – even more than usual. Rather than taking off his mask, his public face, he seems to have attached it to himself even more firmly.

Stephen receives feedback from the group about this. It is impossible to tell whether he has taken it in or not, but the residential weekend is to take place a few days later, so we tell the group that they will have another opportunity then "to show your shadow to the group if you want to."

The following Saturday the group are gathering for their afternoon session in the huge sitting room of the country house where we are holding their residential. It is in a lovely setting on an organic farm in Kent, with extensive grounds where we can lead the group through shamanic chants and moving meditations, or simply take them on country walks. Various members of the group have taken the opportunity to dress up as another aspect of their shadow but Stephen has not yet appeared.

Then he walks in and takes his place in the semi-circle of comfortable old armchairs around the enormous open fire. He is wearing a tweed jacket and flannel trousers and looks, if anything, even more like an Edwardian curate than before. I am a little disappointed. But then I spot that he has pinned to his lapel a star-shaped badge that he has made out of cardboard. On it in bold letters is starkly printed the words "FUCK OFF."

Stephen has really "got it". This is a part of himself that he has kept heavily repressed till now. What is more, his energy seems genuinely to have shifted. On this afternoon, and for the rest of the course, he seems more alive and vibrant than he has ever been before.

****

Some years before this, my own introduction to shadow work is dramatic. It is early in the morning on the final day of an intensive self development weekend. I am standing, in a state of frozen terror, at the front of a room with about eighty people looking at me. We have all been meeting together on one evening a week for a couple of months, and this weekend workshop is the culmination of our course. Most of my fellow course participants are probably at this moment thinking "Shit or get off the pot!" The facilitator is also showing some signs of frustration so he may be thinking the same.

But I will do neither. I am paralysed by fear. I had woken early in the morning in an extremely anxious state, knowing that I had to face this moment but having no idea what "this moment" would be about. Now, as I look at the frustrated faces staring back at me, I still have no idea why I had to volunteer myself in this way. But I suspect that this is roughly how it felt to be the entertainment of Romans just before the lions and tigers were released.

Suddenly the facilitator has a stroke of genius. He cuts off my stuttering and incoherent words which no one, including myself, can make any sense of. Firmly he says "Right! I want you to point at every person in this room that you have an issue with."

Hesitantly I point at someone. He orders them out of their seat and onto the stage, which is behind me. I point at someone else and he does the same. By the time that I have worked my way around the room, twelve people are lined up on the stage. They are wondering what is going to happen next and so am I.

The facilitator leads me up the steps onto the stage and stands me in front of the line. "Now" he says "I want you to stand in front of each person and tell them exactly what your issues are with them. No holding back!"

There is nothing to be done but to obey. I start at the beginning of the line. Schooled as I have been by my upbringing in the ways of passive-aggressive behaviour, and well-versed as I am in the practice of evasion and avoidance, this is the first time in my life that I have "told it straight" to a dozen people. Within a few seconds I am revelling in the experience of genuine free speech. Nine people receive my negative feedback, without flinching or rancour. Three people hear of my admiration, even love for them. This positivity is, to my surprise, the more difficult for me to voice.

No one reacts badly. The ceiling does not fall in. The poisonous pedagogues from my past who had schooled me so throughly in passive-aggression do not rise through the floor or enter from the wings to carry me off to hell.

I feel empowered. I sit down. It will still be a while before I eliminate the habit of passive-aggression altogether from my behavioural repertoire, but at least I have made a beginning. And I will always feel grateful to that facilitator and to those twelve people.

****

Now, after more than thirty years of exploring myself and helping others to explore themselves through "spiritual" and psychotherapeutic pathways, I am still uncertain in many cases about what is effective and what is not effective in helping us to feel more comfortable in our own skins. But a few things stand out as likely to make a significant difference. Shadow work is one of these. The less we recognise, acknowledge and "own" the parts of ourselves that we feel uncomfortable with, the more discontented we tend to be. The more we reclaim those parts and integrate them, the more relaxed in ourselves we tend to become. I have been professionally trained not to give advice, but on this occasion I will afford myself the luxury of writing this:- whenever you get the opportunity to shake hands with your own shadow, it is a good idea to take it.

22. The Shaman Of Sheen

I am lying on a massage table in the sitting room of an unexceptional house in West London. Various crystals have been placed on parts of my body which, I have been told, relate to my major chakras. Sam is sitting on a stool beside me. He is passing his hands over me without touching me and removing from my etheric body the shadowy remains of other crystals that were placed there many years ago when I was an inhabitant of Atlantis.

Apparently I have lived with the curse of these Atlantean crystals for many lifetimes. They have prevented me from fulfilling my potential in important areas of my life. For example, they explain my present inability to find good fortune in love. They also explain "the wall of negative karma" which Sam assesses will take him another four months or so to clear. To help with this process, he teaches me how to visualise making an intergalactic journey. Every night, before I go to sleep, I must leap onto the moon and then, using that as a jumping off point, onto Mars and then out into the stars. By the time I have practised this for two weeks, it has gained an inner reality which seems almost convincing, almost more than imagination. Almost. But not quite.

I am paying Sam a small fortune for this New Age therapy. It is a long drive from where I live to his suburban house, so I have elected to have two full priced sessions on each visit. No discounts. Together, the two sessions take little more than an hour, including the pleasant chat we have beforehand about trivialities, such as which exotic holiday island he has most recently been to with his girlfriend. I think "Yes, I paid for a good part of that holiday." A friend of mine disapproves of my visits. To her I ruefully say "I know. I could be buying a small new car for the money that I'm giving to Sam."

Yet I keep making the lengthy traffic-snarled journey to see him.

The fact is that I am going through a very rough period in my life. I have recently been divorced. I only see my children at weekends and in the holidays. I spend much of my time in a state of low-level depression, punctuated every so often with a few days of mild mania. "My life" I tell friends "moves from ecstasy to despair, from grandiosity to collapse." Unfortunately, each month consists of about three and a half weeks of despair and only three or four days of ecstasy.

I am reluctant to take antidepressants because I believe that it is healthier to work through uncomfortable feelings than to suppress them. For a few days I do swallow down a "natural" remedy for depression, St John's Wort. Then I stop taking it, not because it does not work, but because it works too well. It removes my depression but it also removes my affect, my ability to experience any kind of feeling. I realise that I would rather feel miserable than feel nothing at all.

My existing prejudices against antidepressants are confirmed by the following incident. I have a friend who is instructed by her employer's company doctor to take Prozac. If she refuses, she might lose her sickness benefits. Although she is off work and being treated for depression, she has recently become engaged to be married. After a few months I ask her how she has got on with the doctor's little pills. She says "Well, I put on a huge amount of weight and completely lost my libido." This is only a few weeks before her wedding. "I was depressed before I took Prozac, so you can imagine how much more depressed I got while I was taking it!"

She stops taking the pills and damns the consequences.

Then I watch a TV documentary. It is about a doctor in a small town in America who believes that almost everyone should be taking Prozac because this will make their lives happier and more fulfilled. He has already prescribed it to quite a large number of the townsfolk but he does not yet feel that his work is finished. When patients visit his consulting room, he shows them a flip chart with various questions written on it. If they answer "Yes" to one or more of the questions, he recommends to them that they take Prozac.

The questions include ones like these:-

"Do you ever feel unhappy?"

"Do you ever feel unfulfilled."

"Do you ever feel that life could offer you more than it does?"

The documentary goes on to allege that Prozac is linked to an increased risk of suicide and to acts of extreme violence.

I am delighted to read some time later that the doctor has been officially disciplined for his profligacy with these little pills.

Because of the rigours of the journey to Sam's house, the cost involved and the evanescent nature of any benefits, I sometimes feel like terminating the therapy. But each time that I determine to do this, some phenomenon occurs which makes me feel that something "real" is happening and that it is worth it for me to continue. Once, for example, as I lie on Sam's massage table, I have the distinct feeling that my "consciousness" is not aligned with my physical body. It is as if from my shoulders upwards "I" am lying partly outside my body and at an angle to it. As Sam performs whatever jiggery-pokery he is up to, "I" slide back into my body with a sense of comfort and relief.

I have no idea what to make of this. Moreover I know that, despite whatever stories I, you or anyone else could make up about it, it lies in the realm of the unknowable.

The fact is that amongst the misery of my life at this time, on the days that I visit Sam I simply feel good. Something about the Shaman of Sheen is indubitably healing, at least for me. Nevertheless I cannot help noticing that the time frame for the termination of my therapy keeps shifting. Every time that we approach the end date, it turns out that Sam has discovered more secrets, developed more processes and is able to offer me more spiritual goodies. There are always more entities to be released, curses to be lifted, demons to be exorcised and higher planes of being to be explored.

Moreover, there are hints of conspiracy theory beginning to emerge in Sam's colourful descriptions of what he is doing and I am highly resistant to conspiracy theories. In fact I have two rules for dealing with conspiracy theorists:-

Rule One:- I will not enter into discussion with conspiracy theorists.

Rule Two:- I will not discuss with conspiracy theorists why I will not enter into discussion with them.

The reason for Rule One is that there is no point. The reason for Rule Two is that if someone does not understand why Rule One exists, it is probably because their head is already stuck firmly down the rabbit hole. In that case I have no wish to talk to their waggling white-tailed arse.

Nevertheless, I have a friend who has a framed photograph of David Icke hanging in his sitting room. But either in deference to me, or more probably to make a not very subtle ironic point, he turns its face to the wall whenever I visit him.

So the time comes when I say goodbye to Sam. If I had not, I might still be seeing him to this day. And I might still be driving a very old car. In fact more than twenty years later a friend of mine who knows Sam tells me that he is still discovering more entities to purge and chakric curses to lift. He even now has around him a group of acolytes, some of whom have been going to see him to have their Atlantean spectres removed for over twenty five years. And the conspiracy theories have grown much thicker.

****

Some time later I go with a friend to see Ted in a small terraced house off the Seven Sisters Road in London. Ted is a Native American shaman who is visiting England at the invitation of the owner of the house. He is offering a weekend workshop on shamanism, but I and my friend have decided not to sign up for this. We have chosen instead each to have an individual session of healing with him. He has been highly recommended to us by one of my students.

We are shown into a tiny front room and asked who would like to see Ted first. My friend's needs seem much more serious than my own, so she is taken into the shamanic consulting room next door while I sit down in a shabby armchair to wait my turn. I notice that above my head, suspended from a hook in the ceiling, is a small pyramid made of copper tubing with a few crystals hanging from it by thread.

I suddenly feel unaccountably tired. I shut my eyes and almost immediately fall into a deep, deep state of meditation.

After about twenty minutes I come to, feeling hugely refreshed and highly alert. So by the time that it is my turn to be taken in to see Ted, I am so full to the brim with healing energy that there is simply no room for any more. I lie on Ted's massage table, now under a much bigger copper tubing pyramid. It has large crystals hanging from it, some of them wound round with copper wire. A crystal wand is placed into my hand. More crystals are laid on my chest and Ted begins his shamanic work. And it is the works! He dances and prances around me. He emits guttural grunts. He chants and waves feathers and a smudge stick over me and shakes a rattle near my ears. He bangs his shamanic drum. The air is thick with the scent of burning sage.

I feel nothing. My chakras have already been washed clean by my sit-down in the front room. Today all the healing that could possibly take place has already happened.

Nevertheless I thank Ted, pay him and leave feeling very satisfied.

A few months later, with the same friend, I visit Dan in Herne Bay. Dan is another visiting shaman and like Ted, he is a genuine Native American. I have already attended a public talk that Dan has given. It is stupefyingly boring so in the tea break I mutter an excuse and leave. Nevertheless, one sunny afternoon finds my friend and I drinking tea in the sitting room of the sea side bungalow where he is staying, for we have each booked a one-to-one session with him. This is a measure of the immense inner discontent that we both feel with life at this time. Each of us is desperate and we will try almost anything.

The bungalow belongs to Sheila, the girlfriend of Dan's English pal John, who is sitting on the sofa next to him. John is sharp-tongued and unkind to Sheila's twelve year old son, but Dan is amiable and pleasant. After some social niceties and cake, he takes us into the conservatory and sits us down. He lights a cigarette, takes a few drags on it and then rests it on the side of an ashtray on the floor. He sits back and watches the smoke as it curls towards the ceiling. He is, he indicates, waiting for a sign. Eventually it comes. The smoke weaves about and then wafts unmistakably towards my friend. "Right" says Dan, pointing at her. "You first." He ushers her into the consulting room.

Although my own session with Dan is so insignificant that I can remember nothing about it, I am impressed by the cigarette trick. In fact at this time I am impressed by any kind of augury. One of the things that I find most seductive about shamanism is that it can make even the most trivial event seem portentous. Stepping outside our front door, we find a white feather on the path. Surely it must signify something significant about our life, some lesson that the Universe is trying to teach us. We ignore it at our peril.

****

One weekend I attend a workshop run by an American woman who is a shaman. It is held in a posh hotel in Kensington. Through a process of heightened awareness that she is to induce in us, she will be able to train us as therapists within the shamanic system of her medicine lodge in only a couple of days. Of course we know that the original shamans of the Americas underwent a considerably longer period of training than this, but we allow our Western egos to be flattered by her offer. Many years later I still have the certificate that she awarded me. Of all the certificates and diplomas that I possess, it is the most impressive looking. It has a big gold seal on it. It is also the one for which I had to do the least amount of training.

Towards the end of the weekend, she leads us through a visualisation designed to reveal to us our Native American shamanic name. As I lie on the floor and follow her instructions, my mind becomes like a cinema screen. This is most unusual for me. The screen reveals a stage. Onto this stage comes, high-stepping and with linked arms, swinging elegant canes in a coordinated fashion, a troupe of brown bears. Then in front of them a larger bear appears. He is wearing a top hat, which he doffs as he gracefully traverses the stage with nimble feet.

And so I add another spiritual name to the ones that I have already collected on my journey.

I am to be Richard Dancing Bear.

23. Synchronicity

It is not one of the most noble episodes in my life. I am having an affair with a married ex-student.

It is clear throughout the year while I am teaching her that there is some kind of sparkle between us. Nothing overt happens, but one evening towards the end of her course she turns up at college in her motorcycle helmet just as I am leaving after one of my classes. She is carrying a package which she holds out to me, saying "I've just come to hand in the last assignment that I owe you." We both know that this is a heavily coded act, that she could just as easily have left the piece of work in my pigeonhole, that she has had to study my timetable assiduously to determine that I will be here at this precise time on this precise evening.

So I invite her over to the pub across the road for a drink.

Nothing definite is established at this time, but I notice at the end-of-course meal in a Chinese restaurant that she makes sure that she sits next to me. At one point she rests her hand on my arm in a way which is not appropriate for a student with her tutor. I find that I do not mind. Later, when photographs are being taken, she positions herself next to me. I still have two of those photographs. I am standing in the centre of a group of four women. My arms are around the shoulders of two of them. It is not difficult to determine which is the object of my desire. Nor from the look on her face that I am the object of hers.

As soon as the course is over, my rather lax ethical standards allow me to phone her to discover whether we might like to meet up. But before I can do this, she phones me and invites me out for a drink. We meet on a sunny evening in Regents Park and in an astonishingly short time we are involved in a headlong affair.

We make plans. She will leave her husband and we will live together.

She is slender, beautiful and sensitive. Unfortunately her husband is a thuggish brute. I see a photograph of him and a warning shiver passes through me. I think "Beauty and The Beast". He is thickset with cold eyes and a drooping moustache that makes him look like a member of a Mexican drugs cartel.

Somehow he is on to us. We engineer a trip to Paris together, where we stay with her sister. We take a trip to Versailles, where another sister earns a living with her boyfriend squeezing orange juice for the tourists. It is a good living. They work for six months of each year and travel around the world for the other six. But on our way back to the city we learn from her Parisian sister that her husband is following her over. We have to change our plans pronto.

Looking back, I do not know how we could have thought that our plans would ever come to fruition. Love is blind. In more ways than one.

One day her husband tries to break into my apartment and attack me with a tyre lever.

In these long ago days I am not averse to seeking psychic counsel in times of trouble. But I am most choosy about whom I will go to. Not to any old psychic hoi polloi. I have been before to one of the most renowned psychics in England. He is regarded as the "psychics' psychic". Let us call him Sebastian.

I have been told the following story about Sebastian. He is invited to give the keynote address at a conference of psychics. Everything is being recorded. On the tape afterwards, the introduction by the master of ceremonies can be clearly heard. So can Sebastian's footsteps as he walks across the stage to the microphone. But as he gets closer, a crackling starts. It continues throughout his speech, making it wholly inaudible on the recording. Then, as he leaves the stage, the crackling fades and voices can be heard once more.

Sebastian's psychic aura is so strong that it has temporarily fucked the recording equipment.

I am apt at this time so long in the past to be mightily impressed by such stories. For some reason it reminds me of another story that a Buddhist friend has told me. He is at a public meeting which is being held in Birmingham to host the Dalai Lama. Everyone is of course entranced by His Holiness. Everyone that is except for one man who seems strangely disaffected. He interrupts. He asks awkward questions. He is disruptive. He is to put it bluntly a pain in the arse. At the end of the meeting, as he leaves the building and walks down the steps in the rain, he slips, falls and breaks his arm. My friend tells me smugly that he himself witnessed this event.

Karma? Synchronicity? Coincidence?

I would like to consult Sebastian about my present sorrow. Urgently. Immediately. But there is a problem. Sebastian is so much in demand that the waiting time for an appointment with him is usually at least a month. By then it might be too late. Another tyre lever might have been wielded and this time it might have connected with my skull.

His appointments are arranged for him by a weird old woman, with the meetings taking place in her apartment in a multi-storey block in Swiss Cottage. She looks as much like a witch as anyone I have ever met, but she is a kindly soul. On one occasion she cures my young daughter of tummy ache.

On the off-chance I call her. On the off-chance. Knowing it is hopeless. She picks up the phone. I explain to her that I would like to see Sebastian. As soon as possible.

"It's strange that you've called right now" she says. "I've just had a phone call from someone who's cancelled his appointment for tomorrow morning. If you can come then, you can have his place."

Karma? Synchronicity? Coincidence?

The next day I am sitting in the darkened lounge of her

apartment with Sebastian. He talks about everything under the sun except what is so much on my heart and mind. He gives me thirty minutes of a psychic reading which is almost sublimely irrelevant to my concerns. At one point he recommends that I take up gardening. Oh, the banality.

Finally he asks "Do you have any questions?"

Now is my one and only chance. I briefly outline the situation to him. Of course I include the tyre lever.

Sebastian looks at me seriously and presses his finger tips together in his mannered way. He speaks slowly and insistently, emphasising each of the following words:-

"If you do not leave this affair alone, you will become an old man before you have finished being a young man."

My blood freezes.

But I am stubborn and love is sometimes deaf, dumb and blind. I still cannot quite make up my mind. We are even now finding ways to meet, my ex-student and I.

About two weeks after my meeting with Sebastian, a friend of mine has an appointment with her dentist. His surgery is in Rochester, a pleasant drive from my home. My friend and I have a habit of going on jaunts together so she asks me if I would like to come along. Not so that I can sit in the dentist's waiting room with her, but so that we can have coffee and cake and a good natter after her teeth have been seen to. The centre of Rochester is an island of Dickensian themed charm in a great sea of urban deprivation and poverty. The plan is that I will wander around this "village" area on my own and meet up with her in a cafe after the great drilling has taken place.

I drop her off at her dentist and park my car. I walk down Rochester's picturesque main street. Then I do something uncharacteristic. I wander into a newsagent and start browsing the papers on the news stand. I never usually take any interest in local newspapers, but something about the front page of the 'Rochester Echo', 'Chronicle' or 'Times' – I do not remember the exact title – catches my eye.

For almost the only time in my life, I buy a local paper. I take it to a cafe, order a coffee and sit down. The main story on the front page is about a local tragedy. An attractive woman has left her husband and moved in with her lover. One evening they pull up in their car outside their new home after going to the cinema together. Another car pulls up behind them. The woman's husband gets out of it holding a shotgun. He walks to the passenger side of their car and fires through the window, killing his wife. He then walks round to the driver's side, where the lover is jumping out of the car. The husband tries to fire the shotgun at him, but it jams. The lover wrestles the gun away from him.

When the police interview the husband, he claims that he followed the couple merely to talk to them. It was, he says, the lover who threatened him with a shotgun. They struggled and it went off, accidentally killing his wife.

Unsurprisingly neither the police nor the jury believe him. He is convicted of her murder.

There is a large photograph of the husband on the front page of the newspaper. Something about him seems terribly familiar. He is a thuggish, brutish clean shaven man. I take out a pen and onto his face I draw a drooping moustache.

Now he looks like a member of a Mexican drugs cartel. Now he is the spitting image of my lover's husband.

At that time, I do not know whether or not I believe in psychics. But I sure as hell believe in synchronicity.

I make a clean break.

24. A Pilgrimage

I am at a particularly low point in my life. It is summer time, so I take myself off on a pilgrimage to the West Country. Somehow, I feel, this might be healing.

I start by driving to the southern tip of Cornwall, where I have booked myself in for a weekend stay at a lovely country house. It usually hosts personal development courses and themed retreats, but for a few days it is available for those who just want to hang out and cool out. This period free of any meaningful endeavour is sandwiched between a shamanic week on death which has just ended and a tantric sex workshop which has yet to begin. Thanatos and Eros. When I arrive and get out of my car, the gardener is staring disconsolately at his vegetable patch. Apparently, the wannabe shamans were required to dig their own graves and lie in them for the whole of one night. Some of them exceeded their allotted burial space and encroached on his beds of parsnips and leeks. He is not a happy bunny. Nor right now is he favourably disposed towards shamanism.

I am hoping that I will meet some nice people over the weekend, perhaps even a beautiful and sensitive woman with whom I can drive off into the sunset. But although it has been advertised in alternative magazines, the weekend has proved remarkably unpopular. There are only two other punters and I manage to have a spat with them in the kitchen within half an hour of my arrival.

Kate and Tessa are both students, training in psychodynamic psychotherapy. I am a lecturer, training students in humanistic therapy. At this time, these two approaches to healing wounded psyches are virtually at war with each other. By the time I have taken my first sip from the mug of tea that I have made, Kate and Tessa are expressing outrage at me. This is because I do not agree with them that clients must work through their issues in chronological order, starting with their earliest childhood traumas. It has always seemed more sensible to me to deal with what the client feels is important, rather than what the theories of the therapist assert should be important. But Kate and Tessa view my opinion as highly irresponsible, heretical and probably even dangerous. I get the impression that they would like to report me to my accrediting body, but alas I do not belong to one.

Having pissed off Kate and Tessa, I spend the rest of the weekend mooching about the place, taking a few walks, reading and visiting the fogou, an Iron Age underground chamber in the grounds of the house. As I am packing up my car to leave on Monday morning, the tutors for the tantric sex workshop arrive. They try to recruit me as a participant on their course, explaining to me that I do not need to have a partner in order to enrol. I suppose this means that I can have tantric sex with myself. But I do not much like the look of them so I manage to scarper before their groupies fetch up at the house and the tantric sex shenanigans begin.

I head up the north Cornish coast to Tintagel. My plan is to stay there for one night while trying to ignore the Arthurian claptrap. However, Tintagel surprises. It is true that there are Camelot-themed horrors here. You can buy a Queen Guinevere Burger at the local cafe and get a drink in the Excali-Bar of The Castle Hotel. There are probably Sir Launcelot Pasties and slices of Sir Gawain And The Green Knight Carrot Cake to be found too. Tintagel Castle, said by some to be a residence of King Arthur, cannot fail to disappoint, consisting as it does of a few old stones sticking up through some tussocks of grass. A tourist couple stops me and asks me if that really is the "castle" they have come all the way from America to see. When I say "Yes, I'm afraid it is", the look on their faces borders on grief.

Perhaps they were expecting a Disney King Arthur Experience with holographic knights jousting to win the favour of medieval damsels. Or maybe they just hoped to see a few standing walls.

But as I said, Tintagel surprises. In fact Tintagel is quite magical. A village sitting on top of a cliff overlooking the Atlantic, all the Camelot tat in the world cannot overcome its enormous charm. I book myself into a guest house on Atlantic Road, intending to stay for one night. But I stay for two. Then three. Eventually it is more than a week before I can bring myself to leave. In the back garden of the guest house there is a caravan with a hippy couple living in it. They visited Tintagel intending to stay for a week two years ago and are still here. It seeps into you, this village. It draws you in and it does not want to let you go.

I hang out at the local rock shop and eventually I am taken by a hugely expensive quartz crystal. The bewhiskered old geezer behind the counter spins some story about secret knowledge from Atlantis being embedded in the cloudy impurities within it. I ignore the story but buy the crystal anyway. The hippies at the guest house give me healing and spin a story about my karma and future fate. I ignore the story but feel better for the healing anyway. I walk up to St Materiana's Church at the top of the cliff. I ignore the Christianity but delight in the atmosphere anyway. I decide that one day I would like my ashes to be scattered from this cliff.

Eventually I am able to draw myself away from Tintagel. I still feel wounded by the buffetings of life so I head for Glastonbury where I think that I may be able to find more healing. I am intending to stay at a guest house run by a woman whom I know slightly from courses that we have done together. Both the guest house and the woman have lovely spiritual names, so here I will call them The Bhodi Tree Guest House and Shakti respectively. But when I arrive in Glastonbury, the guest house is full. So instead I fetch up at a solid traditional farmhouse, with a solid traditional farmer's wife serving full English breakfasts. These breakfasts turn out to be blissful and very healing. Later I find out that I have not just had a lucky escape from muesli and alfalfa sprouts. It seems that Shakti has plunged much further into the vortex of spiritual madness since I last saw her. I am told that she has been leading parties of the innocent and the bemused to join hands and circle Glastonbury Tor at dawn, apparently in some kind of attempt to levitate it. No significant signs of physical ascension have been detected, but it may have risen an inch or two on the auric level.

One of my hopes in Glastonbury is that I will be able to meditate in isolation at the top of the Tor. Some recurring thought has lodged in my brain that this will help my progress back to psychic good health. I realise that I will have to overcome my natural laziness and get up very early one morning in order to do this. I climb the Tor in persistent drizzle and sit, wrapped in my rainproofs, outside St Michael's Tower at the top. I meditate for half an hour with the rain dripping off my Gortex hood. Just as I am finishing I hear the voices of the first tourists of the day arriving.

Glastonbury Tor, like Glastonbury itself, seems to me to be a place of both darkness and light. As I sit down to meditate, I am aware that St Michael's Tower, as well as providing me with a convenient back rest, is also more dramatically the location of the disembowelling, hanging and quartering of Bishop Richard Whiting. After the dissolution of the monasteries Bishop Whiting insisted on remaining a Papist and thereby seriously annoyed Henry VIII's enforcer, Thomas Cromwell, with results which could easily have been predicted.

Superstition abounds in Glastonbury. Shakti's attempts to elevate the Tor are founded on centuries of irrational belief. It is held by some that Joseph of Arimathea visited Glastonbury shortly after the death of Jesus, carrying with him the holy grail. There he thrust his staff into the ground, where it miraculously grew into a thorn tree. The first account of his visit did not appear until about a thousand years after this supposed event, and the first report of the miracle of the thorn tree was not made till centuries after that. Nevertheless, the story drew many pilgrims to Glastonbury, substantially increasing the income of the priests. Lamentably it is still taken seriously by some who should know better today. Its monetary value to The Church has probably over the years at least been equal to that of a saint's wizened and blackened finger housed in a bejewelled silver reliquary.

To match its atmosphere of both darkness and light, Glastonbury has two holy and healing wells, one in a dark Victorian "temple", one in a bright airy garden. I visit both and then set about finding more healing for myself. I am carrying with me a piece of paper with a phone number on it given to me by a friend. I ring the number and book myself in for a session with June, a woman who offers Aura-Soma colour therapy. She has a collection of bottles, each with two coloured oils in them. Something about the viscosity of the oils prevents them from mixing together. I have to choose the bottle with the colours that most appeal to me, then lie on June's massage table while she does her magical stuff. I have no idea why, but the forty minutes that I spend with June feel immensely therapeutic to both my body and my psyche. I book another session for the following day. And then the next. And then the next after that. I spend my evenings attending meetings with titles such as Cleansing The Chakras With Tibetan Singing Bowls, Meditating From The Heart and The Coming Earth Changes With Shri Shanti Dev (actually an English bloke from Nottingham). By the time that I head back to London I really do feel that my psyche has been cleansed of some of the garbage that it contained when I set out on my pilgrimage a few weeks earlier.

****

A year or two later I return to Tintagel with a friend. We have not booked a place to stay in advance, so we decide to investigate The Castle Hotel. This is an immense building overlooking the sea from the cliff top at the the very end of Atlantic Road. The only way to get further from the village is along the cliff top path. This is the same path from which, I was told, a hiker fell to his death during my first visit to Tintagel.

The Castle Hotel is a magnificent building. It looks like an actual castle, or a crenellated fort. Unfortunately, as we approach it we see in its right-hand corner a neon sign over a side entrance which really does read The Excali-Bar. Nevertheless we go in through the main entrance with hope in our hearts for two nice single rooms and a bit of Cornish luxury.

At that time, many years ago, the horrors that we find within are difficult to describe. Imagine an infernal mixture of The House Of Usher with the Adams Family's ancestral home. A mouldering Gothic abyss out of Edgar Allen Poe. I can almost hear the tell-tale heart beating from beneath the worn and faded carpets. Are those blood stains that I can see?

Ok, I am of course exaggerating for dramatic effect, but nevertheless, within a few seconds I have decided that I cannot possibly stay here. However, politeness insists that we allow the ancient shambling lackey behind the desk, whose name is probably Igor, to come out and lead us down the dismal corridors to view a couple of equally dismal bedrooms.

Being English, I say "We'll think about it and get back to you" rather than the more honest and forthright "I'd rather chew my left leg off than stay a single night in this hotel." We make for the door as fast as is commensurate with a measure of politeness and book ourselves in to the nice guest house that I had stayed at on my previous visit. Though the gentle hippies with their caravan have moved on, the breakfasts are as good as ever.

A few years after that I return to Tintagel again, this time with my girlfriend. We are staying in a cottage on the outskirts of the village and of course I feel that I must introduce her to the horrors of The Castle Hotel shortly after our holiday begins. It will provide a low point against which everything else will seem magnificent in comparison.

As we walk across the car park, the first thing that I notice is that The Excali-Bar has gone. Surely a good sign. We enter the lobby. Igor has gone too. So has the smell of mould. The hotel has been smartened up and there has been a name change too. It is now The Camelot Castle Hotel. Although it could still do with a few more quid being spent on it, it has at least had a hair cut, a shave and a new suit. It has scrubbed up well and is looking quite presentable. You would not mind introducing it to your mother.

We take the plunge and order tea in the huge lounge. We sink into comfortable armchairs and enjoy the views of the sea.

Then some oddities start to become apparent. On the coffee table there are a few copies of a strange in-house newspaper which prints "positive news" only. One edition has on its front page a photograph of the Hollywood actor Nicholas Cage. Standing next to him with his arm around Cage's shoulders is one of the owners of the hotel. The accompanying story announces that Cage is delighted with his visit to Camelot Castle, though to my mind in the picture he seems to be in a state of shock. My projection, probably.

Then we notice that on the walls of the lounge there are a number of huge paintings. They have equally huge price tags. Some of them are over £1,000,000. To my eyes, and in all fairness I should acknowledge that I know little about art and I offer this judgement entirely as an untutored personal opinion and not as an art critic, they are staggeringly awful. There are a lot of washed out spiritual colours. There is a great deal of pink. Many of them have a butterfly motif. Accompanying literature announces that the artist, the very same hotel owner who to me looks as if he might have taken Nicholas Cage hostage, is being acknowledged by increasing numbers of art critics as the world's greatest living artist. Not Tintagel's. Not Cornwall's. Not Great Britain's. The world's.

It turns out that the hotel has been taken over by a holy trinity of Scientologists. This might possibly explain Cage's presence there. He was, after all, briefly married to a Scientologist, so perhaps he actually has nothing but happy memories of his time spent at Camelot Castle. Nevertheless, because some people allege that Scientologists can be both extremely litigious and vicious, I am not going to name the artist-owner here. I shall simply call him Artist A. Of course if you would like to know his actual name, you will be able to find it quite quickly on the internet and there is nothing that I can do to prevent you. On your own head be it.

More literature on the coffee table tells us that Artist A has also invented a marvellous device called The Light Box. Accompanying comments from members of the public attest that witnessing The Light Box may be a life changing event, perhaps even both transformative and transcendental in its nature. Artist A may be available, we read, to demonstrate his unique invention personally.

Our interest is piqued. We go to the reception desk to find out when we can view The Light Box. As luck would have it, we are told, Artist A is free at this moment and will be with us in a trice.

Artist A appears and jovially ushers us through a door and down some stairs into a basement corridor festooned with ducts and pipes. As the door closes behind us we realise with a shudder that *no one in the world knows that we are here*. If we fail to return, *it will be as if we have disappeared into the Cornish mist*.

Artist A conducts us down the long corridor, which is lined with many more of his peculiar paintings, to a room at the very end. There he asks us to sit down. Then he inexplicably produces a guitar. Before we can see the marvellous device, he tells us, he wishes to sing us a love song. One that he himself has composed.

If embarrassment could kill, I would not be writing these words right now. But as it cannot, we survive the singing of the amorous lyrics and are led into the room where The Light Box is waiting to transport us to a plane of transcendental bliss.

It turns out to be a rather ordinary box in fact, somewhat large, resting on the floor and covered in what may be black carpet tiles. It is actually rather difficult to see because the whole room is very dark, with blackout curtains on the tiny windows. If we are to be hacked to pieces in a bloody Cornish slaughter, this surely is where it is going to happen.

But Sam Peckinpah's 'Straw Dogs' has lodged in my brain too vividly. I can offer a few criticisms of Artist A, but he is not a mad axeman. In some ways he seems to me to be almost sweetly naive. He sits us down again, produces one of his paintings from a large stack, places it on top of the marvellous device and flicks a switch. Light emanates from a slit in the top of the box and illuminates the sickly pink picture from beneath. Artist A wants to know what we think. We make disingenuous noises intended to indicate a measure of some kind of ill-defined pleasure, though to be truthful this experience seems to me to be neither life changing nor transformative nor even transcendental.

Perhaps the word "overclaiming" drifts through my consciousness at that moment. I cannot remember.

Artist A's stack of paintings is very large. And he is not going to miss any out. We get quite fed up with mouthing "Ooo, that's nice ….." in a variety of different ways. But politeness dictates …..

When Artist A has shown us the last painting I experience a measure of relief, but it turns out that the show is not yet over. He intends to display each of them to us again so that we can say which is our favourite. My girlfriend has always been a shade brighter and a bit more quick thinking than me, so as the fourth painting is hoisted back onto The Light Box she hurriedly says "That one!" I catch on to what she is up to and leap in with "That's strange! It's my favourite too!"

Artist A now makes us an astonishingly generous offer. The asking price for that painting, he tells us, is £3,000. But if we close the deal right now, he can let us have it at a fraction of its price.

A tenth to be precise. £300.

The events of the last hour have turned my brains to goo. I feel paralysed and I can think of nothing to say. But my girl-friend (brighter and more quick thinking than me, remember) immediately says "We're going to be in the area for a few more days so we'll think about it and get back to you."

If there is going to be an axe murder, surely it must be now. But no. Artist A seems to take no offence whatsoever. Instead he is quite charming to us as he ushers us up the stairs and back into the hotel lobby. He shakes our hands warmly as we leave.

No hard feelings then.

There are some interesting stories on the internet about the second owner of the hotel, whom I will simply call Owner B, but I am not going to go into them here. You can make your own enquiries if you want to. The third owner is his Russian wife, and she runs the hotel's kitchen. As far as I know her reputation is spotless, but because we are dealing here with Sci-entologists I will just call her Russian Wife C. When I write that "she runs the hotel's kitchen", I doubt whether she stands over the sink in yellow Marigolds scrubbing the pots and pans, for she is rather elegant. But the hotel restaurant's menu is replete with her recipes. And the hotel is offering what looks like a decent three course dinner at a very reasonable price. Including a bottle of wine.

We decide to risk it so we book a table for the last evening of our holiday. The dinner turns out to be rather tasty. I still have some nice photographs of the event. We are a bit worried that Artist A might approach us again with our favourite painting, but if he is even in the building he keeps a discreet distance. And Russian Wife C's recipe for borsch is actually pretty good.

So if you are in the area of Tintagel and you fancy a bowl of borsch, you might do worse than to drop in to The Camelot Castle Hotel for dinner. But if you are thinking of actually staying there overnight, I would take a look at some of the truly astonishing comments about it on the internet first if I were you.

25. Channelling

It is Friday evening at a lovely retreat centre in East Sussex. A group has gathered for a weekend on Science And Spirituality. I have been invited by the organiser to be there to lead two sessions, one on meditation and one on a transpersonal technique called Symbol Therapy. We are sitting in a circle and introducing ourselves to the other members of the group. We have had Anne, Marjorie, Peter. Then, when it is her turn, the woman sitting next to me startles me by saying "My name's Iris and I'm a light worker from beyond the Dog Star Sirius."

As I am leaving after the session, an enthusiastic young woman comes up to me and starts talking about channelling. She is keen to try it. I am politely noncommittal but in her excitement she does not notice this.

The next morning I return to lead the first morning session. As soon as I have stepped through the door the young woman rushes up to me and thrusts a sheet of paper into my hand. It is printed in green ink in a typeface designed to look like handwriting. She explains that she awoke at four in the morning and found herself channelling cosmic wisdom for the first time. She sprang to her computer and typed out the wise words before they were lost for ever. She wants to know – immediately – what I think of them.

I quickly read the green print on the white sheet. It suggests that by and large the world would be a better place if we could only be a little kinder to each other. We should, says the cosmic visitor, stop killing each other and performing other acts of violence. According to he, she or it, we will become happier if we deal with our fears, jealousies and other negative emotions. And at times of stress, breathing is good for us.

I think but do not say "Why are channelled messages from great cosmic beings always so banal?"

I think it.

But I do not say it.

I do not feel good even about thinking it. But there you are. That thought comes. So it goes.

I mutter some bromide such as "This must be very exciting for you" and move away.

It is a thought that comes to me at other times, especially when confronted by similar enthusiasts of channelling. "Why do great cosmic beings or long-dead people travel across the eons of space or all the way from the afterlife to bring us messages of such staggering banality, messages which could be found in any self-help book or collection of high-minded cliches sold at Xmas as stocking fillers? Why never next week's lottery numbers? Or something else about the future that could at least be verified?"

Surely we already know that it would be a good idea not to kill each other or perform other acts of violence. Our natural sense of empathy, evolved over millions of years, tells us that. Surely we do not need an invisible cosmic guide steeped in morality and virtue to tell us it too.

As evidence for this, those of no belief often behave as well as those who have belief. Quite frequently, they behave better. Few people over the ages have committed as great atrocities as true believers.

Some say "It's a question of faith. You must have faith."

But to my mind at this point in my life, faith is for those who have locked their brains away in a box. Faith is a psychological analgesic and a tool which is useful to scoundrels.

****

Some months later, I am at a spiritualist meeting in Kent. The meeting is large but I am not there to talk to the dead. I am helping a colleague make a presentation about transpersonal psychology. The numerous people in the audience listen politely to us, but clearly this is not what they are really here for. They are eagerly awaiting the second part of the evening, when they hope that the spirits will bring them comfort.

There are some truly tragic cases here. One woman has lost both her daughter and her mother in an accident. This happened two years previously. Of course she is still utterly distraught. I feel like weeping when she tells us about her suffering. She is desperate for some message, some sign that there is personal existence beyond the grave. For two years no convincing message has come, but still she clings to hope.

I cannot help thinking, but I do not say, "Wouldn't it be better to have some decent psychotherapy? Wouldn't it be kinder to offer her that?"

In the tea break a woman asks me where I live. When I tell her she says "Then you must know Rosanna. She lives there and she channels all seven members of The Great White Brotherhood." She seems quite confounded when I tell her "No, I've never heard of Rosanna", as though this gap in my psychic network casts a great deal of doubt on my spiritual credentials. "Then you must meet her" she says. "I'll give you her card. All seven of The Brotherhood!"

I think but do not say "Surely one of them would be enough." The phrase "personality disorder" drifts gracelessly through my mind.

****

In a small and isolated village that I know, there are not one but two women who channel great wise beings. I meet one of these women. She has the air of someone who has gone beyond worldly concerns and who pities the rest of us for not doing the same. Her energy is flat and vapid. If I could see auras, I feel hers would be grey. I go to one of her meetings. It is the same bromide as usual. We will be happier if we are not fearful. We should try not to be angry. But in this lonely place where the broadband connection is weak, it is something to do of an evening.

At one time I join a local meditation and psychic development group. To be honest, my motives are not noble. I have no partner at this time and I am attracted to the woman who runs it. I quickly learn that she already has three suitors, two of whom are wealthy. Nevertheless I continue to attend. Here I realise that the desire to develop psychic powers can bring unnecessary suffering. We are led through a variety of quite conventional visualisation exercises. One woman in the group, although she dropped out of formal education at a young age, is bright, attractive, lively. Yet week after week she tortures herself because she simply cannot visualise anything. As the rest of us describe our power animals or the inner wise beings that have come to us as we lie in the sun in meadows next to our imaginary rivers, she falls into deeper and deeper despair at what she sees as her psychic failings.

Later, a friend of mine who is also unable to visualise anything is described as "disassociated" by her tutor at college. She is one of the least disassociated people that I have ever known. Her ability to connect with people is amazing.

One of the members of the group begins to have problems with his balance. His doctors initially diagnose meniere's disease. Our psychic tutor agrees. She reassures him about his health. Quite quickly he dies of a brain tumour.

Then I am invited by a friend to join another psychic training circle. It is held in a Methodist church hall and is run by an almost inconceivably old man who used to work as a shunter on the railways. He teaches us how to contact our spirit guides. Or rather he tries to do this. In my case it is without success although he describes my spirit guide to me. Apparently he is wearing a turban.

Another friend, Gary, goes to a psychic to have his third eye opened. The operation is all too successful. Waves of channelled material flood in. A fan of David Icke, Gary finds himself being rogered one night by a large lizard with a jewel in its forehead. This is clearly during a hypnagogic state so I do not take his story too seriously. I was once murdered by an African woman wearing a tribal headdress during a hypnagogic state, yet the evidence I have strongly suggests that I was not actually killed at that time.

But Gary does take it seriously. For him the lizard has a literal reality so he returns to the psychic and begs her to teach him how to shut his third eye down again.

The fact is that some people have more of a problem with "reality monitoring" than others do. They are less able to distinguish between events in the outside world and events that are internally generated through imagination or visualisation and in hypnagogic or hypnopompic states. They are therefore more liable to confuse their own internal reality with actual external reality.

"Alien abductees" tend to fall into this category. So does Gary.

Then I receive an email from a girl who wants my help. Some years earlier she started channelling. She loved the attention and the feeling of being special and different that this gave her. More and more people contacted her, eager for her to bring them spirit guidance. Now she has grown bored with the psychic intrusions into her mind. Now she wants to have done with them and to be ordinary again. Now she wants the voices to shut up.

But they will not. They will not go away and leave her alone. I have to let her know that regretfully this is not one of my areas of expertise. But I do suggest that she could try simply telling the voices to fuck off.

I know someone who claims that this has worked with ghosts in his spare bedroom. His new wife told them to fuck off and they did.

My partner has a friend who sees dead people and talks to them much of the time. She is eager to bring messages from them to her friends and acquaintances, whether solicited or not. As she moves in transpersonal circles, an unsurprisingly large number of them are happy to be approached by her. They listen entranced to the news that their dead relatives love them.

So far, nothing verifiable has come from this. Nothing. Nada.

If she ever tries this on me, I will use the "fuck off" trick.

****

Then I receive an invitation to speak about non-duality at a conference of psychics and mystics in a town in Germany. I take a look at the organiser's website and on the basis of what I read there, reply "No". I add that anyway I am not available on the conference dates, which is true. He ignores this and offers me more money. I say "No" again and remind him that in any case I cannot attend. He contacts me once more and tells me that the dates have been changed. If I will now agree to go, he can arrange a lift for me all the way to his house with another speaker at the conference. Once there, I can stay with him and his wife.

I think "What can be the harm? It might be fun." I agree to go after all.

The journey there is a bizarre one. My driver is a psychic, a hypnotherapist and a certified master practitioner of Neuro-Linguistic Programming. I have noticed before that certified master practitioners of NLP are ironically often amongst the least competent communicators that I have ever come across. He is a thin quiet man who appears to be serene. But he stops his car frequently to get out and smoke cigarettes standing by the side of the road. This may have something to do with the ferocious wife who sits beside him. She is plump and dark and constantly on his case, nagging, carping, issuing instructions. He barely responds. He seems to have decided a long time ago that apparent compliance is his best option. But really he is not listening. Water off a duck's back. Perhaps helped by selective deafness.

Once at the conference, I quickly realise that the two hundred people gathered there are also only really interested in receiving messages from the dead. Nevertheless they listen to my presentation politely. Afterwards two of them come up to me to tell me how much they enjoyed it. One hundred and ninety eight of them do not. The rest of the weekend is spent on psychic channelling, hypnotherapy and messages from aliens. The last are brought to us by a Swiss man with piercing eyes. He has an attractive young girlfriend with him who adores him. He wants to know if I can put in a good word for him with my publisher.

I cannot.

I do not attend most of those other sessions. Instead, I am outside the conference hall walking around the quiet lanes or drinking coffee and reading a book at the local inn. But I walk back into the hall just as my chauffeur has hypnotised a plump young woman. At what looks like some risk to his own health, he picks her up in his arms and staggers across the stage at the front of the room with her as if she is flying. Apparently he has hypnotised her into believing that she can actually fly. When afterwards she is asked, she claims to believe that she was indeed flying. Then he waves a bottle in front of her eyes. She claims that she can see nothing. Apparently he has hypnotised her into not seeing the bottle.

He is a hypnotherapist! I struggle to understand what the therapeutic benefit of all this can be for the plump young woman.

But he is very popular with the audience. Unlike me, this is not the first time that he has been asked to speak at the conference. And unlike me, it will not be the last.

In the evenings, we are entertained at our host's house. There are about a dozen of us in quite a small sitting room. Everyone is smoking except for me. My host and a friend of his are smoking large cigars. The combined effect is to produce a fug which is awful. I have noticed before that many healers and psychics smoke, some of them incessantly. I remember that my friend and teacher Terry Dukes, who was a heavy smoker, used to say that smoking was only harmful if we breathed in impure thoughts with the smoke. He was one of the most physically fit men that I have ever met. He ran his own martial arts school and taught kempo karate. In his early sixties he died of heart failure.

The attractive young girlfriend talks to me excitedly about the latest book of alien revelations that her boyfriend is working on. I try to feign interest. I do not want to appear rude, not least because she is attractive.

My host talks to me about Electronic Voice Phenomena. This is a means whereby the voices of the dead are captured on various recording devices, thereby offering absolute proof of survival after death. Apparently someone in Germany has built a new and hugely sophisticated machine which is achieving remarkable results. It sounds from my host's description as if whole speeches from the dear departed are being recorded on it. Perhaps Shakespeare himself might come through the static and add another tragedy to the cannon. My host wants to know what I think.

He is jovial and he has been hospitable. I do not want to appear ungracious or ungrateful. He has after all paid me quite a lot of money to come to Germany and talk to two hundred people, most of whom are frankly not remotely interested in what I have to say. He may already have received feedback from some of them and he may already be regretting his decision.

I try to sound noncommittal. But in actuality I am not non-committal. In fact I am thinking that Electronic Voice Phenomena is utter nonsense, yet another sign of our great tendency to credulity and of our failure to think critically.

I think that I have got away with it and we part on good terms. But when I am back in England my host contacts me again. He would like to conduct an interview with me for a spiritual newspaper that he publishes. I agree to this and he sends me a list of questions by email. I answer them as well as I am able to. The last one is about survival after death.

He likes the answers that I send him very much. Except my response to his last question. In this, I write that it is impossible to know whether anything at all happens after death. And if it does, it is impossible to know what it might be. So all speculation on the subject is baseless. He disagrees strongly with this, reminding me that the evidence from the new Electronic Voice Phenomena machine in Germany has provided indisputable evidence of life after death. So I must be wrong. In view of this, would I like to send him a revised answer to his question?

I would not.

I tell him simply to cut the last question out. I cannot be arsed to get into a disputation over this.

Later I am listening to a radio programme about psychology. The presenter is discussing the topic of Electronic Voice Phenomena and the claims of its enthusiastic proponents that it brings evidence of messages from the dead. On air he conducts a fascinating experiment. He plays a recording, a mixture of static and interference. There is no doubt that it is simply random noise. There is no message that can be heard in it. Then he suggests a specific message that might be discernible and plays it again. This time the message that he has implanted in our minds seems quite clearly to be there. In fact, it is impossible not to hear it.

Seek and ye will find. But what ye find may simply be confirmation of thine own prejudices. I must confess that my own prejudices are confirmed by this radio programme.

Channelling

****

At some time in my story I am invited to a meeting by a spiritually inclined acquaintance. This is to hear a presentation by an Australian lady, Donna, who spent some years as a devotee of a popular guru. Unfortunately certain of his sexual shenanigans were eventually exposed, so Donna became disillusioned with him. She set off to find a replacement spiritual guide.

She has been successful in her search and now she is on a tour visiting various countries, including England, to share news of her very exciting spiritual discovery. I am lucky enough to have received an invitation to find out more. Rather against my better judgement I decide to accept it.

There are about fifteen of us gathered in the sitting room of an apartment in North London. Donna starts by peddling an American conspiracy theory to us. It is the usual toxic mixture of the New World Order, the coming economic apocalypse, the end of civilisation as we know it and the need to keep enough food for two years in rat proof containers and invest in Canadian gold maples. And we must live at least two hundred feet above sea level. Or is that meters? It is heavily laced with the lightly concealed antisemitism that nearly always accompanies these theories.

I sit there wishing more people would read Norman Cohn's book 'Warrant For Genocide'. This gives an account of the Okhrana's successful plot to libel the Jewish people with a fraudulent document, 'The Protocols Of The Elders Of Zion'. The Okhrana were Tsar Nicholas II of Russia's secret police and the document that they cooked up purported to prove that there was a Jewish conspiracy to take over the world. Although it is so obviously a fake that an intelligent child of fourteen should be able to see through it quite easily, many adults who should know better still believe its lies today. I suppose that this can only be because they want to. The Okhrana's plot was so dishonourable that even the Jew-hating Tsar Nicholas refused to sanction it. They went ahead with it anyway. A direct line can be traced from their document to the Nazi genocide in Europe, although to be fair to the Okhrana, their own plot was itself built upon centuries of shameless antisemitic propaganda disseminated by the various Christian Churches. In this, The Holy Roman Catholic Church, the Orthodox Churches and the Protestant Churches seem to have been in competition with each other as to who could come up with the most poisonous lies.

As I sit listening to this conspiracy theory garbage, I feel slightly ashamed that I do not voice any objection to Donna over it. But I am after all a guest in someone else's home. They have made me tea and offered me cake, so I do not want to risk causing a fuss and embarrassing or upsetting anyone.

Then Donna gets on to the real business of the evening. She tells us about a great spiritual being that has recently made its appearance on the planet. It is immeasurably old and wise. In so far as it has any gender, it appears to be male, but it has chosen to reveal itself to us through the body of an American woman. Because Americans can be extremely litigious, I am not going to name either the great being nor its host here. I shall simply refer to them as The Great Cosmic Being and The American Woman.

Donna is so impressed with The Great Cosmic Being that she has brought news of him to Britain and Australia so that we too can learn from his ancient wisdom.

We watch a video of The Great Cosmic Being addressing an adoring crowd in the USA after he has possessed The American Woman's body. He stomps mannishly around a large enclosure, orating wisdom that only a great cosmic being could have gleaned from a lifetime stretching over many millennia. "Be kind to each other. Deal with your fears. Be more loving."

The crowd receive this advice reverentially. It seems that none of it has ever occurred to them before.

The most remarkable characteristic of The Great Cosmic Being, and the one which makes him hilarious to watch, is that in spite of his profound cosmic wisdom he does not seem to know what century he is in. He speaks a kind of cod medieval English such as you might come across in a very bad Hollywood movie about knights of yore. He struts about, addressing individual members of his audience and referring to them archaically as "thee" and "thou".

When he vacates her body at the end of the show, The American Woman appears exhausted, as well she might be.

There is something in all of this which is charmingly reminiscent of Lobsang Rampa, the disincarnate Tibetan Lama who inhabited the body of West Country plumber Cyril Hoskins in the nineteen fifties, sixties and seventies. Lobsang Rampa wrote the book 'The Third Eye' amongst many others and spoke English with a cod Tibetan accent. Mysteriously, he was completely unable to understand Tibetan itself.

Actually many channellers speak in voices quite unlike their own. In Albuquerque I came across Caroline, a large woman who channelled a being called Barnabas. Or maybe it was Bernard. Or perhaps Bertram. He too came from the other side of the cosmos to be with us on some Sunday afternoons in a suburban house in a moderately well-off part of the city. Once he had invaded her body, Caroline spoke in a way that was deep, slow and pompous. This was not at all like her usual voice.

Many channellers seem genuinely puzzled by this phenomenon and take it as evidence of the authenticity of their alter egos. Their psychological naivety about this is surprising yet somehow also rather charming.

26. Angry Nuns and Lamas

In a secondhand bookshop I buy a copy of a book by Karen Armstrong called 'Through The Narrow Gate'. It is about the experiences that she has in the convent which she joins when she is eighteen years old. She stays in this convent for seven years. They are not happy years for her.

In the book she goes into the physical and psychological abuses that she suffers. These include some of the sadomasochistic practices which can regularly be found within The Catholic Church, particularly in cults such as Opus Dei. I should make it clear that "sadomasochistic practices" is my term and implies my judgement, not Karen Armstrong's. As far as I can remember, she does not use these words. As well as whipping herself and wearing a spiked chain around her arm, she is punished for disobedience by being forced for two weeks to sew at a treadle sewing machine which has no needle in it.

The sheer vacuous idiocy of this punishment reminds me of the penalty that we receive as boys for various infringements of the rules at my school. We have to write out the first six hymns of the school hymn book. Even at the age of sixteen I think that few things could be more calculated to put us off religion. Is my apparently Christian school run by closet atheists, intent on destroying any budding faith that we have before it can blossom? How much more intellectually fruitful might our punishment be if we were required to write an essay on "Humanity's Existential Dilemma" instead. I believe that quite a few reasonably bright teenagers would be able to compose something interesting about that.

One of the things that Armstrong's fascinating book makes clear is that we can tell little about the temperament of those who profess a religious vocation from their surface behaviour. Among cardinals, bishops, priests, monks, nuns and others who lead a religious life, a great deal of energy is so often dedicated to suppressing any sign of the shadow. This means that for much of the time what is apparent on the surface may give no clue at all to what is going on beneath. It is possible that the kindly face of a priest may conceal a child rapist, while his saintly-looking bishop may be colluding with him, covering up his crimes* and transferring him to a distant parish where he can go on to ruin the lives of other children. The placid expression on the face of a nun, carefully composed in public, may conceal a simmering anger and perhaps the cruel beating of children supposedly in her "care". Many who were brought up in orphanages or educated in schools run by those who choose to serve the Christian god of love can testify to such abuses.

Remember that those who live a religious life are often under absolute instruction from their superiors to appear serene at all times.

****

One day a group of Tibetan lama monks comes to London. They are here in order to construct a sand mandala. This is a beautiful religious artifact, made by painstakingly arranging millions of brightly coloured grains of sand into intricate patterns. This is achieved by applying the sand in a gentle flow down small funnels. The lama monks are to spend a week creating this mandala. When it is complete they will carry it to

---

*Since I wrote those words, a former Archbishop of Canterbury has been forced to resign his honorary positions within The Church Of England because of his involvement in a case where information about a paedophile bishop was not passed on to the police. I have no idea whether this retired Archbishop's behaviour may have constituted an attempt to pervert the course of justice, a crime which in English law carries a maximum life sentence. I am currently waiting to see whether the police will be investigating this possibility, but I fear that I will have to wait for a very long time. Or as they say outside ecclesiastical circles "Don't hold your breath!"

the River Thames and destroy it by sweeping it into the flowing waters. This action will signify the transient nature of all things.

At the time I am still flirting with Buddhism, so with my good friend Sheena I go up to the centre of Town to watch part of this ceremonial creation. Some of the monks are sitting cross-legged around the mandala. Trickles of sand run down the funnels and tiny patches of bright colour appear. Other monks seem to be sitting on the reserve benches, ready to take over when needed.

At a certain point, all the monks form a line and start processioning around the room blowing impressively large brass horns. I find the deep resonance of the sound rather wonderful. I am struck by the profound spiritual nature of these men. I turn to Sheena and say something to that effect.

She looks at me as if I am slightly balmy. "Well" she says, "I think they look very angry."

I look at the lamas again. It is certainly true that they are somewhat red in the face, but I have assumed that this is because they are playing brass. I look more closely. From their appearance they could be angry, or perhaps just out of breath. Is Sheena projecting an anger that is not there onto their faces or am I projecting a holiness that is absent? I cannot be sure, but I know from experience that Sheena sometimes correctly spots subtleties in people's behaviour that I have missed.

Initially I think "What could these holy men living such a spiritual life have to feel angry about?" But then the mists of my naivety start to clear away and my mind begins to ponder a few possible answers to that question.

Here are some of them.

These are traditional lama monks. All or most of them will have been brought up from a young age in Tibetan monastic communities. Let us not beat about the bush. As Jimmy The Saint says in 'Things To Do In Denver When You're Dead', "Give it a name." Although lama monks are under instruction to be celibate, we now know that the rape of children sometimes occurs within Tibetan monasteries. There are those who claim that this happens frequently. So when they were boys some of these monks may have been sexually abused by older monks. It is also quite probable that they were beaten. These could be two potent reasons for anger. And the abused sometimes become abusers, so it is at least possible that some of them may have gone on to commit their share of assaults on children in the monasteries in their turn. Abuse tends to beget guilt and guilt is another potent fuel for anger.

Where the rape and beating of children by those living a religious life is concerned, not to give it a name should have us weeping bitter tears. Conrad's character Kurtz in 'Heart Of Darkness' is much too often quoted, but here surely it is justified. "The horror! The horror!"

At the time of the sand mandala ceremony many years ago, such musings on my part might have seemed fanciful. But now, with the pervasive presence of the World Wide Web, the evidence of child rape and other abuses within Tibetan Buddhist monastic communities cannot be denied. I am not going to go into the details here, but a few minutes on the internet will apprise you, through first-person testimony, of the heart-rending stories of young men who have had the great misfortune to be designated reincarnate lamas when they were very young children. In a way never before known in human history, they are now able to make their suffering public and to blow the gaffe on their corrupt communities. They can give it a name.

These monks now in London will probably have been brought up in an atmosphere of harsh discipline and may have been beaten for their misdemeanours. They will have spent their childhood sitting for long hours memorising and chanting sutras. They will have been deprived of comfort. They may have had little time for play. They will have learnt nothing which would fit them for life in the outside world should they ever wish to disrobe. Their heads will have been filled with superstitious beliefs. They will have been sold a story that they are superior to the villagers whose hard work supports them. Stephen Batchelor gives an insight into the lama monk mentality when he describes how one day, after spending some time training as a monk in a monastery, he challenges one of the senior lamas over the truth-nature of his beliefs. The lama is appalled because, as he says, if the beliefs are not true then the monks are no better than the ordinary villagers. He does not seem to realise that this is precisely Batchelor's point.

Now here are the sand mandala monks in the heart of London, surrounded by hedonism. Vacuous hedonism maybe, but perhaps attractive hedonism nevertheless. Elegant well-heeled cosmopolitans have come to gawp at them. A little like we might gawp at those other llamas, the ones that may be found not far away in London's Regents Park Zoo. Cosmopolitans who enjoy pleasures that the monks can only dream of. Not that I am asserting that the monks do actually dream of them. How would I know?

Perhaps some of this provides potent reasons for anger. Perhaps not.

****

Where there are communities of supposedly celibate men with access to children, there is a risk of child rape. It makes no difference whether the community is monastic or not. It makes no difference whether the community is of Buddhist monks or of Catholic priests or of men from other religions, sects, or denominations. It makes no difference whether the abbots and bishops are in Dublin or Boston or Sussex. These places have all seen their share of serious sexual assaults against children by those living a religious life. So have many, many other places. The list is, sadly, almost endless.

Sexuality is a potent force. You can push it into the shadows but one way or another it will have its say. One Catholic priest has admitted to sexually abusing at least one hundred boys.

Just one priest. One hundred boys.

Parents, when celibate priests are about, take your children by the hand and run away with them as fast as you can.

Who in their right mind would entrust their child, unaccompanied, to a celibate man? To the one person who can be guaranteed to have no normal experience of adult sexual relationships. To a man whose own sexual psyche has probably been frozen in time at the developmental stage of an adolescent.

****

But if you want reassurance on these matters, you have only to look to The Vatican. It has conducted a thorough investigation into itself and to the surprise of no one it has concluded that it can exonerate itself. The comforting word from Rome is that celibacy in the priesthood does not contribute to the risk of child rape by the clergy. There is a particularly egregious article by William Oddie on the Catholic Herald website to this effect under the title 'Clerical child abuse has nothing whatever to do with celibacy' (www.catholicherald.co.uk 19th December 2014).

Well, although I have never applied for a position in the priesthood and probably never will, I am aware of one or two of the requirements for these posts and also of the opportunities that they offer:-

Requirements:-
Applications for these posts will only be accepted from men.
Successful applicants will not be permitted to have sex with women.

Opportunities:-
Successful applicants will be given almost unlimited trusted access to children.

Call me a naïve fool if you want to, but it occurs to me that such positions might attract a higher than average number of applications from people who:-

are men.
do not want to have sex with women.
would like to have almost unlimited trusted access to children.

As the Americans say "You do the math."

****

I cannot leave this chapter without noting that in Bhutan the health ministry is now making condoms available to Buddhist monks. This follows the diagnosis of sexually transmitted diseases, including AIDS, among the monks. The youngest monk diagnosed in this way was twelve years old. In an official statement the health ministry acknowledges that monks engage in "thigh sex". Without going into the details and just for the record, a monk cannot contract AIDS from "thigh sex".

As Jimmy the Saint says "Give it a name."

27. Gestalt

Twenty three of us are sitting in a circle on the floor. This number includes Shirley, an elderly, very experienced and somewhat intimidating Gestalt therapist from Canada. Making us sit on the floor is intended to regress us to a younger age. About five years old. It is quite effective in doing this.

One person is in the centre of the circle. This is Lawrence. Shirley is doing her best to work with him.

There is a pithy sentence that Fritz Perls, the psychiatrist who originated Gestalt Therapy, sometimes came out with when the person in the "hot seat" was not coming up with the psychotherapeutic goodies. I have mentioned it once before in this book.

It is "Shit or get off the pot."

For some time now we have all been desperately hoping that Lawrence will do one or the other. But so far he has resolutely refused to do either.

In groups there is a tendency for individuals to behave repeatedly in certain ways that result in them being labelled by the other members of the group. Often they can be stuck with these labels and therefore with specific roles for the lifetime of the group. The roles may include among others "the first and best", "the last and worst", "the rebel", "mother's little helper", "queen bee", "the mystic", "teacher's pet", "the joker", "the space cadet", "the earth mother", "the clown", "the fairy child" and "the wise one".

Lawrence has been labelled "the most stuck" in our group. This is because he shows very little evidence of any emotional intelligence or self-awareness. As we are collectively members of a postgraduate humanistic psychology training group, this is quite strange. Our group includes Tom, an elderly secondhand book dealer who can only feel emotion for his dogs, not for his wife or children, and Colin, who has so reconstituted himself as a feminist New Man that he mentally beats himself up whenever he notices an attractive woman on the street. But Lawrence seems by far the most out of place and by far the most out of his depth.

Shirley is trying to encourage Lawrence to work with a dream that he has had. In the way of Gestalt, she is doing this by asking Lawrence to take on the role of various aspects of his dream, to act each aspect out, and to "speak from that place." It is hoped that this might bring the light of self-understanding to Lawrence.

The justification for this Gestalt approach to dreamwork could be summed up in the following way:- as it is your dream, everything in it represents a part of yourself. If you dream that you are running down a street to escape a monster wielding an axe, then you are the monster, the axe and the street as well as the "you" who is running away. So you may be asked to enact or dramatise each of these parts to see what insights this might bring you.

Lawrence's dream contains various elements which he has acted out in a dull and stilted way. Shirley is hoping for some kind of emotional response, some kind of breakthrough, but so far nothing. Now she moves on to the rabbit.

At some point in Lawrence's dream there had been a rabbit. Shirley says to Lawrence "What was the rabbit doing?"

Lawrence replies "It was hopping."

"Ok" says Shirley, "then hop."

Lawrence crouches, bends his arms in front of him like a cartoon bunny, and hops.

"How do you feel?" asks Shirley.

But as usual Lawrence does not feel anything.

Then Shirley says "Was the rabbit doing anything else?"

"Yes" says Lawrence after a little thought. "It was nibbling a lettuce."

"Ok" says Shirley. "Nibble the lettuce."

Lawrence mimes a rabbit nibbling a lettuce.

Still nothing. No reaction. No insight. No breakthrough. Perhaps the rabbit is Lawrence's mother. Perhaps the lettuce is his father. It seems like we are destined never to know.

It is then that Shirley utters the words that should be immortalised in Gestalt lore.

She says "Ok Lawrence, become the lettuce!"

And Lawrence becomes the lettuce. Shortly after this Shirley calls "Tea break."

By now we recognise that she does this, like some other Gestalt therapists, when the pain of banging her head against a brick wall has become too great for her to bear.

Some time later I am in a Gestalt group in which the therapist is an elegant Swiss lady, Ingrid. The group has been incredibly stuck for some time. It is the afternoon and getting a response from us has been like pulling teeth. Suddenly Ingrid jumps to her feet and barks at us "I do not know what you are doing to yourselves as a group! Well, you do what you like! I am going to have tea!"

She storms out of the room, leaving us feeling chastised. And about four years old.

One summer I spend two weeks in Greece as a member of a Gestalt group facilitated by an elderly American, Max Furlaud. Helping Max to run the group is an attractive young English woman. There are hints that they may have been lovers, but the ambiguity about this is never quite cleared up. During the sessions she is sometimes quite critical of his interventions in a way that we, the group participants, do not dare to be.

Max has an unusually large collection of spectacles with him. One by one he puts them on, finds them wanting, tries another pair, swaps them over, then occasionally hurls them across the room in frustration.

Max lives in Paris and describes himself as "a retro-gestaltist". By this he seems to mean that he will have nothing to do with newfangled developments in the field, like the recent fashion for combining gestalt with spiritual psychotherapies. He tells us that he lived for a while with an enlightened man. He says that he did this because he wanted to find out what it would be like. However he also ensures that we know that he was keen to have sex with this enlightened being at least once, so there was probably something else going on as well. But he makes it clear that he did not succeed in this. Or perhaps in telling us about it, he is simply trying to shock us into some kind of reaction.

At this time I believe with wide-eyed credulity that there are indeed enlightened beings on the planet. So does the rest of the group. We are eager for Max to tell us what living with this wondrous human was like.

But all Max will say is "It was incredibly frustrating. We couldn't plan anything. He just did exactly what he wanted to do at any moment of the day. He was so spontaneous that anything we arranged fell apart. He was impossible."

Max passes on to us a quotation from the enlightened being that I still treasure. Apparently he said "I don't know what the big deal about enlightenment is. We're all enlightened when we're dead. It's just more chic to be enlightened while we're alive."

One morning Max has us doing trust exercises. Each of us in turn allows ourself to fall backwards with eyes closed into the arms of someone standing behind us. We have to do this several times each. I am a gabby little beggar at this time and I find it necessary to give every one else in the room a detailed report of my innermost thoughts and feelings each time I prepare to fall.

After a while, Max interrupts my almost eternal monologue and says in quite a kindly way "Listening to you, Richard, is producing in me a kind of exquisite boredom that I have never experienced before."

It is like a slap round the face but with a velvet glove.

I still have a great fondness for Gestalt. And, although he his dead now, for Max. Later on I warmly recommend to my own students that they participate in a gestalt group if they ever get the chance to do so. I feel that this might shift long-ingrained self-destructive habits of feeling, thought and behaviour in a relatively short time, and bring genuine insight into the hidden nooks and crannies of their psyches.

I also tell my students that at the very least, and even if they actually get nothing else from it, "It's likely to be more entertaining than anything that's on the television that day."

28. How Does Matter Think?

"The human brain .... remains by far the most mysterious object known to science. It is still completely unknown how 3lb of wet jelly, plus tiny electrical currents powered by the energy we release from our food, can give rise to consciousness. But it does." Michael Hanlon

I am having an argument with my girlfriend. I am claiming that science will never explain consciousness. By consciousness I do not mean a mysterious effluvia which permeates the universe, nor some personal quality which we can develop through assiduously following a spiritual path. I simply mean experience. I am asserting to my girlfriend that science will never explain how a physical universe gives rise to subjective experience.

Actually, the word "subjective" is redundant in that last phrase. Many people do think of experience as divided into objective, outer experience and subjective, inner experience. A table is considered to be objective and a feeling of happiness to be subjective. But in a very real and obvious way, all experience is subjective. It belongs to you or to me, the subject.

Some people prefer to use the word awareness to experience but that can sow confusion. Awareness can be taken, like consciousness, to refer to a mysterious universal effluvia or a personal quality that can be developed. This can lead to all sorts of tiresome and stressful teachings designed to increase our awareness or to raise our level of consciousness, when actually all we need to do is wake up in the morning and there awareness is. The ultimate free gift.

The gift of experience.

Experience of what? Experience of phenomena. Experience

of phenomena is all that we have.

So the question that my girlfriend and I are arguing about is "How can physical matter give rise to experience?" The neatest way of putting this that I have ever come across is "How does matter think?" This is such a good question that I wish I had thought of it myself.

We can phrase the problem in other even more perplexing ways. "How does matter have emotions? How does matter feel empathy? How does matter love? How does matter hate?" These questions indicate that the mystery is very deep indeed.

My girlfriend believes that science has already solved the problem of consciousness. She points out that neuroscientists have greatly increased our understanding of what goes on in the brain when experiences happen. They have mapped electrical impulses and neurotransmitters. They have even determined in certain cases which specific brain cells are firing when a particular phenomenon, such as the colour red or the scent of a lemon, is experienced.

Philosophers of consciousness call an individual experience a quale. So when we look at an apple, we experience the quale "redness". When we sniff a lemon, we experience the quale "lemon scent". Other examples of qualia (the rather unexpected plural of quale) are the sensations of a kiss or of a toothache, the feeling of happiness at seeing a sunset or of sadness at losing a friend, the warmth of a cup of coffee held in the hand or the coldness of an ice cube touched to the lips.

I say to her "We know that the firing of neurons gives rise to qualia or experiences, but how this happens is a mystery. And this mystery has no solution, at least at present."

My girlfriend says that the firing of neurons and the experiences that they generate are the same thing so there is nothing to explain. I say that they cannot be the same thing, because we can never be directly aware of the firing of neurons in our own brains, whereas we are directly aware of our own experiences.

In this crucial way, even if in no other, they are clearly different.

My girlfriend thinks that I am arguing with her only because of my obtuseness. Or my stubbornness. She cites Daniel Dennett. Daniel Dennett agrees with her and he is a highly paid American philosopher. He is possibly the highest paid philosopher in the whole world. He has even written a book agreeing with her.

I tell her that many scientists, philosophers and psychologists agree with me, even though they may not earn as much as Daniel Dennett. Though probably between them they do. They recognise that the problem of consciousness is extremely difficult to solve. They actually call it "the hard problem". Sometimes they refer to "the explanatory gap" to indicate that something is missing in our understanding. What is missing is any coherent theory of how physical phenomena such as the firing of neurons can give rise to experience or qualia.

They have written books too.

I think that Daniel Dennett is a highly paid fool.

Perhaps I think that my girlfriend is stubborn. Or obtuse. But I do not say so because I value her love.

I do actually have one area of sympathy with my girlfriend's view and that is concerning woo woo. I believe that some scientists and philosophers deny that the hard problem exists because they recognise that it is a doorway through which all kinds of superstition may be able to rush in. Once it is acknowledged that experience or consciousness or awareness is a mystery and that we have no real idea how it occurs, a huge number of irrational ideas from spoon bending to angel channelling and from quantum healing to talking to the dead may be able to get a foot in the door.

Nevertheless, I believe that intellectual rigour demands the recognition of the hard problem. And that we can still bar the door to superstition.

My girlfriend and I also argue about religion. I feel that

her view of The Church is overgenerous because she has been contaminated by her Catholic upbringing. I believe that she privileges The Church in a way that she does not do with other organisations. But she feels that I am unduly harsh in my judgements of The Church and of religious beliefs in general.

Ironically, on this subject it is Daniel Dennett and I who are in agreement and my girlfriend who is out of step.

Eventually I say to my girlfriend "I think we should agree not to talk about consciousness. Or about religion. We'll never see eye to eye about either of them and it just makes us angry. So what's the point?"

But our arguments leave their small scars. This may be one of several reasons why she is no longer my girlfriend.

****

Many philosophers, neuroscientists and psychologists acknowledge that they have no idea how physical brain activity gives rise to experience, consciousness, qualia. They do not really even have any workable theories about this. And no way to test them if they did have.

Some scientists and philosophers claim that consciousness may be explained through quantum physics. Probably the best known of these at the time of writing this is Roger Penrose, who has theorised that consciousness might be caused by quantum activity in "microtubules" in the brain.

But as one critic has pointed out, Penrose's theory has about as much explanatory power as declaring that consciousness is caused by pixie dust*.

Some philosophers posit the theoretical possibility of zombies. A zombie in this philosophical sense is a being which

---

*"Pixie dust in the synapses is about as explanatorily powerful as quantum coherence in the microtubules." Patricia Churchland

behaves exactly as you and I do in every way, but it has no inner life. For a zombie there is no experience, no consciousness, no qualia. In other words, the lights are not on. There is nobody home.

There seems to be no reason, at least in theory, why such zombies could not exist, nor any reason that we know of why physical brains should give rise to the experience of consciousness at all.

Actually, of course, we each only have direct experience that we ourself are not a zombie. But it seems reasonable to give others the benefit of the doubt.**

Some philosophers and neuroscientists think that the problem of consciousness will never be susceptible to a scientific explanation. I agree with them. By its nature any scientific explanation would have to be physical, and by its nature consciousness consists of non-physical subjective experience. This is that damned "explanatory gap" that I referred to earlier. Of course we know that the physical structure of the brain greatly influences how consciousness is experienced. For example, the kind of subjective experience that we have can change radically

---

** Since writing this, I have developed a more sophisticated theory to account for Daniel Dennett's obtuseness where consciousness is concerned. It may be that Dennett is himself a zombie – in the philosophical sense, not in the voodoo sense, of course. In that case, lacking any internal subjective life, the notion of qualia would naturally make no sense to him. A philosopher friend of mine has suggested that Dennett's "mind" may in fact be a sophisticated AI-bot. But of course so might my mind. Or yours. However let's not disappear too far down the rabbit hole at this point.

And if you object to such a rankly amateurish philosopher as myself going up against a highly paid professional like Daniel Dennett, you could refer to some of Sam Harris's YouTube videos and writings. Harris offers a much more sophisticated critique of Dennett's case than I do, notwithstanding the fact that Dennett is a friend of his.

when the brain is damaged by accident or by Alzheimer's disease, or when its chemical balance is altered by drugs. But what the actual connection is between the physicality of the brain and consciousness itself remains a mystery.

And is likely to remain a mystery for a very long time. Or for eternity.

29. Grimstone

One New Year's Eve finds me in a sweat lodge on Dartmoor. It is midnight and there is a little snow on the ground. Earlier in the day a group of us had built the lodge, as well as the fire pit outside it where the rocks for the lodge have been intensely heated for many hours. There are about twenty of us crammed into the lodge, naked and chanting and sharing our intentions for the coming year. What burdens do we want to shed from our lives? How do we want to grow in spirit over the next twelve months? We invoke the help of Father Sun and Mother Moon. Apart from the red glow of the rocks it is completely dark. Every so often someone goes outside and returns with a laden shovel to the cry of "Hot rocks coming through." Every so often we all go outside and hurl ourselves onto the snow, spread-eagled and panting, until we are ready for another roasting.

The building of the sweat lodge has been directed by Leo Rutherford, who regularly leads shamanic workshops. I enjoy this week spent drumming and chanting and studying the medicine wheel with Leo at Grimstone Manor, an impressive Georgian mansion surrounded by the moors and run by a community as a retreat centre. So the following Christmas I return for another week arranged by Leo in the same place.

But now there is a problem. At this time, Leo actually runs two organisations. One offers training in shamanism and is therapeutically orientated. The other is for funsters, pranksters and jokers who just want to have fun. It is a kind of playgroup for adults. So one half of the large group, including me, which gathers at Grimstone the day before Christmas Eve is made up of sensitive souls, most of whom have been through psychotherapy. Several of us actually are therapists.

What is more, many of us are going through a very tough time in our lives, which is why we have chosen to escape from family this Christmas and go to a retreat instead of facing the turkey, brussels sprouts, crackers and Uncle Steve telling inappropriate jokes. The other half of the group want to creep up behind us and shout "Boo!" or squirt water in our faces from plastic flowers pinned to their lapels. They find it incomprehensible that we do not think that this is hilariously funny and that we are not awash with simple glee in any case because it is Christmas. "What's wrong with you!" they seem to be thinking, genuinely puzzled that we have not yet realised that a plastic red nose can cure any psychological or emotional ill.

I upset the apple cart more or less straight away. On the first afternoon we sit in a large circle in Grimstone's huge lounge and each introduce ourselves to the group. The "talking stick" is passed around and reaches a French woman, who announces that she is a psychotherapist and that she is here to help and support us all. "I just want to love each of you" she tells us. There is something about her tone that I find immensely patronising. Unfortunately at this time I can be a confrontative little bleeder and I believe that the point of a group like this is to be open and honest and relatively uncensored in our communication. About half of the people in the room agree with me. Like me they have probably spent many hours sitting in similar "open groups" where this is precisely the culture. In fact, in such a group there is always a high risk that you will be "processed" by the other participants and by the facilitator if they think that you are holding your thoughts and feelings back.

So when the "talking stick" reaches me, I share my reaction with the French lady as directly as I can. I am not expecting what happens next, which is that she bursts into tears. Maybe they do these things differently in France.

The psychotherapeutic half of the group take this in their

stride. Most of them will have seen far worse than this many a time before.

The prankster half of the group go into a state of shock.

Leo seems to feel called upon to intervene, though he could just as easily have left it to the group to sort out. He calls the French psychotherapist and me out into the middle of the floor so that we can "work on our issues" with each other. This does not really go anywhere and after a few minutes he gives up. I do not really feel that I have any issues with her, except that I do not want to be patronised by a group member, especially when she is a psychotherapist and so, I think, should know better. The subpersonality in me that still wants to "please Daddy" tries to make something up to satisfy Leo but it is pretty half-hearted.

About half an hour after the end of the group, while we are waiting for our Grimstone supper which will turn out to be heavy on lentils, stewed vegetables and brown rice as meals usually are in such places, one of the pranksters comes up to me.

"You have" he informs me "ruined the weekend for everyone."

Some of the sensitive souls approach me to tell me exactly the opposite.

The next few days become more and more socially interesting, particularly for me. I have given a lift to Grimstone to Sally, who is a girl friend of mine but not my girlfriend. We have left her car locked in my garage for safekeeping back in South London. This piece of information probably seems both trivial and irrelevant at this point but it will become important later on.

On the second day, after a swim in the indoor heated swimming pool, Sally and I are showering. There is only one group shower, so this involves being naked together. This may sound a little louche to the English reader, but remember that we are on a vaguely hippy retreat. Sally chooses this moment to let me know that she would like to be my girlfriend, not my girl friend.

Embarrassedly, I stammer out that this is not what I want. Cue awkwardness all round. Suddenly being naked together does not seem to be as ok as it did a moment before.

To make matters worse, there is a girl on the retreat, Lizzie, who I am attracted to. We have already chatted to each other in the coffee queue and arranged to go for a walk over the moors in the afternoon. This goes well. We seem to have a lot in common.

Meanwhile the tendency for the pranksters to prank goes on. If anything it gets worse as they sidle up to us and shout "Boo!" even more loudly than before, or suddenly grab one of us from behind and attempt to swirl us around the floor in a grotesque and unwanted dance.

By the evening of Christmas Day itself, the atmosphere has become so uncomfortable that Lizzie and I decide to escape for an hour or two to the nearest pub, which is a short drive away. We have been told that it is open even though it is Christmas. We sit in its traditionally dark and dour bar, have a drink or two and pass an agreeable couple of hours excoriating the retreat and its unholy coupling of sensitive lost souls with boorish comedic bores. When closing time is called, we look at each other and realise that we are each thinking the same thing.

"Let's elope!"

We decide that instead of returning to Grimstone, we will drive into the nearby town and find a hotel room. In this way, we will both escape the horror of dealing with the clowns and also be able to enact the lascivious desires that have been forming in each of our minds. It does not occur to either of us that eleven o'clock on Christmas night may not be the easiest time to find a hotel with an unbooked room.

Within half an hour we are banging on the imposing but locked oak front door of the only hotel we can find in the town. For a long time nothing happens. Then we hear a muffled voice from behind the door bark at us "We're closed!" We shout through the panels, intimating our desperation. The voice suggests that our best hope is to head for the nearest city. Plymouth. At least an hour's drive away.

I believe that by this point we are each more in the grip of our wish to act on our lustful intent than our need to flee the pranksters. So we clamber back into my car and head as fast as we can for Plymouth. But we do have the presence of mind to stop at a garage on the way to buy condoms. And toothbrushes.

We do not have to drive around Plymouth for long before we spot a hotel. It is new and large, and it looks very expensive. But most importantly, it is open. I park the car, leave Lizzie sitting in the passenger seat, and walk nervously into the foyer. I am acutely aware that it is now one o'clock in the morning and I have no luggage. Except a toothbrush. And a packet of Durex. As I approach the reception desk I notice a sign on its shiny new surface with the cost of a double room printed on it. It is huge. Not the sign. The cost.

But at this time in the morning, if the uniformed man behind the desk does not sell a room to me at a bargain price, he is unlikely to sell it to anyone else at any price. I prepare to haggle.

However I do not have to bother. He understands the economics involved in this transaction as well as I do. He looks me up and down, quickly calculates what he thinks I can pay by the cut of my gib, and offers me a room at a huge discount. I accept and we even strike a deal for a second night.

The next morning, it occurs to me that we should telephone Grimstone to let Leo know that we are safe. Otherwise, I fantasise, a search party may spend hours scouring the moors looking for us in every crevice and eventually call in the police. I leave a message for him, saying that we will return to collect our luggage on the last day, and also a message for Sally, reassuring her that I will be there to give her a lift back to London. What could possibly go wrong?

We pass a pleasant couple of days. We explore Plymouth, which at that time is an astonishingly ugly city. By the time we need to return to Grimstone, we have decided that we are better off as friends than as lovers. This is a decision that we will reverse and reverse again several times over the next few months before finally settling on friends.

We drive back to Grimstone. No one there comments on our disappearance.

Except Sally.

Sally is simmering with a quiet rage. It seems that Lizzie and I were the only people on the retreat that made it bearable for her. Our disappearance left her bereft. She wanted to flee from Grimstone and return to London but she was faced with the apparently insuperable obstacle that her car was locked in my garage. So she had to sweat it out – two more days with the oafish and obnoxious pranksters. It seems that my thoughtlessness is unforgivable.

The long drive back to South London is not a happy one. Once there, I unlock my garage. Sally gets wordlessly into her freshly liberated car and drives off. We do not see each other again.

****

I visit Grimstone once more to attend a residential course run by Anthony, a psychotherapist. I have come across Anthony before when he facilitates a two day workshop for a humanistic psychology course that I am a student on. I am impressed by him, especially by his fearless way of handling the expression of anger and the exploration of conflict within our group. At one point he sets up an exercise which I will call "the circle of rage". This is not its official title and I describe it here as best as I can remember it, which is not perfectly.

Half of the group sit on the floor in a circle. One person at a time becomes the focus of attention. Everyone else in the seated circle hurls a barrage of negative feedback at them. All yelling at once, they shout out at them without censorship every critical thought that comes to them. The task of the person who is the focus of this anger is to shout it all back, not to let it in, not to let it affect them. To give as good as they get.

Meanwhile the other half of the group stand outside the circle. They move around it and whisper into the ears of the ones who are seated any negative feedback that comes to them. Amidst the cacophony the whispering can be heard, especially if what is whispered is particularly germane. Any phrase that stands out, any phrase that particularly hits home and is remembered, is likely to be good feedback.

At this time my relationship with my girlfriend is in turmoil. As in many relationships, one of us seems to hold the overt power while the other exercises covert power. One bangs the top of the table, the other twists the short and curlies underneath the table. The one phrase that I hear loud and clear when it is whispered into my ear among the din is "Under the thumb!" When I am in the outer circle, I hit home equally effectively with a whispered "Queen Bee!"

This group exercise may sound like a form of torture which should be banned under the Geneva Convention. But in many cases it produces a considerable sense of empowerment, an increase in confidence and an ability to resist and reject criticism that is not warranted. This is certainly preferable to taking on unjustified criticism and collapsing under it, as many people are prone to do. Throughout the exercise, Anthony keeps a careful and sensitive eye on what is happening. He immediately stops the process if he sees that the person who is the focus of the group energy is not able to confront it with sufficient strength.

At Grimstone, I settle down to enjoy a few more days with Anthony and the lovely moorland setting. What is more, Grimstone appears to be a place where I have good relationship karma. Once more I find myself in the coffee queue on the first afternoon chatting to an attractive girl. We seem to be interested in each other and arrange to go for a walk on the moors. As we stride along in the sun, we discover that we have much in common. All seems to be going well. Until she reveals to me that she is in a committed relationship. With a woman.

She is, many years later, still in a relationship with the same woman. But now they are married. This would not have been legally possible at the time that I first met her. Somehow I find this change in the law very pleasing.

****

There is a strange coda to my experience of Grimstone Manor. A year or two later a student of mine, Thomas, tells me the following story. He is a participant on a rebirthing weekend at the Georgian house on Dartmoor. One morning before breakfast he is swimming in the pool. The only other person in the pool is his roommate. After a while, Thomas gets out, dries himself off, dresses and goes to breakfast. He expects his roommate to join the group in the dining room a few minutes later. Time passes. He does not appear. More time passes. Eventually some concern is expressed and someone goes to check on him. His roommate is found dead in the pool, having drowned.

I have a memory of having already read about this accident in the national press and about the criticism it brings down on the rebirthing movement. Their response is that the victim was practising a technique in an unauthorised way, one that he had been warned not to do unless a therapist was present to supervise him. Strangely, I can find no reference to the tragedy now on the internet. Maybe I imagined the newspaper articles. But I did not imagine Thomas or his story.

30. Green And Away

I am spending four nights in a field under canvas experiencing Green And Away, an ecologically minded organisation which runs "Europe's only tented conference centre".

Actually I am not strictly speaking "under canvas". My tent is what is know as a "nylon nightmare". In the social pecking order of the green festival-goers, eco-enthusiasts and hippies who surround me, "nylon nightmares" are at the bottom of the heap. The fact that I own one already casts doubt on my ecological credentials. Who knows how many fertile valleys had to be turned into desert to manufacture my two person Eurohike.

At the top of the heap are yurts, followed by teepees and then anything else made of proper actual canvas. An old fashioned Boy Scout's tent will do.

Later I meet a couple who are about to have a baby. They also have a twelve year old son who has learning difficulties. They have sold their house and are going to move permanently into a yurt, albeit a yurt with an additional "pod", whatever that is.

Quite frankly, I think that they are mad.

My eco credentials are further damaged by the fact that I have arrived by car. If I cared one whit about the planet I would have walked, cycled or roller skated to this camp in the middle of nowhere.

At three of the Green And Away Camps that I eventually attend, about six or seven in all, the same Australian family is there. It consists of mother, father and two children. They all fly from Australia at who knows what cost to the planet to be with us each time. They arrive at the camp, having driven from their temporary home in England, in a decrepit gas guzzling

Volvo. Mother then delivers a talk in which she tells us that we should all walk everywhere to save the planet, just as she does when she is back home in the bush. She is unspeakably smug as she lectures us on green issues. But I can almost see the layers of CO_2 building up in the atmosphere around her while she speaks. This ecologically minded family may be racking up nearly as many air miles a year between them as the average CEO of a Fortune 500 company.

Neither camping nor a commitment to ecological issues come naturally to me. One day I am drinking coffee on the terrace of the cafe in my local park. I cannot help hearing the conversation of a group of six twenty-somethings at the next table as they plan a summer holiday together. After a long discussion of their options which is producing no agreement, someone says "Well, I suppose one of us has to mention the C word." An attractive blonde girl immediately barks "I am NOT going camping!" and the topic is dropped. I empathise with her.

On another occasion I am having dinner in a restaurant with a group of friends. Sitting opposite me is Chloe, the fourteen year old daughter of Hazel. At this time Chloe is a militant vegetarian and eco-fundamentalist. She is arguing with me about the impact on the environment of eating meat. Finally, having no sound arguments, I say to her as I order my steak "There's no doubt that you've got all the moral high ground, Chloe, but what you have to remember is that I just don't care."

For a fourteen year old, Chloe takes this in remarkably good spirit.

By and large, I keep my sceptical views on green issues to myself while I am at Green And Away. I have no desire to end up staked out on an ant hill with honey smeared on my buttocks. I do not tell my neighbours in the teepee next door that I consider their fervour for recycling in essence to be a lifestyle choice. Although I obediently put my recycling out in green boxes as my local council demands of me, I suspect that this makes little ecological sense. A Swiss report has recently claimed that the recycling of paper creates masses of toxic chemical waste and that the benefits of recycling glass are dubious. Apparently, only the recycling of aluminium cans has clear ecological benefits. Paper, the report says, should be burnt. The resulting carbon is taken up by the trees which are grown to make new paper, a carbon neutral cycle.

But I am hugely impressed by the camp itself and by the people who run it. Before arriving I had imagined them to be an enervated bunch of hippy stoners but they turn out to be remarkably well organised and extremely good at putting up sturdy marquees. There are several tents for holding meetings in, a kitchen tent and a lovely bar tent full of hay bales covered in rustic throws for us to lounge around on while we drink too much fine organic beer and cider.

Best of all are the willow showers. These are individual showers constructed from willow boughs, offering privacy while being open to the sky. There is plenty of hot water – if you arrive at the right time of day. It is heated ingeniously. Water from a pipe is fed through old radiators balanced against each other to make an inverted V. A wood fire beneath them heats the water as it passes through on its way to collect in a great iron container. This has been anthropomorphised by a name written on it – it is "Billy Boiler" which makes our showers possible. It is a wonderful feeling to stand in the middle of the willow boughs washing off the mud from the camp while steam rises towards the blue sky overhead.

One afternoon a friend asks me to go with her to check out another camp nearby. It too has an ecological theme and we are thinking of moving on to it when the Green And Away camp ends. We drive around the countryside till we find it, park the car and walk across the field to the "Welcome Tent". But here the organisers actually are all lying around stoned – far too stoned to do much welcoming or anything else. They have not even managed to lay on a water pipe to the camp site yet. We return to Green And Away with a renewed sense of gratitude at how well everything works there.

****

The second time that I go to Green And Away, I meet the woman who will become my lover for the next ten years. In the summer of several of these years we return to Green And Away together, to attend the regular conferences hosted there by 'Resurgence Magazine' and Satish Kumar. At one of these Resurgence camps we listen to a lecture on alternative medicine. My girlfriend is not amused. She is highly sceptical and is much more likely than I am to munch down a few pharmaceutical pills if she has a headache. After the talk I find myself sitting in the middle of a bench, bookended by her and by Noel, a distinguished looking man in his seventies. He has the hallmarks of an ageing hippy. He has long white hair, tied back in a ponytail. He has beads and crystals on leather cords tied round his neck and wrists. He is wearing a tie-dyed T-shirt, shorts and sandals. His angular face bespeaks a fine but alternative intelligence. I have every hope that he is going to support my side in the ongoing discussion about homeopathy, magnets, acupressure and the like.

My hopes are misplaced. It turns out that Noel is a retired physicist and even more contemptuous of alternative medicine than my girlfriend is. I find myself under fire from both ends of the bench. Their incredulity at my medical naivety and super-stition is vast.

At one point I start listing for them some of the alternative ways that I have tried to improve my health and peace of mind. I do not give them the extensive list which is below. In fact, unless you are obsessive about such matters, you should prob-ably skip the next paragraph yourself. It is included here only for the sake of completeness. In my defence I should say that I have experienced some of these treatments only once or twice, and that was sometimes just as a guinea pig to help out a friend who was in training.

I have had two long homeopathic treatments, stretching over some years. I have also tried at one time or another acupressure, acupuncture, affirmations, Alexander Technique, aromatherapy, Aura-Soma therapy, Ayurvedic medicine, Bach flower therapy, biodynamics, bioenergetics, Bowen Technique, chiropractic, craniosacral therapy, crystal healing, Hopi ear candles, hypnotherapy, iridology, kinesiology, macrobiotics, magnets, massage, moxibustion, naturopathy, osteopathy, past life therapy, polarity therapy, radionics, rebirthing, reflexology, regression therapy, Reiki, Rolfing, shamanic soul retrieval, shiatsu, Tibetan medicine, Traditional Chinese Medicine, Vita Florum Water and vitamins, as well as numerous psychotherapeutic and spiritual techniques.

As I begin to count off some of these treatments for Noel and my girlfriend on my fingers, I start to find the list rather depressing. I realise that I have very little idea which if any of them have ever been helpful to me.

Except the magnets. They definitely worked.

The discussion on that bench is the beginning of the end of my love affair with alternative medicine. From that point on my scepticism grows.

I begin to suspect that some of the principles at work among alternative practitioners may not be entirely wholesome. After all, it is in their interests to find me sick, or at least less than fully well, and to keep treating me for as long as possible. And whether I get better or worse or stay the same, they will probably declare their treatment a success. If my symptoms improve, then their therapy has clearly worked. If my symptoms worsen, the treatment has provoked a healing crisis, so their therapy has also been effective – either that or I have not followed their instructions zealously enough. If my symptoms do not change, they will quite possibly tell me that I am resisting their treatment because I have an unconscious block, and that I do not really want to get better.

Even my death might be hailed as simply a rather intense healing crisis. Or as the result of my unconscious death wish. The ineffectiveness of my practitioner's treatment will never be to blame. I know of someone who, diagnosed with cancer, chose homeopathy over conventional treatment. Even now, years later, his friends are still very angry about his premature and probably unnecessary death. An acquaintance of mine, who has weakened and ailed progressively as she has followed her naturopath's extreme dietary advice, is at last starting to realise that it may be the advice itself which is hastening her towards her grave. I hope her realisation has not come too late.

Of course alternative practitioners also benefit enormously from the fact that many physical ills are self-limiting and will therefore eventually get better of their own accord. It is not uncommon for practitioners to take both the credit and the pay for curing an illness which in actuality time itself has healed.

One principle which underlies much of the practice in the alternative health field is that few people are regarded as being at peak health. Therefore there is usually scope for improvement in my "energy", that hottest of hot words amongst practitioners and patients. So if I go to a variety of practitioners and say "I feel pretty good, actually. But I guess I could feel even better", many of them will take me as a patient. Then unsurprisingly they will inform me that it is precisely their treatment that I need. The iridologist will prescribe iridology, the acupuncturist will tell me that acupuncture will do me good, while the reflexologist's diagnosis will reveal that I need reflexology. Each alternative treatment will have its own overarching and all inclusive theory to justify why it is appropriate for every possible ailment. These theories will not be testable by any normal scientific means.

Few alternative practitioners will turn me away because their treatment is inappropriate for me *or simply because I am not sick.*

Many practitioners, left to their own devices, will never reach the point when they will discharge me. They will go on treating me in perpetuity, unless I decide for myself that I would rather have a new hat or until my death deprives them of an income stream.

In short, it is in the interests of private practitioners to find me unwell and to treat me for as long as possible. This means of course that I am at risk of receiving unnecessary treatment for their profit.

Private health care, whether alternative or orthodox, works according to principles quite unlike those governing our own dear National Health Service. The NHS in fact operates in a way which is a little like the health care system rumoured to have been provided long ago to certain Chinese Emperors.

It is said that a Chinese Emperor would pay his doctors only so long as he was well. When the Emperor became ill he stopped paying them. This of course gave the doctors a startlingly effective incentive to cure the Emperor of whatever ailed him as quickly as possible.

This seems like an admirable scheme to me. In the NHS, while the system is not identical, my doctor is nevertheless paid simply because I am registered with her. She does not derive extra profit from declaring me to be sick, nor for giving me as much treatment as possible for as long a time as she can. If I am ill, it is in her interest as well as in mine that she cure me quickly so that I am off her hands. It is not in her interest to give me as many expensive and possibly invasive tests and procedures as possible, as it is for private practitioners whether orthodox or alternative.

In this way, and as long as I keep myself out of the hands of private practitioners, I may be escaping a good few iatrogenic problems* that might otherwise occur. After all, one simple way to avoid getting a perforated bowel from colonic irrigation is not to have colonic irrigation.

So I do not know about you, but I have come to feel that I am not in favour of any system that rewards health practitioners only when I am sick and not when I am well.

On the bench at the camp, Noel and my girlfriend pretty much wipe the floor with me.

****

At the first few Green And Away camps that I attend, before the organisation moves to a new site, we are invited to talks in Jack's house. Jack has built his house out of straw bales at the edge of the field we are camping in. It is a lovely structure, with a verandah and a huge comfortable living room heated by a wood burning stove.

Jack has no planning permission for his house. He just bunged it up. He knows that one day he will have to demolish it and he is phlegmatic about this. It cost him only a few thousand pounds to build it. By the time that he has to abandon it, he will have had more than his money's worth in the rent that he has saved from living there.

Jack tells us the following story.

A man had built a straw bale house without planning permission in a nearby county. The planning officer visited him and told him that he would have to demolish it. The man did not comply. The visits continued, the planning officer became more insistent, court orders were sought. Still no demolition. The planning officer made one more visit. This time the man felt sufficiently cornered to reach for his shotgun. He shot and killed the planning officer.

---

*Iatrogenic problems are problems that are caused by medical or surgical interventions.

"Since then" says Jack, who does not own a shotgun, "planning officers have been much more polite."

****

At one Green And Away camp I say a terrible thing. My girlfriend and I are having a friendly conversation with a nice girl who lives in an experimental commune in Northumberland. She is enthusiastic, but also realistic about the problems which are involved.

Then we are joined by a friend of hers from the same commune, who is cut from quite a different cloth. She is smug and evangelical about her self-appointed role as green saviour of the Earth. In fact she is an eco-nazi. I cannot remember what it is that she says which gets my goat, but I mutter something that obviously casts doubt on my commitment to her cause. In an instant she has rounded on me and demanded angrily "Don't you want to save the planet!" Before my mind knows what my brain is thinking, my ears hear my mouth bark back at her "I don't give a fuck about saving the planet!"

My girlfriend, who is quite an eco-freak herself, takes a long time to forgive me for this. She considers my lack of commitment to ecological issues to be just one of several signs of my lamentable shallowness. If I am lambasted by eco-nazis it can only be because I deserve it. All that I can do is reply to her in a rather feeble way "Yes, but you have to remember that I had to explore great depths in order to to become this shallow."

****

One summer the Association for Humanistic Psychology Practitioners holds a conference at Green And Away. My girlfriend and I attend. The conference is almost abandoned before it starts for there has been major flooding in that part of the country, nearly wiping out Green And Away's summer programme. The organisers have managed to rescue the campsite by an almost superhuman effort but it is still a sea of dangerously slippery mud. Although straw has been scattered over all the paths, walking anywhere on the site is hazardous and some of us are taking two or three falls a day. Land Rovers are sent foraging to the nearest town, returning with a job lot of smart green wellies.

John Rowan, the well known psychotherapist and writer, is one of the figures stamping around in the mud. He is an elder statesman of the humanistic psychology movement and the main keynote speaker at the conference. In the past I had been drawn to his model of "subpersonalities", but now he seems to have lost interest in it himself, even though he has written a book about it. These days, he tells us, he prefers something called Integral Theory, which is the brainchild of an American writer, Ken Wilber.

I do not know much about Wilber at this point except that he seems to consider himself to be something of a tough guy and a head honcho on the transpersonal psychology circuit. I have seen him described as "the fastest gun in the transpersonal West", the theorist that everyone else has to either take on or line up behind. But many years ago I read a book by him, 'Grace And Grit', about the death of his wife. I thought this book was honest and moving. So for the moment at the conference I am inclined to give him the benefit of the doubt.

Perhaps it is because I am not really paying attention, but I get only a very hazy idea from Rowan's presentation of what he is talking about. So when I am back at home I do a little research into Wilber's Integral Theory. It is at this point that the benefit of my doubt begins to disappear quite fast. I discover that Integral Theory is a collection of transpersonal psychological models of immense complexity. However it does not seem to me to contain any great originality. In fact it appears to be a cobbling together of most of the spiritual and psychological theories that anybody else has ever come up with in the entire history of the world, and an attempt to stitch them together into a kind of giant metaphysical American quilt.

I cannot see the point of building this hugely complicated intellectual structure, appearing as it does to me to rest rather heavily on superstitious grounds. So I am not surprised when I subsequently discover that Wilber's theories generate a great deal of criticism on the web. John Heron, who developed the first university-based centre for humanistic and transpersonal psychology in Europe, is particularly critical of Wilber. I admire Heron very much and some years ago I studied at the centre that he founded, so I feel that I am in good company. I read among other judgements on the web that Integral Theory "is largely ignored in academic circles" and that Wilber "is mostly ignored in the field of religious studies." It seems to be difficult to find an objective commentator who takes him seriously.

As I go on to read more of Wilber's work, I recall the comment supposedly made by Samuel Johnson to the author of an unpublished book:- "Your manuscript is both good and original. But the part that is good is not original, and the part that is original is not good."

Wilber clearly has an encyclopaedic mind but he seems to me to have little ability to put this to good purpose. Coincidentally, a friend of mine has been reading Wilber's book 'Integral Theory'. I ask her what she thinks of it. She rolls her eyes and replies "He hasn't written a book, he's written a telephone directory."

One of the key notions that is central to Wilber's theories is "evolutionary enlightenment". This is a kind of enlightenment treadmill, on which spiritual seekers may be kept tramping for years on end. They are told that enlightenment is constantly developing or evolving, so they must forever go on working to keep up with it. This may have the benefit of guaranteeing some teachers of evolutionary enlightenment a continuing income stream.

The concept of evolutionary enlightenment appears to

have been developed by Wilber with a friend of his, a Western guru-figure named Andrew Cohen. Some commentators allege that Cohen has an ego which has skidded alarmingly out of control. His own mother, Luna Tarlo, has written a book, 'The Mother Of God', in which she describes her "harrowing spiritual bondage to …. Cohen" when she became his "slave-like disciple". Stephen Batchelor, author of the excellent 'Confessions Of a Buddhist Atheist', has also written an excoriating article about Cohen, calling his starry-eyed followers "Androids". Batchelor's article appears as the introduction to another book which heavily criticises Cohen, William Yenner's 'American Guru'. I warmly recommend Yenner's book to you both as a very entertaining way of passing a wet Sunday afternoon and for its insight into the dangerous transference and countertransference that can sometimes go on within guru cults.

Eventually, with ex-followers lining up to take a pop at him, Cohen is abandoned by many of his acolytes and falls spectacularly from grace. His organisation collapses. There are then rumours that he has retreated into the wilderness for a period of soul searching and reflection. Certainly his previous lively presence on the internet goes very quiet for a while. At the time of writing this, I am waiting with interest to see how he might reinvent himself.*

Although, or perhaps because, "evolutionary enlightenment"

---

* I wrote that sentence about Andrew Cohen some time ago. Since then, his rehabilitation and return to public life has begun, with meetings scheduled in various European countries. There is also a nice new website, on which you can read that "Andrew has begun to rediscover the gift of awakened consciousness" and "has woken up to his own flawed humanity." If you would like to accept his invitation to help "shape ….. a very new direction for spirit in the 21st century" you can find the details by the usual means. But I am going to respond to his reformulated spiritual offer by having a nice cup of tea and a biscuit instead.

is a highly speculative theory, it has become yet another modern-day religion, complete with its own doctrines, high priests and devotees. It asserts that it can explain everything in the universe, including even physics. When those who are not physicists write about physics, they take a big risk and often make fools of themselves pretty quickly. So Wilber and Cohen may be treading on dangerous ground in this. To avoid the peril of falling through the same thin ice myself, I will write nothing more about that here except to quote the philosopher of science Karl Popper:- "A theory that explains everything explains nothing."

Sitting at home with the copy of Wilber's 'Integral Theory' that a friend has lent me, I quickly reach the end of my patience and decide that I simply cannot wade through its numerous complexities as my sock drawer needs my urgent attention. Later on I try another book by Wilber, 'The Spectrum Of Consciousness', and watch a video in which he laboriously explains some aspects of his theory. Same result as before. My sock drawer has never been tidier. For me Wilber represents almost the apotheosis of a kind of spiritual writing that offers maximum difficulty with minimal reward. I begin to regard him as the transpersonal equivalent of a postmodernist and recall the only joke about postmodernism that I have ever come across:-

What do you get if you cross a mafia boss with a postmodernist?

An offer you can't understand.

Then for a little while I try to be more charitably disposed towards Integral Theory, thinking "Well, at least it's not doing anyone any harm, I suppose." But quite quickly I discover that whole cohorts of transpersonal psychotherapy students are having to study Wilber's immense books when they could be doing something more useful like painting each others' finger nails. I have for a long time believed strongly that psychotherapy training should be highly experiential, so immersing students in these seas of intellectual and spiritual abstractions seems to me to be precisely the wrong way to go.

Up to this point I have had a fondness both for transpersonal psychology and for transpersonal psychotherapy. But now I am starting to suspect that they are each awash with superstition and dogma.

Although my own patience with Wilber is by now worn thin, if you are interested in finding out more you will be able to read many detailed and in some cases extremely harsh criticisms of his theories on the internet.

Then I discover that many transpersonal psychotherapy students are also having to read the immense works of another contemporary teacher, A H Almaas. He is the director of his own school which teaches his Diamond Approach to spiritual development. I watch an interview with Almaas, during which I am astonished to hear the announcement of his most recent project. Now I have to confess that it is possible that I misunderstand him – you can do your own researches into this if you like – but he seems to be troubled by the thought that after his death, the teachers and students in his school will miss out on his invaluable guidance. To avoid this happening, he appears to be currently working out how he can continue to tutor them from beyond the grave.

I cannot remember whether the phrase "spiritual narcissist" drifts through my mind at this point. I hope not, for it would be a thought that is neither generous nor warm hearted, and in any case may be entirely inaccurate. Nevertheless that phrase might have come to me.

To be honest, by this point in the interview I have become rather confused. Almaas begins to talk about a disincarnate yogi called Babaji. Many years ago Swami Yogananda wrote about a spiritual guide named Babaji in his well known book 'Autobiography Of A Yogi'. Babaji pops up again in the folklore of the rebirthing movement via a connection with Leonard Orr. So this may be the same great being that Almaas is referring to.

CONFESSIONS OF A SEEKER

Almaas seems to be saying either that he is now in actual communication with Babaji, or that he hopes to be in contact with him in the near future. Apparently, Babaji has already mastered the art of interfering in the affairs of the living from the realms of the dead**, so he may have a lot to teach Almaas. But by now I feel as if I am rapidly losing the will to live and that I am in danger of becoming disincarnate myself.

I may have entirely misunderstood the point, but if I have not then I hope that whether you are one of Almaas's students or one of the teachers in his school, he does not haunt you after his death.

Complex spiritual systems, whether ancient ones such as the Kabbalah or modern ones such as the Diamond Approach or Integral Theory, could in some ways be considered to be like prisons. Once we have entered inside one of them, there is a good chance that we will become entrapped there. Their leaders could be regarded as the metaphorical prison wardens. Of course those of us who become the "prisoners" have all volunteered to be there. No one has coerced us. But if we spend many years in a prison, albeit voluntarily, we are likely to become institutionalised and to find it difficult to leave even though the door is wide open.

But the clear fresh air of freedom can only be found outside.

I ask myself what can be the attraction of immensely complicated spiritual systems like these, systems within which people sometimes willingly incarcerate themselves for twenty years or more. Then I remember some wise words that Carl Jung wrote:- "People will do anything, no matter how absurd, in order to avoid facing their own souls. They will practise Indian yoga and all its exercises, observe a strict regimen of

---

**Astute readers who have come across Babaji before may complain about my description of him, claiming that he is not considered to be actually dead, but merely "disincarnate". To me this is a moot point which I do not want to pursue here.

diet, learn theosophy by heart, or mechanically repeat mystic texts from the literature of the whole world – all because they cannot get on with themselves and have not the slightest faith that anything useful could ever come out of their own souls."

****

Back at the Green And Away camp, another keynote speaker at the conference announces that after many years he is not renewing his accreditation with the British Association for Counselling & Psychotherapy. He is old enough to retire and do without it, so he can finally wave two fingers at their bureaucratic procedures. He seems to take some delight in telling us this. But ironically he was himself one of the original chief architects of the BACP's tiresome accreditation system, so this announcement causes a lot of disaffected mutterings among the more junior therapists there, who still have to suffer its depredations. These juniors think that his repentance has come too late, so they give him a very hard time. He then leaves the camp rather hurriedly. There is a lot of further muttering among some small groups of young psychotherapists and counsellors about how difficult it is to turn a buck in the profession. Too many therapists, not enough clients.

At the end of the camp, the president of the AHPP gives a charming speech in which he confesses that this has been his first experience of camping. He has, he says sweetly, enjoyed it very much, before adding "but not enough to ever do it again."

****

There is a strange coda to the AHPP event at Green And Away. After it, I have a bizarre row with its chief keynote speaker, John Rowan. Rowan attends one of my talks about non-duality in London, and afterwards writes an article attacking my views, as well as the views of some other speakers on the subject. This article is published in an obscure professional journal, 'The Transpersonal Psychology Review'. To be fair, although Rowan is considered to be a holy cow by many in humanistic and transpersonal circles, when I ask for a right of reply the journal's editor concedes this and publishes my response in full in the next edition.

****

A year later my girlfriend and I again attend the AHPP summer conference. This time it is held at a "personal growth centre" in Dorset, Osho Leela.

Once more my prejudices lead my expectations astray. In the past I had not been much impressed by Osho. I saw him give a talk only once and that was on video. He seemed to me to have some of the characteristics of a charismatic charlatan and although I was attracted at that time both to charisma and to charlatans, this was not enough to carry me off to India or America to join in the herpes and AIDS fests there. The devotional and sexual shenanigans simply did not appeal to me. My loss, perhaps.

So driving down to Osho Leela I am expecting the community that runs the rambling country house to be a centre of lunacy, a group of maladjusted sociopaths and neurotics with superstitious notions about the way the universe works on a par with David Icke's shape-shifting giant bejewelled lizards. However, when I arrive I find that, as on certain other occasions, I have to adjust my prejudiced views very quickly. It turns out that the group in charge of the centre are charming, grounded, well organised and attentive to our needs. There does not seem to be a trace of lunacy, except perhaps in my own febrile brain. Maybe, I think, if I am so wrong about his followers, I should adjust my view of Osho himself.

I remember once seeing a short video clip of Osho being driven around his Oregon ranch in the back of one of his many

Rolls Royces. While the thousands of adoring devotees straining to get a glimpse of him seemed to me to be both hypnotised and hysterical, Osho himself sat unmoved, enfolded by the luxurious leather upholstery. If I could read anything on his face it seemed to be that he honestly did not give a fuck. Not about the Rolls Royces. Not about the adoring chelas. Not about anything. "Rolls Royces come? Let them come. Rolls Royces go? Let them go." Non-attachment. This, anyway, is what I imagined him to be thinking.

But I could well be wrong. I have come across folk who certainly believe that I am.

Then I read an anecdote which also improves my disposition towards Osho. It claims that while living in Oregon he became addicted to nitrous oxide, aka dental gas. One afternoon, under the influence of his new drug of choice, he is reported to have giggled out the words "Thank goodness I don't have to pretend to be enlightened anymore!" Or something very like that.

I have no idea whether this report is accurate. But I want it to be. And I begin to like Osho a little more. It is true that some within the small group who controlled his community in Oregon were sociopaths who were planning to murder a U.S. attorney and poison the local townsfolk with salmonella. But I suspect that Osho himself was not in on these plots*. And in any case, it is virtually inevitable that in a large spiritual organisation like Osho's it will be the sociopathic control freaks who take over. After all, they are the ones with the desire to run everything and no one else can be bothered to stop them.

---

*That was the view that I held at the time, shortly after my visit to Osho Leela. But in fairness I should add that there are now many people on the internet giving the opposite view, and they would probably consider me to have been quite naïve back then. If you make your own enquiries, you may very well come to a different conclusion yourself and decide that Osho knew perfectly well what was going on.

****

My girlfriend and I spend one morning of the conference at Osho Leela in a field with a woman who is running a workshop about equine therapy. This is a form of therapy in which horses are enlisted to help unhappy people, although there are also practitioners who offer therapy to help unhappy horses. As we enter the field, my girlfriend and I both have a positive and cheerful disposition towards horses and we are looking forward to the session. But it turns out that the relationship skills of horses are very limited. When the farm cat wanders into the field to investigate what is going on, we realise that her relational skills are much more advanced so we spend some quality time with her instead.

Unusually for us, we pass an uneventful, quiet weekend without conflict and drive back to the Home Counties in peace.

31. An Existential Weekend

I first come across Ray Billington, Professor of Philosophy, at The City Lit, the wonderful adult education college in central London. I attend some of his one day courses on Oriental philosophies.

Ray is a great teacher, erudite, intelligent, stimulating and fun. He tells us the following story:-

While a minister in the Methodist Church in the early nineteen seventies, he writes a book that casts doubt on core Methodist beliefs. As a result, he is accused of heresy. He has the distinction of being the last Methodist minister to be formally tried as a heretic in this country. He is found guilty and defrocked.

After the trial, he tells us, an elderly minister who has voted for his defrocking approaches him and says "Three hundred years ago we would have been able to burn you."

From the tone of his voice, Ray implies, the elderly minister thinks that it is a great pity that they cannot burn him today.

This increases Ray's stature in my eyes, even more so because since then he has turned virulently against religion, as I have done myself.

Ray has also written a book called 'Religion Without God'. My girlfriend scowls at this and says that she would prefer a world in which there was "God without religion."

Every year, Ray and his partner organise a trip to Paris. For a few days he and his students wander the streets and visit locations where famous existentialists used to hang out. There Ray lectures on different aspects of existential thought.

This sounds to me like the perfect city break. Paris *and* existential philosophy! What's not to like? So I sign up. When she hears about this, my girlfriend, who is even more keen on existentialism than I am, forgets her scowl and signs up too.

Ray tells us another story. As a young man he is studying for his postgraduate degree in Paris. Naturally he wants to meet Jean-Paul Sartre. One evening he is told that if he goes right then to such-and-such a bar, not only will he find Jean-Paul, but the actor Peter O'Toole will be with him as well. Ray hot-foots it to the bar where he does indeed find Sartre and O'Toole sitting together. Nervously he approaches them and introduces himself. "Unfortunately" he finishes the story "they are both so drunk that neither of them can say a single word."

About twenty five of us fetch up on the first afternoon at our Paris hotel. Most of the others are long term fans of Ray. They follow him about and attend lots of his courses. They have committed themselves to a life of philosophy whereas I have committed myself to a life of psychotherapy and spiritual searching. Consequently I find them a rum lot. They find me pretty rum too.

I have never before spent a sustained amount of time with a group of philosophers. I suppose it should not have surprised me that I find them overwhelmingly stuck in their heads. Brains on legs. Most of them seem to have developed excellent cognitive skills but almost no emotional intelligence whatsoever. They are quite unlike Ray. Ray is passionate, whereas they are dry as dust. Ray's conversation is juicy, whereas their bones rattle when they talk. During one of Ray's discourses I ask a question about existentialism that borders on the dangerous country of feelings. The brains and dry bones turn to look balefully at me as if I have lost my senses. "Why is this mad idiot asking about feelings?" they seem to be saying. "We didn't come all the way to Paris to talk about feelings! Feelings don't have anything to do with any stuff that's important!"

At dinner on the second night, I finally find myself talking to a couple of the philosophers who seem to have developed some real heart and an understanding of feelings. Because of my experience of the weekend so far this seems strange to me, but after a few minutes conversation I learn that they have each also been through an in-depth psychotherapy training. Then it makes sense. Unlike the others, they are committed to more than philosophy.

The regulars know Ray well, and they have learned that if they want to have some fun and watch fireworks explode, all they have to do is point Ray in the direction of religion, light the blue touchpaper, retire to a safe distance and wait. We are at supper on the first night and I am recovering from a frustrating discussion about education with a brittle desiccated man whose views on this subject are antithetical to mine in every possible way. Ray is standing at a table and is about fifteen minutes into his first lecture when one of the old-timers decides to have a bit of fun. He interrupts Ray with a question about religion and children. Ray is quickly red in the face and spluttering with anger.

"I think" he says, thumping the table in front of him to stress each word, "that to bring up a child in a religion is one of the most immoral things that a parent can ever do!"

I agree with him. I warm to him even more than before.

There are schools in Britain, in the twenty-first century, run by an American based fundamentalist Christian organisation. Children in these schools are "taught" by being placed in individual booths with no contact with other children – or with teachers for that matter. On their own they work through textbooks which teach them that evolution is false, that homosexuality is "learned behaviour" and a "corruption of God's plan", and that the proper role of women is to be subservient to men. Some commentators accuse this organisation of grooming girl pupils to accept marriage to much older men within its hierarchy, and claim that pupils leave its schools with "qualifications" which are virtually useless in the outside world. Yet astonishingly, until recently the British government's official schools inspection body, Ofsted, assessed some of these schools as being "good" or "outstanding". Now, after fierce criticism, Ofsted has changed its tune.

As I discover more about this organisation, I do not know whether to weep bitter tears or howl with manic laughter.

****

My own experience of the existential weekend descends into unexpected drama. It becomes clear very shortly after we arrive in Paris that my relationship with my girlfriend is in crisis. She is going through an internal crisis of her own and she is alternately flirting with me and pushing me away. On the Saturday afternoon, when we take a break from the group and go for a walk on our own to get the dusty smell of philosophy out of our nostrils, she sprays perfume over me coquettishly, dances around me and says "Play your cards right and you might get lucky tonight!" Ah, the romance! But later, when we are at supper in a restaurant with the group, she angrily pushes my affectionate hand away and glares at me. I glare back. After that, we enter into a rapidly deteriorating downward spiral. By the time we are on the Eurostar for our return journey to London twenty four hours later, our relationship is at an end. After some frantic texting over the next couple of days we recover, but our existential trip to Paris leaves its scars.

During the weekend we listen to lectures by Ray at some of Sartre's favourite places – Cafe Flore, La Coupole, and for some reason that I cannot remember Napoleon's tomb. On Sunday morning we stand in the open air at Le Cimitière du Montparnasse beside the grave of Sartre and Simone de Beauvoir. An attendant tells us proudly that there was competition for their corpses among the cemeteries of Paris but that "We always knew that we'd get them! They belong to us!" One in the eye for Le Cimitière du Père Lachaise, the other main contender.

On a later trip to Paris, I return sentimentally to their grave. On it is a single dead rose, a cigarette, several notes and a few stones like small tribal totems. As I stand there lost in thought for some moments, a young couple come and stand on the other side of the headstone. The girl looks like a caricature of a Parisian existentialist. She has short straight black hair, a wan face and scarlet lipstick. She is wearing a beret, a horizontally striped T-shirt, tight blue jeans and stilettos. She is holding a single red rose, a fresh one, which she places reverentially on the grave. Then she and the young man each solemnly light and smoke a cigarette, before she places the rest of the pack on the grave too.

For the dead must also have their smokes.

I do not know whether somewhere in Central Casting there is a stockroom stacked with shelves of philosophical caricatures. About a year later I am accompanying my existentially minded girlfriend to an afternoon lecture on Jacques Lacan. I guess that I must owe her a big favour. The lecturer is as stunningly awful as Ray is brilliant. I have long been involved with training lecturers in experiential teaching techniques, sometimes known as "facilitated learning", and I did not know that such terrible lectures were still available within British academia as a great testament to its contempt for students and for progress itself.

The lecturer walks into the room, sits down behind a desk and opens an exercise book in which he appears to have written out his lecture verbatim in spidery longhand in blue ink. He starts reading it in a monotonous tone without once looking up at us, his audience. After about thirty five minutes of his mind-numbing and incomprehensible mumbling, the organiser of the session stands up at the back and tells him that he has ten minutes to conclude "so that we can have some time left for questions."

At this, he looks up for the first time and says peevishly "But I haven't finished my introductory remarks yet!"

The only point of interest in the lecture comes about fifteen minutes after it has started. The door opens, and flamboyantly late a girl sweeps into the room. She could be the identical twin of the girl at Sartre's grave, dress sense and all. She has the beret, the jeans, the scarlet lipstick, the straight black hair, the stilettos, the striped T-shirt. Central Casting has come up trumps again. At the end of the afternoon she goes off with the lecturer and his chums. She is obviously a mate of his.

Or perhaps she is his mate. Intelligence – helping unprepossessing men have sex since the discovery of fire.

I still do not know whether her entrance was a stunt. Perhaps we have been subjected to a bizarre psychological experiment, designed to see how far a lecture audience can be pushed before it finally breaks.

My girlfriend and I stumble mind-befuddled out into the late London afternoon in desperate search of alcohol.

32. Men Who Hate Science

I have a memory that I cherish. I am sitting in a friend's kitchen in Wales drinking tea. Paul is a hippy who has devoted much of his life to avoiding work. In some ways he has expended more energy dodging and weaving his way around the benefits system than a light job would have consumed. But never mind, by his own lights he has done well. He has lived life on his own terms. He may not have beaten The Man, but he has not allowed The Man to beat him. He has made the system work for him. In his own eyes he is an existential hero.

Paul is expounding his views on science to me. Science, he tells me, is not to be trusted. Science is dangerous and full of folly. Science wants to do us down and do us in, microchip us, barcode us, control us and force dangerous vaccines on us for the profits of capitalists.

He interrupts this exposition of his views on science while he texts a friend on his mobile phone. Let me repeat that in italics:- *while he texts a friend on his mobile phone.* Then he boils a kettle on his electric stove to make both himself and me another mug of tea. That deserves repetition in italics too:- *Then he boils a kettle on his electric stove.* While decrying science. The irony of this is lost on him. It is not lost on me. I hope it is not lost on you.

Paul tells me that he has watched a televised discussion between three religious luminaries and a scientist. The priest, the rabbi and the imam patiently explain to the scientist, who is too thick to realise this for himself, that science is fatally flawed. This is obvious to them because science keeps changing its position and revising its theories. Therefore it is not to be trusted. It cannot offer us the immutable truths that religion can. Much of what science took for reality one hundred years ago has had to be discarded. But what religion knew to be true two thousand years ago and more still holds good today. According to Paul, the scientist cannot answer this powerful argument. The representatives of religion have won the debate and in Paul's eyes they have exposed the scientist as a fool.

But according to me, the representatives of religion have entirely misunderstood the nature of science and in my eyes they have exposed themselves as fools.

I say to Paul "The difference between science and religion is simple enough and obvious enough to be written on the back of a postcard."

"Go on!" He challenges me. "What is it then?"

"Science is evidence based. Religion is not" I say. "It's as simple as that."

Paul has a quick and sophisticated mind and so he is rarely bested in an argument. But on this occasion, just for once, he is silent. Then he changes the subject and rolls himself a joint.

****

When it comes to our attempts to understand the physical realities of the world, our only choice is between superstition or science. There are no other options. When crops fail, we can sacrifice a virgin or we can understand plant genetics. When crops fail we can pray to one of the innumerable gods or we can understand insect physiology and biochemistry. When crops fail we can invoke the help of nature devas or we can understand weather patterns and irrigation systems. When crops fail we can choose religion and starve or we can choose science and eat.

"Why" we might ask ourselves "is religious superstition so seductively alluring?" The answer is partly because it is easy enough for any fool to understand. But very few of us understand science. Many of us are so ignorant about science that we do not even know what it is that we do not know. Some scientists, following Wolfgang Pauli's lead, describe those of us who have this deep level of ignorance about science as "Not even wrong."

Yet even though we may not be able to understand even quite fundamental mathematical equations, many of us will happily make fools of ourselves by claiming that quantum physics explains consciousness or proves the existence of paranormal phenomena and spiritual forces.

****

Some time later I am once again drinking tea. I seem to spend much of my life drinking tea. Only now I am not in a kitchen in Wales but in a nice cafe in Leeds, talking to another friend, Robert. I first met Robert at university and I have known him for about forty five years. Robert is a huge genial man who is well suited to his job as a senior social worker. He is intelligent and well educated and he is one of my oldest friends. But although we agree about many things, at this moment we are having an argument. It is a friendly argument, to be sure, but still it is an argument.

Robert is telling me how arrogant scientists are, how pumped up with hubris. According to him, their assumptions that their theories tell us anything truly important about the world are simply outrageous.

I ask him "Who do you think are the more arrogant? Scientists or religious leaders?"

"Scientists" he answers unhesitatingly.

I ask him why.

"Because scientists lay down the law about how the world is supposed to work" Robert says. "They cling to their theories, even when they're wrong. If something can't be explained physically, to them it doesn't exist. So they miss out on all the stuff that is truly important."

"Can you give me any examples?" I say.

"Yes, poetry and romantic love, for example" he says.

Frankly I am baffled. I have never come across a scientist who denies the existence of either poetry or romantic love. I have even come across one or two scientists who claim to appreciate the first and to have experienced the second.

To my mind, no one is more arrogant than religious leaders who assert that they know what God thinks and how God wants us to behave.

Robert remarried six years ago and now he has two young children, his second family. During this discussion, they are playing with lego bricks in a corner of the cafe, for this is a child friendly establishment. Robert's children have been vaccinated against certain childhood diseases. Childhood diseases which can sometimes prove fatal. Or seriously disabling. They have been protected from these diseases by vaccines which have been created by scientists.

Not by priests. Not by rabbis. Not by imams.

By scientists.

I say to Robert "I think that science may be the one and only genuinely self-correcting method of human thought and endeavour. When a scientist publishes a new theory, other scientists immediately jump all over it to see if it really holds up. If the theory is flawed, this usually gets exposed very quickly and it is abandoned.

"For example, when Pons and Fleischmann announced that they'd produced energy through cold fusion, it took other scientists less than two months to test their findings and show that they were wrong. But when The Catholic Church threatened to torture Galileo because he noticed that the earth revolves around the sun and not the other way round, it took The Church three hundred and fifty years before it could bring itself to apologise. I know which I'd say is the more arrogant!"

As so often in these cases, we get nowhere. Neither of us will give any ground. So we just have another cup of tea and change the subject. Then Robert goes home with his two children. His two children who are alive and healthy. Quite possibly because of the good offices of science.

****

In my experience, there is a high degree of correlation between those who decry science and those who take conspiracy theories seriously. Here is a simple way to tell the difference between a scientific theory and a conspiracy theory:-

If a scientific theory does not fit the evidence, you discard the theory.

If a conspiracy theory does not fit the evidence, you discard the evidence.

33. Stripper On A Train

I am in an attractive town in the north of England. From the windows of the cottage where I am staying I can see the dry stone walls on the surrounding moors and the sheep peacefully grazing. I am in this town because I have been invited here to hold a meeting about non-duality. After the meeting has ended, I feel that overall it has been a success. Once or twice my answers to questions may have seemed a little harsh but several people have come up to me at the end to express their appreciation.

Not the people I have been harsh to, though. One woman has questioned me remorselessly about life after death. She very much wants to believe that she will enjoy some kind of an afterlife in heaven. She is hoping for my reassurance that this is the case. She is not impressed when I fail to give her this facile comfort.

I prefer this brief anecdote instead. It seems to me to express everything that we need to know, or indeed can know, about death:-

A student goes to his teacher, a Zen master, and says to him "Tell me, master, what happens after death."

The master simply shrugs his shoulders and says "I don't know."

The student looks shocked and stutters out "But you're a Zen master!"

"Yes" replies his teacher "but I'm not a dead Zen master."

At one point while talking to this anxious woman, I introduce into the conversation the first fictional character to appear in this chapter, dead Aunt Mabel. Some people may want to believe that she is happily playing bridge in heaven. After determinedly searching for some comforting words from me that are not going to be forthcoming, the anxious woman finally demands "But what about dead Aunt Mabel!"

"Dead Aunt Mabel is having a bloody good time on the other side!" I retort. Perhaps this is not one of my finest moments. Nor one of my most empathic ones.

At another point in the meeting, a man rather tetchily interrupts me and says "You sound to me like someone talking about a religion. I can't see much difference between what you're saying and any religion!"

"The difference" I tell him, "is that I don't give a fuck."

Perhaps I could have put this more gracefully too. Or more empathically. What I mean by it is that when people talk about a religion they often have an agenda. Frequently they want to persuade us to share some superstitious beliefs that they have. In other words, they do give a fuck. But I do not care what anyone believes. Beliefs have no purchase on non-duality. The only agenda that I have is to enjoy myself at this meeting if possible and perhaps to get to the chocolate biscuits in the tea break before they are all gone.

Nevertheless the majority of the audience seem happy. So does the woman who has arranged the talk and put me up in her traditional two-up two-down stone cottage. She has even induced me to appear in a little video about the event. We appear to part on good terms.

We appear to. But I notice afterwards that she does not invite me back. Then, some time later on the internet, she denounces the interpretation of non-duality that I have given in my talk. Though to be fair to her she does not mention me by name. And after all, everyone is entitled to change their mind.

****

When it is time for me to leave her cottage, she drives me to the station and I catch a little local train to the nearest city. In the old days it would have been a characterful puffer and not a boring diesel, the equivalent of a bus on rails. Next I change onto the big intercity train for London, settle into my seat at a table and wait for it to depart. I relax, for I love long train journeys. Once the train is rolling and I and the other passengers are suspended between departing and arriving, I can luxuriate in what the Tibetan Buddhists might call a bardo. Nothing to be done but watch the world go by.

Just before the train sets off I am joined at the table by two other passengers, both young women. One of them is rather beautiful. For the purposes of this story I will call her Lisa, because I am pretty sure that is not her name.

Lisa, it turns out, is a member of an evangelical fundamentalist Christian cult. By coincidence, a little while before my visit to the north of England, I had watched a documentary about this cult on television. Though I am sure that its members do good work amongst the drug addicts of the more poverty-stricken areas of London, they are so militant that I do not wish to name their organisation here. I do not want to wake up early one morning to hear them marching up the hill towards my house with staves and pitchforks and flaming torches chanting "Kill the beast!"

The other young woman, Sue, has applied to join the Royal Air Force and is on the train because she is going to her interview. She is very enthusiastic about this and I hope that she succeeded. For the half hour before Sue leaves us at the next station, Lisa evangelises her with shining eyes and the words of the Lord. I look out of the window and occasionally smile wanly but I do not join in. Nevertheless, by the time that Sue gets off the train, I have learnt that Lisa used to be a stripper but her soul has been saved by the love of the sweet Lord Jesus, so she has given up her stripping ways. Now she wants to devote the rest of her life to bringing prostitutes to God in order to save them from themselves. A member of her cult, an ex-prostitute, is living in a northern city doing just that right now. Lisa has been visiting this city to learn from her how best she can save the prostitutes of London. Now she is returning to Cult Central with her new savvy. That is why she is on this train.

Immediately after Sue has left us, Lisa turns her evangelistic attention to me. I let her know that I am willing for us to have this conversation but I also warn her that if we do, I will not pull my punches. She should consider carefully whether she wants to go ahead. We are still a long way from London.

My friend and teacher Terry Dukes, who was a Buddhist, used to say that we should not argue with someone about their faith. If we do and their faith weakens as a result, we become responsible for them in some way. That is what Terry said. In the past I had agreed with him, but not anymore. As far as I am concerned now, if you want to take me on, on your own head be it. Sauve qui peut. I have given Lisa fair warning.

Lisa cannot resist taking up the challenge. As I suspected that she would have to do.

We rehearse all the usual tedious arguments. As always, the case for the Judeo-Christian God is tendentious and flimsy-thin, as are the arguments as to why Jehovah should be given any more credence than the innumerable other Gods that have been dreamt up by the imagination of human kind. I will not insult your intelligence by repeating these arguments here.

At a certain point one of my imaginary friends joins us at the table and I introduce him to Lisa. His name is Rashid and he is a Moslem. He was born of Moslem parents, brought up in a Moslem culture and unsurprisingly he is just as convinced of the truth of Islam as Lisa is of the truth of Christianity. Rashid knows that Lisa is destined for hell if she does not embrace his religion and acknowledge that Mohammed is the last and greatest prophet of God. In the same way, Lisa knows that Rashid's fate is to end up in the fiery pit if he does not mend his ways and take Jesus into his heart as the one and only Son of God and his sole hope of salvation.

Both Lisa and Rashid are, of course, utterly sincere.

Lisa seems quite nonplussed by Rashid's fictional presence at our table. Frankly, she does not know what to make of him.

At one point Lisa throws at me rather challengingly "Well, what do you believe in then!" Because I am on my way back from holding a meeting about non-duality, I have a few copies of my first book with me. It has the rather unsettling and easily misunderstood title 'I Hope You Die Soon'. At this point I have to go to the loo, so as I get up to leave the table I put a copy into Lisa's hands and say "This might give you some idea." She starts leafing through it.

When I return a few minutes later, Lisa seems to be in a state of shock. Or perhaps I just imagine this. Like I have imagined my friend Rashid. She hands the book back to me and makes no reference to it.

Eventually we pull in to our London terminus. I wish Lisa well with her prostitutes and she takes her bag down from the rack overhead and leaves. During the whole of our journey, a young man across the aisle from us has been sprawled out across the seats asleep. Apparently asleep, as it turns out. Now that the train has reached its final destination, he stirs, stretches and sits up. He looks at me and says "I really enjoyed that! Especially your friend Rashid!"

"I thought you were asleep" I say.

"No. I heard every word of it. Great show! I loved it all."

****

There is a bizarre event a few months later. I am giving a talk in London. During the tea break, a young man says to me "What have you done to piss off The ********?" He is referring to the Christian cult that I will not name. "They really don't like you!"

he continues. "It's on their website. They're warning their members not to have anything to do with you!"

I can only assume that Lisa has reported me to their Thought Police. I go onto their website to try to discover what they have written about me, but it is a large and complex site and after searching fruitlessly for twenty minutes, I give up.

****

My friend Angus is a Buddhist chaplain. He lives in Birmingham and he has an excellent way of dealing with proselytisers. One day I am visiting him when a pair of Jehovah's Witnesses come knocking at his door. He talks to them on the doorstep and for a while I join him. To my surprise, he actually seems to be pretty interested in what they are saying. After a while I get bored and drift away.

Nearly two hours later he is still talking on the doorstep. It is starting to get dark and the four other Jehovah's Witnesses who have been working the area have joined the first pair. They seem rather desperate to get their friends away from Angus.

Eventually Angus wishes them a polite goodnight and comes back into the house. "Why do you waste your time with these people?" I ask him.

"Ah" he says, grinning. "You don't understand. We're under instruction from our abbot. He tells us 'Whenever the Jehovah's Witnesses come knocking on your door, you must keep them talking on the step for as long as possible to stop them spreading their lies down the street.' "

****

In my local park one day I am approached by two clean-cut besuited young Mormons. I stop and talk to them. They play Good Cop, Bad Cop, one of them nodding empathically at everything I say, the other implying that my eternal soul may be in deadly peril. Eventually the Bad Cop asks me sternly "Aren't you religious in any way?"

I look deeply at him and say "I do not have a religious cell in my body. But ...." I pause and gaze into his eyes, "I am very .... very .... very " another pause "spiritual."

He seems confused at this so I leave him pondering it and I go on my way.

****

I have difficult audience members in other places than the North of England. At the first talk that I ever give on non-duality, generously hosted by a friend in her sitting room, a man springs to his feet after listening to me for five minutes, stares coldly at me for a few seconds and then stomps out without saying a word. At another meeting in a private house at the seaside, I am about ten minutes into my talk when a man named Bill, who is sitting very close to me in the front row, suddenly shouts at me at the top of his voice "You are the most arrogant person I have ever come across!" Then he stops, sits silently for a few seconds looking blank and red-faced, jumps up and rushes out of the house. The next day my host, who is a friend of his, tells me that Bill has contacted him to say that he experienced a major breakthrough of some kind after this event. I think rather gracelessly "Well, he might at least have come back to say thank you!"

In London I go into one of my meetings to find a lanky young man ostentatiously sitting more or less with his back to me, his legs flung over the side of his chair. I immediately think "Hello! You're going to be trouble!" He does not disappoint in this. His name is Ben. I find out later that Ben has been brought to the meeting by his brother, who is in despair about him and thinks that one of my talks might do him some good. How wrong he is. Within minutes Ben is challenging me and interrupting me with irrelevancies and after a short while I can sense that other people in the room are already getting pissed off. Ben says that he wants me to talk about Kirkegarde. Knowing more about Kirkegarde, he suggests, might do me some good. At one point he misunderstands something I say to him and asks "Are you throwing me out?" "Not yet" I reply "but I'm seriously thinking about it."

I feel that this is a good enough shot to put across his bows and that it might calm him down. But he cannot help his psychopathology and it drives him on to more and more facile interruptions. Eventually I lose patience. "Now" I tell him "I am throwing you out. You can have your money back. Please leave now." He seems utterly shocked – and to have completely forgotten about my earlier warning.

Later I talk to his brother about him. I tell him that I think Ben has a personality disorder. "Funnily enough" says his brother "that's exactly what Ben says about you!"

At another meeting a Frenchman accuses me of holding my meetings just to make money. I gesture at the pathetically small audience. There are barely enough people to cover the cost of the hire of the room and my train fare. I make another gesture, this time of despair.

One afternoon I am holding a meeting in a house in another seaside town. It has been arranged by a lovely woman who is very keen on what I have to say about non-duality. She has enthusiastically invited many of her friends. Unfortunately, she has not taken into account the fact that unlike her they are all still deeply involved with spiritual and New Age beliefs. One channels the dead, one sells power crystals, one reads tarot cards, one balances people's chakras for them, they are all wedded to powerful beliefs in reincarnation and karma and most of them probably own at least one copy of 'The Secret'. The room is awash with superstition and the atmosphere quickly bristles with barely suppressed hostility.

At a meeting in Hamburg, a young man with staring and possibly psychotic eyes lurks around at the end of my talk until everyone else has left the room so that he can say to me "What you are saying is complete bullshit! There are a thousand different people inside your head!"

One afternoon I am present at a talk about non-duality given in London by another speaker, Nathan Gill. After the meeting he is harangued and almost physically attacked by a member of his audience. The man is a follower of Ramana Maharshi and he seems to feel that Nathan has not been respectful enough in talking about his beloved guru. Fortunately a burly friend of Nathan's, Jack, is present. Jack more or less picks up the disgruntled Ramana devotee by his collar and throws him forcibly out onto the street.

I wish Jack had been present at the worst haranguing that I ever receive at one of my talks. In London one Saturday afternoon I am shouted at and told to "Pipe down" and then to "Fuck off" by a practitioner of Dzogchen Buddhism. Lionel from Finchley, if you are reading this you know who you are.

But after a meeting in Berlin, Andrea, a young woman who seems at first to be quite hostile, comes up to me. She stands over me as I am still sitting in my chair and demands challengingly "You talked about unconditional love. What about dog shit? Does unconditional love also include that?"

"Sure" I reply. "Unconditional love includes everything. Otherwise it wouldn't be unconditional."

Andrea breaks into a big smile. "That" she says "is what I wanted to hear!" Then she bends down and gives me a warm hug.

Andrea is actually far more representative of audience members at my talks on non-duality than the account that I have given so far might suggest. In fact I would say that the people I have met at non-duality meetings, whether my own or those held by other speakers, are in general among the warmest, most open and most accepting people that I have come across. A friend once said to me "The trouble with holding non-duality meetings that are open to the public is that the public come." But I do not agree with this view. While it is true that these meetings will inevitably occasionally attract trouble makers, including the personality-disordered, the psychotic and the psychopathic, most of the members of the public that I have met through my meetings have been an absolute delight.

34. In Wales

For many years I have a love affair with Wales. I am fortunate in having several friends who live there so I can visit often, sometimes for weeks at a time. My friends are scattered from the extreme hippy strongholds of wild West Wales, through the green eco-warriors around Machynlleth in Mid Wales and on up to the Welsh Nationalist centres of the North. These last start around Dolgellau and reach as far as the furthermost tip of the Lleyn Peninsula, where you can see anti-English graffiti scrawled on barns and along stone walls. When I first start visiting, it is the stark message in Welsh "Dal dy dir". I am told that this means "Stand your ground!" or "Hold onto your land!" Then someone suggests a more interesting translation to me. "Show them your arses!" In later years the graffiti is the starker "Colonists out!"

This reminds me of the years, now gone, when Welsh Nationalists were burning down homes owned by the English in North Wales. It gave rise to a poor joke in bad taste. "Come home to a real fire. Buy a cottage in Wales." As far as I know, in the sparsely populated towns and villages of North Wales, where everyone knew everyone else and what they were up to, there was not a single arrest and conviction arising from these arson attacks. So much for the investigative powers of the local police and of the Welsh criminal justice system.

On one of my early trips I have arranged to meet my friend Fiona in Corris, a village built around a now-defunct slate mine. Neither of us has ever been there before. She has fetched up there earlier than me and I phone her to make the final arrangements for meeting up. Breathlessly she tells me down the phone that she has fallen in love. Knowing Fiona as I do, I imagine that this must be with some hippy wild man living in a caravan or a yurt and devoting his life to eco-warfare against the local capitalists. But no. She has fallen in love with Corris itself.

As soon as I arrive in the village I understand why. When the sun is shining it is one of the jewels of Wales. With its steep wooded hillsides, its traditional slate cottages and houses and the mountains of Snowdonia in the background, it is stunningly beautiful. When the sun is shining. Which it does not do very often. I contemplate moving to Corris but I am told that on the "wrong" side of the valley I will not see the sun from September through to April. The "right" side of the valley is not much better.

Depression lurks in such geology.

Another friend has moved onto the Lleyn Peninsula. A neighbour remarks to him as he moves in to his new home, an ancient cottage built out of huge rocks, one November that it has rained on each of the previous eighty days. But ho hum, "There's no such thing as bad weather. There's only bad clothing."

Remote places often bring out extremes in the psyches of those who live there. Corris is not an exception. I am told that there are regular drunken lock-ins in the pub till the early hours of the morning, that drug taking is rife and that the sex life of the local hippies makes 'Beyond The Valley Of The Dolls' look respectable.

With Fiona I make a trip to West Wales to stay with friends in a large shabby apartment in a huge rambling country house. They are hosting a party for some local musicians. When I slide off to bed at about 1.30 a.m, they are playing guitars and smoking weed around the ancient wooden kitchen table. In the morning, when I get up, most of them are still there, still playing the same repetitive riffs. Fiona is having a bad time at this point in her life and needs to get out and about so that she can have some "car therapy". This is therapy that takes place while driving around nice country roads in a car. It can be remarkably effective, although I recommend that it is the "therapist" who does the driving rather than the "client" and that a stop for tea be regarded as a vital part of the treatment.

We end up taking a long drive across country to Tenby and are away from the West Wales kitchen for about five hours in all. I will swear on whatever holy book you choose that when we return the musicians are still sitting in the same places around the kitchen table, still playing the same few riffs, apparently locked in an experimental enactment of Nietzsche's "eternal recurrence". If we could bottle and sell the palpable sense of inertia in the room, we would be able to afford a luxury yurt.

****

As I have mentioned, remote places often beget extreme psyches. And extreme psyches sometimes retreat to remote places. I ask myself "Do the people I know in the wilds of Wales move here because they are already a little bit more crazy than the rest of us, or has living here sent them crazy?"

I decide that it is a little of each. If we are seriously uncomfortable in our own psyches, remote places can seem to offer us a more gentle and an easier way of life. But the actual exigencies of living there are likely to make our psychopathology even more extreme than before.

Not enough reality checks, you see.

I have an argument with Suzie, the eighteen year old daughter of a friend. Suzie looks terrifying. She has tattoos and dreadlocks and there are various bits of metal sticking out of her face. I suggest to her that the people we know living in the sundry cottages, caravans, tree houses, communes, teepees, yurts and camper vans round about are just that little bit crazier than the folk in London.

"You must be the crazy one if you think that!" she explodes at me. "London! London! People in London are *absolutely* crazy!"

I stick to my guns. "Of course" I say "there are more crazy people in London than there are down here. That's because there are lots more people in London overall. But as a percentage of the population, I reckon that there are more crazy people here. In London we just can't get away with the kinds of delusional thinking that you can. You see, we're much more likely to come up against someone who'll pull us up short and tell us that we're talking nonsense. Down here you're all feeding each other's weird beliefs, all colluding with each other about conspiracy theories, giant alien lizards and angels. No one challenges anyone."

We end up agreeing to disagree and Suzie makes me a cup of tea. She may look like a character from 'Mad Max Beyond Thunderdome' but she has a kind heart.

The kitchen in which we are standing belongs to a friend who seriously believes that the world is ruled by David Icke's shape-shifting twelve-foot high bejewelled lizards. Perhaps you do too, but if that is the case you really should not be reading this book. His ex-partner drives from her home to a nearby village every few days to collect water from a spring in a huge plastic container, having been convinced that drinking tap water will imperil her health and may shorten her life. Unsurprisingly, the woman who has convinced her of this has also sold her an expensive water filtration system. Presumably this is so that she does not become seriously ill or die from the bugs which might have contaminated the spring water, for the fact is that sheep piss nearby. Yet most of us drink tap water and our longevity continues to climb remorselessly upwards. Her next-door neighbour channels angelic healing forces and a friend across the road is the mouthpiece for a spirit guide who dispenses cosmic wisdom every Thursday evening. Just up the street lives a lady who regularly goes on a detox diet of such savagery that it deserves to be classified as an eating disorder. If you greet her with a hug, you find yourself holding bones. The man a few houses along from her meditates for up to eight hours a day. If he meets you in the village, he may grunt and nod, but he will not join in any conversation lest it distract him from his spiritual path. Many of the local parents go in for Home Education, which as one of my friends caustically asserts "Down here should really be called No Education." The parents keep their children away from school and instead gather with them regularly at coastal coffee bars. There they ignore the children, who are left for hours on end to re-enact 'Lord Of The Flies' on the beach. One of these parents is receiving succour from an entire health care team, including psychotherapists and social workers. She seems to have made it her mission in life to seduce each of these in turn. In this she has so far been remarkably successful.

And then there is Robbie. I have a friend who says "We each have our own individual islands of psychosis." But in Robbie's case, it is more like whole continents. In theory Robbie should be one of the more sane people that I come across in Wales, because he is one of the few who actually has a real job with a salary. He is a social worker, mentoring young people. But Robbie's house is up a long muddy track in the hills far from any other dwelling and this among other things has done for his sanity.

Robbie has obsessions. His current obsession is with the illegality of the council tax. He has convinced himself that under some Royal Charter of 1347 or an obscure codicil to The American Declaration Of Independence or a minor amendment to Le Code Napoleon, it is illegal for the council to charge him for emptying his bins when they are full, sending fire engines to his house if it is on fire, providing police to protect him should thugs threaten him, and lighting and paving the long road that leads to his track. Robbie lives far from any centre of civilisation, so council employees actually have to travel a great distance to service his property. Ironically, some of us feel that in view of this he should actually pay more council tax than the rest of us, rather than the "Nothing at all" which he considers to be fair.

Robbie has done his research and like many obsessives he has files of paperwork to prove it. He stopped paying the tax some time ago and he has been bombarding the council with letters and documents since then. On more than one occasion he has gone to their offices to present his case in person. At the moment there is a standoff. Robbie takes this to mean that he has won and that the terrified council will have to back down. Consequently, the government will be forced to abolish this illegitimate tax throughout Great Britain. Perhaps representatives of a grateful nation will carry him shoulder high through the streets, lauding him and treating with more respect his other ramblings, the ones about alien abductions, the faked moon landings, the Illuminati and the Bilderberg Group.

In fact of course the council are slowly moving things towards their inevitable conclusion. Robbie will eventually receive a summons to court and a fine and a visit from the bailiffs or a brief prison sentence, or he will cave and pay the tax. Of these possibilities, the last is by far the most likely. When push comes to shove, Robbie may be crazy but he is not actually insane.

Though if Robbie knows anything about the Scientologists, this might give him heart. In America The Church Of Scientology has defeated the Internal Revenue Service over demands that it pay billions of dollars in back taxes. After years during which The Church drowned the IRS in documents and legal cases, the IRS has eventually thrown in the towel, cancelled the back taxes and granted the Scientologists the tax exempt religious status that they have been demanding.

This might give Robbie heart but it should not. The Church Of Scientology is alleged to have more liquid wealth than The Holy Roman Catholic Church with which to pay its numerous lawyers and accountants. Whereas Robbie has only a decrepit house half way up a track in Wales, a collection of ramshackle outhouses and a twelve year old Ford Mondeo.

How do I know so much about Robbie's battle with the council? And his psychopathology? Not from choice, but because one evening I am sitting with five other people in the same kitchen where Suzie made me a cup of tea after telling me that the people round here are not crazy. We are listening to Robbie while he jabbers at ninety miles an hour and explains that King Richard III or King Edward II or maybe it was Pope Pious IV or the Emperor Charlemagne granted the people of Britain forever and in perpetuity the right to ignore any tyrannical council which wished us to pay for electric street lighting and diesel fire engines whenever in the future they happened to be invented.

After about twenty five minutes, I can take no more of this. I leave the others to Robbie's ravings and retreat to the sitting room where there is a stack of old videos. The choice of titles is awful. I choose the least bad one and watch it. It is terrible. But it is still a lot better than listening to Robbie.

When it is over I go back into the kitchen. Robbie is still jabbering so I go to bed.

****

As well as more craziness, I am convinced that there is a higher quotient of broken relationships down here in the wilds of Wales. One day I am driving friends of mine, a couple, out of the fantastically cute village where they have lived for about twelve years. We are going on a trip to the coast. They keep on pointing out houses to me, always with the same comment.

"That's where Jim and Annie lived till they broke up. That's where Pete and Susan lived till they broke up. That's where Kevin and Rosie lived till they broke up. That's where Mat and Beverly lived till they broke up."

In this quite large village, it seems that more than one tenth of the houses once contained friends of theirs whose relationships have now fallen apart.

Extreme psyches and places beget extreme difficulties. Not enough reality checks. Too much time on too many hands. Not enough distraction and entertainment. Not enough work. Boredom. Too many extreme beliefs and conspiracy theories. The devil makes work for idle hands.

When all else fails,
Try an affair in Wales.

A year later my friends' own relationship becomes another casualty of village life when it emerges that he has been having an on-off affair for nine years with her "best friend".

****

Two of my friends in Wales, Bill and Ellie, bring their child up in the Yequana way. If you are old enough to remember this and you were interested in unorthodox approaches to child rearing you may have come across an influential book called 'The Continuum Concept' that was published in the mid nineteen seventies. It was by Jean Liedloff, who had spent some time living with an Amerindian tribe in the Amazon rainforest. I once met Jean as a co-participant on a weekend residential course. She was an impressive woman. Bill got to know her much better than I did and embraced the Yequana way of child rearing wholeheartedly, at first in theory and later, once he had himself fathered a child to experiment on, in practice.

Jean's recommendation to young urban parents was that we adopt the child rearing ways of the Yequana Indians, in so far as this is possible in a Western environment. For the first eighteen months there should be the "in-arms phase". Essentially, for this period the child should never be out of physical contact with the mother, day or night. A sling would help in this endeavour. This first principle turned out to be highly effective at producing guilt in young Western mothers who simply could not comply, and anger in sex-starved Western fathers who simply did not want their partners to comply.

After eighteen months, the child is put down onto the floor of the hut in the jungle, or the semi-detached bungalow in Bexley Heath, and then pretty much ignored and left to its own devices. It can play with dangerous arrows or sharp knives on the edge of the fire pit or the fireplace, or play on the cliff top or the kerb side. The child's inner wisdom and innate sense of danger will protect it. It will intuitively know what is dangerous so it will not approach poisonous snakes with wooden sticks or electric sockets with metal forks. The older children, aged three or four years and above, will look after the younger ones. The child will naturally recognise that it should not explore beyond its growing capabilities.

Thus the child will grow up confident, resilient and wise. Or it will not grow up at all having tumbled into the fire pit or shoved a knife into a fifty amp electricity supply.

This approach to parenting should not be confused with the "child-centred approach". In fact, after the "in-arms phase" it is virtually the opposite. Once these first eighteen months are over, the parents pay little attention to the child. They certainly would not do what my friend Harry does. Harry, a child-centred parent and left-wing social worker, on one occasion spends more than five minutes using reason and logic to try to persuade his three year old son to get into a car. It is a Range Rover and three adults ready to go on a picnic are already sitting in it on a hot summer's day. They are probably fuming. And thinking "Just pick the little bastard up and strap him in!"*

---

*On the subject of child rearing, I have a friend who gives this advice:- "All new parents should have two samplers embroidered, framed and hung on either side of their bed. One should say 'If you let them, they'll eat you alive', the other 'Whatever you do, you'll fuck them up anyway.'"

Bill and Ellie's son Tom has been brought up as far as possible according to Yequana principles. Bill is actually happier to let Tom scamper along the very edges of dangerous cliffs than Ellie is. Ellie still seems wedded to a bourgeois preference for individual survival rather than the Darwinian imperative of the survival of the herd. Or perhaps she simply does not trust Tom's inner wisdom as much as Bill does. Or maybe she is just not as lazy as Bill.

Tom, completely unschooled and undisciplined, can by the age of six sometimes be a thoroughly obnoxious child. His behaviour is at times so invasive that he drives the couple in the next door apartment into moving away. His father will take no responsibility for Tom's behaviour at all. After all, among the Yequana the tribe's children are essentially the responsibility of everyone. Which as Bill interprets it, means of no one. Or at least not of Bill.

In fairness I should add that years later Tom has become a nice young man. He has survived the cliffs, the snakes and the electric sockets and he does seem resilient, reasonably confident and self-reliant. He will probably do well at anything that does not require many numeracy or literacy skills. He is ready to take his place as one of the many hippy wild men of Wales.

****

I must have mixed karma with Celtic countries. One day I find myself in Scotland quite near Findhorn, the community founded by Peter and Eileen Caddy, where nature devas help humans to grow giant cabbages in unpropitious soil. I have been holidaying with my wife and two children on Iona, Mull and Skye, and Findhorn is not far from our route home so we make the detour. Once there we discover that we can sign up for a half day "Findhorn Experience", consisting of a tour, a talk and the opportunity to meet some Findhornians.

The Findhornians, we discover, speak mostly in spiritual whispers, for the ethos of the place is one of peace, love and harmony. All traces of the shadow are therefore strangled at birth. Consequently, by the time that we leave the place I feel as if I am suffocating.

I wonder whether my reaction to Findhorn may be ignoble, evidence of my spiritual depravity. So I talk to my friend Tim about it.

Tim is a sweet gentle person and the leader of a meditation organisation, so I trust his spiritual acumen. He also has more experience of Findhorn than I do, having attended their week-long "Findhorn Experience".

"How did you like it?" I ask him.

"Well, the best way I can sum it up" says Tim "is that after it was over I wanted to run along the middle of the road and jump in the air screaming 'Fuck! Fuck! Fuck!' over and over again at the top of my voice."

****

One weekend I am holding meetings in a rural part of Ireland. Before the first session has even started I spend ten minutes backed up against a wall while a woman jabbers at me about her local community's "faery tree". She is a She-Robbie. She explains that the locals tie talismanic objects to the branches of this tree to ask for intercession from the faery folk in their hopes and troubles.

"A little win on the horses, maybe?"

"A little cure of a cancer, perhaps?"

The faery tree has become so overladen with these intercessionary devices that its health is now imperilled. So she has assembled a party of villagers who are spending much of their weekend unburdening the tree. They are collecting and disposing of sacks of the talismanic trinkets.

At some point she catches the glint of scepticism in my eye. She solemnly assures me that those who disrespect these trees, which apparently flourish throughout Ireland, receive drastic karma-uppance. She tells me the story of a farmer whose land had a faery tree in an inconvenient spot on it. So he uprooted it with his tractor. As a consequence, within a month he, his wife, his many children and probably his aunts, uncles, nephews and nieces as well were all dead from a series of tragic and wholly to be expected accidents.

"Why did I agree to come here?" I wonder as I listen to her. Remote places beget extreme psyches.

Her story reminds me of the chaplain at my school. Although he is a Reverend, he is an unlikely man to hold this post. Much too much of a freethinker, you see. He was brought up in a small village in Suffolk where, he tells us, "There is to this day a faery tree which the locals still sometimes make use of." According to our chaplain, they dig out little holes in the trunk of the tree and insert small animals into them to invoke the help of the faery folk.

I also remember him saying to us one sunny afternoon "Now boys, whenever you're out walking in the countryside, remember to take a pair of wire cutters with you." This is so that we can pare away any wire fencing that the local farmers have used to illegally block the public footpaths.

****

One evening I am in a restaurant in West Wales with some local friends. One of them, Pat, says to me "Are you still thinking of moving down here to join us?"

"Oh no." I say. "I've got a very clear idea of what kind of person flourishes down here and it's not people like me."

"Well, who does flourish down here, then?" Pat asks.

"Oh, crafts people for example" I say. Pat is a carpenter and makes beautiful furniture. "And artists." Pat's wife is a painter. "Hippies, eco-enthusiasts, eco-warriors. Anyone who wants to own some woodland and live illegally on it in a shack. Anyone looking for a simpler life near rivers or in the mountains or by the sea. People who want to tune in to nature and avoid the big city. People who need to heal some psychic wound or other."

"So what are you, if you're none of those?" asks Pat.

"Me? I'm an effete metropolitan intellectual" I reply. "I don't fit in here at all."

Pat laughs and says "It's been a long time since I've heard anyone round here use the word 'effete'."

"You make my point for me" I say. And I order myself another cappuccino.

35. Free Will

"Free will is a malign myth." James B Miles

An easy way to start a row with someone, should you ever want to, is to suggest to them that free will does not exist.

This will not work with everyone, of course, as some of us are already aware that free will is an illusion. But most people still believe in the existence of free will and many will respond to the assertion that there is actually no such thing as if it were a deep insult to them. The denial of free will seems also to be a denial of much that we consider to be most important and most cherished about ourselves, our lives and our values. To challenge the notion of free will can be to strike at the very heart of our sense of meaning and purpose in life. Morality itself, or at least the conventional view of morality, is on the line.

You may be able to have particular fun in this way with priests and vicars.

Yet in some ways it is surprising that the notion of free will has such a powerful hold over so many of us individually and over our culture as a whole. For it is in fact very easy to dismantle free will philosophically and logically. The argument, which is simple enough for a reasonably intelligent fourteen year old to follow, goes like this:-

Either the universe is wholly deterministic or it is not.

If the universe is wholly deterministic, there is no place for free will because all apparent "choices" and "decisions" are entirely determined by prior causes. These prior causes include both inherited and cultural factors, or a combination of "nature" and "nurture".

If the universe is not wholly deterministic, then there are only two other possibilities. Either it is partly or wholly random. But a "choice" or "decision" made partly or wholly at random does not involve the exercise of free will in any meaningful sense.

So whether the universe is wholly deterministic, wholly random, or some mix of deterministic and random, there is no possibility of free will.

Of course no sane person actually believes that the universe is wholly random. The evidence of our everyday experience denies that. I have only included the possibility of an entirely random universe here in order to complete the argument. While Sir Isaac Newton ruled over physics, the smart money was betting that the universe was wholly deterministic. But the discoveries of quantum physics have muddied the waters. It now seems probable that there is randomness afoot at least at some level in the universe. But I am not going to risk making a fool of myself here by writing anything more about quantum physics, a subject which not even quantum physicists understand.

Many philosophers, known in the trade as "libertarians" and "compatibilists", insist that free will does exist. They refuse to acknowledge that this is an impossibility because they do not like the ideological implications of this conclusion. Their arguments for the existence of free will tend to be highly complex, convoluted and arcane. This is in itself a clue to the fact that they are trying to pull the wool over our eyes, because in essence these arguments can be boiled down to one or the other of the following brief and simple sentences:-

either *"I must have free will because I feel as if I do."*

or *"The feeling that I have free will is a good enough substitute and an equivalent for actually having free will."*

These two sentences are so patently false that they do not deserve any further comment here.

Many of these libertarian and compatibilist philosophers are driven by their ideology. They tend to be neo-liberal right-wing free marketeers. Their insistence that free will exists suits their ideological beliefs, which are exemplified in the foundational American myth of "From Log Cabin To White House". This is also sometimes known as the myth of "The Self-made Man". "As we have free will," they argue, "anyone can succeed and become rich in a free market economy, no matter how unpropitious the circumstances into which they are born. Therefore there is no need to 'level the playing field' through social, economic and political action."

The problem for these ideological neo-liberals is that if they acknowledge the illusory nature of free will, they will be contradicting their most deeply cherished beliefs and attitudes about society. Then, heaven forfend, they might have to support reform.

Another group of philosophers, known as "illusionists", know perfectly well that free will is an illusion but advocate that we do not let the hoi polloi know this in case they get uppity. Philosophers can be trusted with this knowledge, they argue, but the common herd may start rioting in the streets if they find out. This group of philosophers is also mostly composed of neo-liberals.

One philosopher, Galen Strawson, puts his attitude to free will in a remarkably straightforward and pragmatic way. In a radio interview he acknowledges quite frankly that free will cannot exist. But he goes on to say with great clarity that in daily life it is impossible for him to feel this to be the case.

This of course is the actual experience of most people. It is one of the reasons why it is so easy to start a row about free will. To deny free will seems to be a direct assault on the reality of our everyday experience. It also seems to be an assault on our sense of morality. As the neuroscience researcher and writer Dick Swaab puts it "Our sense of morality accounts for the idea that each individual is responsible for his or her own deeds ....." before he adds "illusory though this is."

Swaab also points out that moral behaviour is actually hardwired into us by millions of years of evolution. So there has always been an important human characteristic which could be termed "natural morality". Therefore we do not need religious precepts to induce us to behave morally. In fact religions come along and hijack morality much later on in our development. They then assert that religious believers exhibit more moral behaviour than non-believers.

There is of course no evidence for this assertion whatsoever. It would probably be easier to demonstrate the opposite. Swaab quotes Arthur C Clarke:- "The greatest tragedy in mankind's entire history may be the hijacking of morality by religion." We could add to this the words of the Nobel prize winning physicist Steven Weinberg:- "There will always be good people who do good things and evil people who do evil things. But to get good people to do evil things, for that you need religion." And Christopher Hitchens, in one of his great blasts against religion, reminds us that "religion has caused innumerable people ..... to behave in ways that would make a brothel-keeper or an ethnic cleanser raise an eyebrow."

****

Essentially free will is an incoherent idea. No one has ever been able to explain in a satisfactory way who or what exercises it or in what manner they do so.

There are a few books worth reading about free will. One of these is 'The Free Will Delusion' by James B Miles. He is a poor writer and maddeningly repetitive and his book is also marred by his own personal anger at the social implications of his subject. However, if you want the arguments fully spelled out in a comprehensive way, 'The Free Will Delusion' is the bee's knees.

By the way, if for some reason you are not impressed by the simple argument against free will presented above, you might like instead to look into the new neuroscience. A mass of direct evidence has been accumulating for some time now from the world of neuroscience that there is no possibility of free will, nor of a central self which could exercise it even if it did exist. In fact the sense that "I am choosing to do this" seems to be added on after the event, after our "decision" has in actuality been made by unconscious processes. In some cases these processes have already taken place several seconds before we become consciously aware of the decision. It is only at this later point that the impression forms that we have chosen that decision.

Interestingly humanity is in a way turning full circle with these recent discoveries, as twenty-first century neuroscientists give us a view of the non-existence of the self which is surprisingly close to views expressed millennia ago by mystics.

And if we think that the experiments being conducted by neuroscientists are too arcane and technical for the layperson to follow, then we might notice that even a popular newspaper like 'The Daily Mail' is on to them. In fact it has been on to them for several years. What is more, it understands what these experiments imply about the non-existence of free will. In 2008 'The Daily Mail' published an article by its science editor, Michael Hanlon, under the headline "Is Free Will Simply An Illusion?" After describing one of the relevant experiments, Hanlon wrote "The implications are hugely significant, because the experiment suggests that what we think of as a 'conscious decision' may, in fact, be no such thing .... Our 'conscious self' .... is merely a passive observer, lazing back in his chair and watching it all happen. It is as though what we are actually aware of is no more than a film show, and the decision-making is made purely unconsciously."

36. Satsang With The Holy One

I am sitting in a hall in London waiting for the appearance on stage of a holy woman. Although she is American, she has a lovely Indian spiritual name. She is scheduled to appear with her consort.

To be honest, I am suspicious of Westerners who assume Eastern spiritual names. This may be just one of my many irrational prejudices but it partly accounts for why I am sitting in the hall somewhat reluctantly. In fact I have been brought along here by a friend who wants my company and I have been promised that if I sit through this satsang and behave myself fairly well I will be rewarded with food and drink afterwards in a nice cafe.

After a while a woman walks onto the stage. This is not The Holy One. Rather it is her advance guard who has been sent into the hall to instruct us in the proper modes of decorous behaviour that we must adopt when The Holy One and her lover finally appear. We must sit quietly. We must close our eyes and meditate for five minutes – or I suppose at least pretend to do so. After The Holy One has spoken we may ask questions by raising a hand and then waiting to find out whether we have been fortunate enough to be selected. At the end of the session, when The Holy One and her lover depart from the stage, we must continue to sit quietly for a further five minutes before getting up and ourselves leaving the hall. This last instruction, I think rather uncharitably, is probably so that the couple can avoid the risk of running into us in the car park in case they are bickering. For the spiritual rumour mill has been working and it appears that all has not been well recently in their relationship with each other.

At this point all is not well in my relationship with myself. I feel oppressed in this atmosphere of sanctity. I believe that the nice cafe may not be sufficient reward for the suffering that I am about to undergo.

Eventually The Holy One appears in a floaty gown and delivers some spiritual bromide. I spot a man in the audience that I know. Being aware of his beliefs and attitudes, I am surprised that he is there and I wonder what he is making of her talk. After about seven minutes I get a clue when he stands up and walks out. Then some deeply troubled people ask a few questions, focussing on their unhappiness with life. The Holy One gives them a little therapeutic processing in front of the rest of the audience.

I have never been keen on "therapy-lite" as public spectacle. But I notice that many modern spiritual teachers like to indulge in it.

The Holy One and her lover eventually leave the stage. We obediently sit there as we have been told to do until they are safely gone from the vicinity. To me there is the stench of suppression in the air. It feels stifling. It feels suffocating. It feels like a prison. To be fair, some of the other people in the hall seem to be in a state of exaltation, rejoicing at having spent an hour or so with their spiritual heroine. But I feel that I have witnessed a great exercise in projection. Onto The Holy One the audience have projected all the perfection that they deny in themselves and all their spiritual yearnings.

The meal afterwards with my friend in the nice cafe is pleasant. But I am not sure it is worth the price I have had to pay.

****

A few months later I am visiting a friend in her little cottage in a tiny village in Wales. Fiona is quite open to spiritual matters but I know that she is also grounded and pretty hard-headed.

As we sit at her kitchen table waiting for the vegetable soup to heat up for our supper, I start to tell her about my visit to The Holy One. Within a few moments Fiona has summoned her up on her laptop. She turns the screen towards me to show me the start of a short video.

"Is that her?" she asks.

"Yes" I reply and Fiona stops me saying anything else while she watches and listens. She does not want my views to influence her. She wants to make up her own mind.

After about three minutes she turns to me.

"What do you think of her?" I ask.

There is a pause and then she says vehemently "I just want to kill her!"

Ah, I think. Not just me then.

37. Among The Benedictines

I am spending an afternoon at a Benedictine Monastery. This is an unusual thing for me to do. In fact I have never done it before. Nor have I ever done it since. I have been invited by a friend to be a guest at part of a weekend retreat for members of the Bede Griffiths Sangha. This is a community of people who seek to combine Western and Eastern spirituality as Bede Griffiths, a Benedictine monk, himself did. Although a Roman Catholic, he helped to set up an ashram based partly on the Hindu model in Kerala, and lived for many years in another ashram in Tamil Nadu. He took a Sanskrit name and became known as Swami Dayananda.

I sit through discussions, a sing-song, a meditation and an exercise in which we are divided into subgroups and given a handout. On it there is a series of quotations for us to con-template. We each have to choose a quotation from Side One of the handout. In turn we will read our quotation out to our subgroup and then talk briefly about why it has particularly touched us. Edward, who is our subgroup leader, explains that these anyway are our instructions, but he is a liberal-minded leader of a liberal-minded group, so we can interpret them as liberally as we like.

I warm to Edward.

I particularly like a quotation on Side Two of the handout. It is quite recognisably about non-duality, a topic which fascinates me. So when it is my turn, I ask my subgroup to turn their pieces of paper over so that they can follow it while I read it out.

Edward immediately intervenes.

"You were asked" he reminds me sternly "to choose a quotation from Side One. Would you please follow the instructions."

His liberality has mysteriously disappeared. His tone implies that because of such insubordination, Empires might crumble. And that because I am a guest, almost an interloper, my wilful refusal to follow the instructions that were so clearly given to me is even more heinous. If not prevented, I am likely to unleash the hounds of chaos and threaten the very order of the world.

Apparently, the quotations on Side Two of the handout are for a session the following day. I have just been prevented from sabotaging that session. A narrow squeak indeed.

I cool to Edward.

I understand more deeply the phrase "an iron fist inside a velvet glove".

I am later told by my friend that Edward suffers from depression. I am not surprised. Nor am I surprised that several other individuals at the retreat also experience bouts of depression and that in my four or five hours with them I get the impression that they are a deeply troubled group of people.

At that time I believe that "repression leads to depression." I still believe it now. At that time I believe that "the fastest way to freedom is to feel our feelings." I still believe that now too. What I mean by this is freedom from psychological ills, not freedom in any philosophical sense. This route to freedom is sometimes referred to as "experiential non-avoidance" by psychotherapists. I hope that phrase speaks for itself.

The participants on the retreat are self-consciously virtuous and moral people. They are committed to intentionally doing good and to intentionally avoiding harm. But as I listen to their discussions, what strikes me is how agonised many of them seem, what little peace they have found. Edward is merely an extreme.

Their problem seems to be that they have seen through the falsehoods that they were told by The Catholic Church during their upbringing but, in spite of their anger at this, they are still too enmeshed in The Church's propaganda to break entirely free.

In short, they are mightily conflicted. And still to some extent hypnotised. The sound of cognitive dissonance is almost audible as it buzzes around inside their heads.

We are not talking of Fundamentalists and Evangelicals here. These Sangha members are intelligent, thoughtful people. They have recognised many of the absurdities that lie at the heart of Catholic doctrine as well as some of the terrible harm that has been perpetrated by their Church:-

The ante partum, in partu and post partum virginity of Mary?

Mary's physical ascension into heaven, perhaps before the corruption of death has taken place?

(Catholic theologians argue about these first two points. Take a little time to let that fact sink in. Intelligent well-educated human beings, some of whom probably have doctorates from respectable universities, argue about these first two points.)

The actual real transubstantiation of the communion bread and wine into actual real human flesh and blood?

The centuries of bloody slaughter? Slaughter piled on slaughter? The slaughter of the pagans? The slaughter of the Cathars? The slaughter of the Jews? The slaughter of innocent women accused of witchcraft? The slaughter of the Huguenots, perhaps twenty thousand massacred on St Bartholomew's Day and during the weeks afterwards?

The Children's Crusade?

The Inquisition? The torture and execution of heretics?

The rape of children by priests? The beating of children by nuns and priests?

The three hundred and fifty years that it takes for The Church to apologise to Galileo, to acknowledge that he was right and that astonishingly the earth does revolve around the sun?

The centuries of slanderous falsehoods against the Jews? The blood libel? The pogroms and the bloody murders?

The interdict against barrier contraception? The Church causing syphilis and AIDS to be spread around the world? Especially amongst the poor and badly educated, as middle class Catholics in the well-heeled West have the sense to ignore their Popes, at least on this issue which affects them so directly.

All those false promises? Promises that only homo sapiens is intelligent enough to be fooled by? (As Yuval Harari writes, you cannot convince a monkey to give you a banana in return for a promise of limitless bananas after death in monkey heaven.)

All those books proscribed? All those shackles placed on the human mind? The near-total destruction of Classical learning, with Western civilization being set back by perhaps a thousand years?

All those protection rackets that The Church has presided over? The sale of indulgences? Tithing? "Give us your money or you'll be tortured in purgatory." All that extortion?

Nonsense piled on nonsense. Dangerous nonsense. Nonsense which causes good people to do terrible things. "The first thing a man will do for his ideals" writes Joseph Schumpeter "is lie."

And The Protestant Churches no better in much of this.

What well-meaning, intelligent person would want to belong to clubs like these? And yet the members of the Bede Griffiths Sangha cannot quite break free.

Instead of breathing the pure air of freedom, they cling to whatever fragments of their faith they can maintain. They fear that if they let go completely, they will drown.

Yet if they let go completely, instead of drowning they might find themselves floating free.

****

Later, I try to talk to my friend about my experience of the members of the Sangha. She is not pleased. In her childhood, she was infected by the same virus as they were. Although she is fiercely intelligent and could be described as utterly lapsed, she too cannot quite break free of the baleful influence of The Church. She even denies to me that The Church interdicts barrier contraception. Well, perhaps we could argue over the words, but I have witnessed a lupine South American cardinal stating directly to the camera, in contradiction of the scientific evidence, that "In any case, condoms do not give any protection against AIDS. The latex has holes in it large enough for the AIDS virus to pass through."

Is he stupid? Or is he lying? One of these must surely be the case.

Nonsense piled on nonsense. Falsehoods. Dead women. Dead babies.

The Church imposes its own punishment for what it sees as sin. The wages of sin shall be death.

Ultimately, my friend and I have to agree to disagree, though the tension that this generates between us never quite disappears.

I am not invited to the Bede Griffiths Sangha again.

38. A Spiritual Potpourri

Tell Me Who You Are

I am attending an Enlightenment Intensive weekend on the out-skirts of a town somewhere north of London. I spend much of the day sitting uncomfortably on the floor facing a partner. They say to me "Tell me who you are." I tell them who I am. Then they ask me the same question again. And again. And again.

Sometimes, instead, I say to them "Tell me who you are." Then they tell me who they are. Every so often we swap part-ners and perform the same exercise with somebody else.

This seems to be some kind of a test, but there are no clues as to how to pass it. All we know is that this is a very junior exercise. We will individually move on to a more senior exercise when we have succeeded at this first one. We are not allowed to know what the measure of our success will be, but if we suspect that we might somehow have accomplished the task, we can consult The Wise Person who sits in an impressive chair at the front of the room. He is so wise that he can determine from what we say whether we have passed the test or not. If we have, he will give us the next exercise.

After two and a half days I am still stuck on "Tell me who you are." I am so far from any breakthrough that I have not even been to the front of the room to consult The Wise Person. Not once. Several other group members have consulted him, some of them more than once, but they have mostly been rebuffed. My friend Rosemary has spoken to him after going through an amazing shamanic experience. She became an eagle. She soared high over the landscape and looked down with an eagle's eyes. Now she knows what it is like to perceive as an eagle perceives.

I am impressed. But The Wise Person is not. Whatever it is that he wants to hear, this is not it. Transcendental experiences are not what he is looking for.

Although it is not overtly stated, clearly the stench of Zen hangs over this place.

Over the course of the weekend only two of the group, Pauline and Ray, receive the stamp of approval from The Wise Person. But they are not allowed to tell us what it is that they have experienced. Or maybe not experienced. For the rest of the weekend they try not to look unspeakably smug. Or perhaps that is just my projection.

When we are not telling someone who we are, we are doing The Wise Person and his wife's housework for them, digging their garden and chopping and bringing in their firewood. At mealtimes they feed us tiny amounts of bean sprouts, grains, dried fruit and nuts.

We have each paid quite a lot of money to be treated like this. So from their point of view this is a good wheeze. But as there is a well known saying in Zen about chopping firewood, it is probably worth it.

And after the weekend I am for a while remarkably sensitised. The clamour of ordinary life seems extraordinarily raucous to me. I cannot bear to watch television or listen to the radio. I can only listen to classical music and to haunting South American pan pipes. Driving about in my car, I play 'The Flight Of The Condor' over and over and over again.

Looking back, my guess is that Pauline and Ray each had a moment of sartori, a momentary complete disappearance of the sense of self. But I have long ago lost touch with them, so I suppose I will never really know for sure.

****

Spiritual Encounter

The group at the Enlightenment Intensive know each other well. We have all been studying humanistic psychology together for over a year. "Studying humanistic psychology" has not involved us in reading many books by Carl Rogers, Abraham Maslow or Rollo May, nor in writing many essays. Instead we have been jumping up and down, shouting a lot and hugging each other. For ours is an experiential course. Now there are many unresolved issues in our group. Issues of love and hate.

To try to resolve some of these issues, we spend a weekend together doing a "Spiritual Encounter" workshop. The facilitator is The Wise Person's wife whose housework and gardening we did. She is an excellent facilitator and I still admire her many skills.

During this weekend we are encouraged to express everything that we think and feel about each other, with no holds barred short of physical violence. That is the "encounter" part of the weekend. But we are also encouraged to "hold the other person in our heart", to be open to the possibility of a breakthrough, to achieve a resolution with them from a transpersonal perspective. That is the "spiritual" part of the weekend.

Too often, when we become interested in the spiritual, there is a tendency for us to deny and suppress our shadow as we embrace and try to live up to some false ideal. Denied and suppressed in this way, our shadow may slowly poison both ourselves and those around us. This is one of the reasons why evangelical preachers are sometimes caught in motel bedrooms with hookers and piles of cocaine and why supposedly celibate priests sometimes sexually assault little boys and girls.

The idea of our "Spiritual Encounter" weekend is that rather than suppress our shadow, we should let our shadow rip. And to encourage us, our facilitator uses a wonderful phrase to describe the behaviour of someone who hides their shadow behind a facade of spiritual nobility.

It is "sugar on shit".

This phrase alone is worth the price of admission for the weekend.

****

Kriyas

Occasionally I go to Swami Muktananda's Siddha Yoga ashram in South West London to join in the meditation sessions there. But it is not always a restful place to meditate. Here is the reason why.

In his autobiography, 'Play Of Consciousness', Swami Muktananda has written about his own spiritual awakening and about how the kundalini energy moved through him, manifesting in "kriyas" and purifying him spiritually.

Kriyas are spontaneous movements and sounds caused by kundalini awakening. The movements may include spasms, shudders, jerks, shivers, twitches and contractions as well as shaking, vibrating, trembling and swaying. The sounds may include howls, barks, shouts, screams, laughter, crying, snorts, growls, screeches, roars, snarls and groans.

Kriyas are thought to be auspicious. Some people believe them to be a necessary precursor to spiritual awakening. I fear that, when it comes to the manifestation of these signs, a certain competitiveness may have developed amongst Swami Muktananda's followers. This could be summed up as "The bigger the spasms and the louder the howls, the greater the spiritual advancement."

Consequently, meditation time at Swami Muktananda's ashram sometimes resembles a monkey house.

Some people might claim that in certain cases at least an alternative word for kriyas could be "hysteria". If that sounds unduly sceptical, consider this. There comes a time when Swami Muktananda announces that kriyas are no longer necessary for spiritual development. Rather suddenly all the kriyas stop. Meditation time at the ashram is no longer like feeding time at the zoo.

Perhaps Swami Muktananda himself simply got fed up with the din.

****

A Health Scare

I am sitting at a table in the garden of Swami Muktananda's ashram in Ganeshpuri. My hand is being held by a Greek lady, Helena.

But this is not a romantic episode. Instead, we have agreed to exchange two of our therapeutic skills. I have already read Helena's hand for her and from it I have analysed her character and the likelihood of certain events happening in her future. Now she is scanning my hand for indications of my state of health. Helena is a naturopath and this form of diagnosis is one of her specialities.

All seems to be going well. So far she has seen no serious threat to my physical wellbeing. Perhaps I could take more exercise, eat more fruit, cut down on dairy products, avoid wheat but this is all the quotidian stuff of her naturopathic advice.

Suddenly Helena frowns. Her grip on my hand tightens. She peers intently at an area of my palm. Then she looks up at me, a palpable look of concern on her face. Dramatically she speaks. She utters the following immortal line.

"Bananas are killing you!"

****

Lizards

Like most of us, I have experienced a few disappointments with people. Here is one of them.

One afternoon I am drinking tea with someone who gives talks about non-duality. We are taking a break during the filming of a discussion which is to appear on an internet TV station. We are two of a panel of three.

I like my co-panellist. He is pleasant and interesting to chat to. Our views on life seem to coincide in many respects. We are getting along well. I am even beginning to regard him as "my new friend".

Suddenly and apropos of nothing, he starts talking about David Icke. Not to trash him, declare him a fool and deride him, as I would do. No, my new friend actually admires him. David Icke, according to him, has realised important truths about aspects of reality that most of us have failed to notice. In fact David Icke has secret information about who or what is really controlling the world. Lizards. Giant shape-shifting lizards.

I despair. And call time on my new friendship.

****

Finding Deep Truth

At a certain time in my life I consider doing a training course to become an Interfaith Minister. After two years of part-time study in London, I will be able to baptise, marry and bury people. If they want me to.

The central purpose of the course seems to be to discover the deep truth that exists at the heart of all religion. To this end, students make a serious study of the world's major faiths.

Finding the deep truth that exists at the heart of all religion appeals to me at this time. But the circumstances of my life are

271

not propitious. My children are still too young to be left alone for the many weekends of attendance that the course requires. I decide to put my ministerial ambitions on hold for a couple of years.

But during the following two years, something terribly irreligious happens deep in my soul. I have a dawning realisation which prevents me from ever doing the course.

The dawning realisation can be expressed in the following question.

"What if, after two years of expensive, demanding and intensive study, instead of the deep truth that exists at the heart of all religion, I discover the deep nonsense that exists at the heart of all religion?"

What a waste of time, money and effort that would be.

****

A Problem With Slugs

Sometime after this I meet an actual Interfaith Minister. She is standing in her garden. This too is not a romantic assignation. She is a very old and very lovely Sinhalese woman and she has spent many years creating great floral beauty in the garden. She is also a Buddhist.

A friend of mine is with us, a keen gardener herself. She says to the Interfaith Minister "I know that you are a Buddhist and committed to not killing any creature. So how do you stop the slugs from eating your flowers?"

"Well" says the Interfaith Minister "as you say, we Buddhists are not allowed to kill any creature. So what I do is I put slug pellets down. Then I say to the slugs 'You can either move to my neighbour's garden or you can commit suicide.' Unfortunately, most of them decide to commit suicide."

****

Jesus In Glastonbury

Sometimes my tongue runs away with me. Because of this, on at least one occasion, I make an enemy astonishingly quickly.

I am on a retreat and chatting during a tea break. One of my fellow retreatants, John, starts talking to me excitedly about a theory that he has recently come across in a book.

The theory is this. Jesus survives his crucifixion. He is taken down from the cross while still alive and nursed back to health. With his pregnant lover, Mary Magdalene, he escapes from Palestine and crosses the seas to Britain. He visits Glastonbury. Mary Magdalene gives birth and the bloodline of Jesus continues to this day. This is the true meaning of "the holy grail".

John wants to know what I think.

What I think is that I am exasperated beyond belief by this theory. I snap at him much too brutally "I think that it's nonsense piled on nonsense. I have no time for such rubbish."

John looks at me. And if looks could kill ….

I do not believe that John has ever forgiven me.

****

Traditional Chinese Medicine

During a tea break at a tai chi class, a discussion about the relative merits of Western medicine and Traditional Chinese Medicine breaks out. One woman, June, decries the ignorance of Western medicine and its insistence on "merely" treating symptoms and ignoring the deeper causes of disease. Traditional Chinese Medicine, June declares, goes to the root of problems and is much to be preferred.

I mutter that some of us might prefer penicillin and sterile operating theatres to powdered rhinoceros horn and dried tiger penis. So might the rhinos and the tigers.

Because I am in a mood to make mischief, I also mention microwave ovens. I have an internal bet with myself that June will dislike them, just as she dislikes Western medicine. So I tell her that I always make my morning porridge in a microwave oven, which is in any case the truth.

June does not disappoint me. She quotes Dr. So And So who asserts that microwave ovens "destroy the molecular structure of water." I very much doubt whether Dr. So And So has done the legitimate scientific research that would prove this extraordinary contention. But even if he has, I do not really care.

The conversation ends. I have won my bet.

****

Richard's Razor
or
Three Ways To Deal With Woo Woo

Occam's razor states that the simplest satisfactory explanation of a phenomenon is more likely to be correct than competing explanations which unnecessarily multiply complexities.

Hitchens' razor states "What can be asserted without evidence can be dismissed without evidence."

Richard's razor states "Any assertion of a dubious nature can be legitimately countered with a gently murmured 'Or not.' No other comment is necessary."

For example:-

"You can only be saved by the love of the sweet Lord Jesus." "Or not."

"Apricot kernels cure cancer." "Or not."

"The world is controlled by shape shifting lizards." "Or not."

Richard's razor can also be used as a mantra. Simply repeat

the words "Or not" quietly to yourself several times a day, especially when confronted with superstitious assertions.

****

Another Triumph For Alternative Medicine

I receive a phone call from a woman who wants to talk to me about non-duality. Her name is Sarah. Among other things, Sarah tells me that she has always lived a charmed life. She is in her early forties, and is considered to be very beautiful. She lives in a large house by the sea in a peaceful and democratic country with her husband whom she loves. She owns expensive fashionable clothes and jewellery.

Now she has stage four cancer.

Suddenly I understand why she has spent the first half hour of our conversation talking to me about death.

She is finding it very hard to face up to the reality of losing all this beauty while still young. She expected, she tells me, to live for perhaps another forty or fifty years.

When she was first diagnosed with breast cancer, a close family member wrote to her strongly advising her not to have orthodox treatment. She told Sarah of cases where near-miraculous cures had taken place through the drinking of particular juices, the injection of specific vitamins and the eating of special diets. She bombarded Sarah with emails almost daily providing details that she had gathered from the internet of more and more cures that had been effected in these ways.

Sarah allowed this close relative to sway her decision about her medical care. She chose not to have the treatment that her doctors had offered her, and instead embarked on a number of alternative therapies.

Now, of course, she deeply regrets this.

To make matters worse, Sarah feels that this member of her

family has always been very jealous of her. She is now wondering whether the advice may have been given with the conscious or unconscious intention of causing her harm.

Sarah's doctors tell her that they could have treated her cancer successfully with chemotherapy in its early stages, but now that it has spread to her bones, it is too late. There is nothing that they can do except to offer her palliative care.

In our long conversation, I say what I can. But this is not very much. After about an hour and a half, we say goodbye and I hang up. I am left wondering how many people have already been killed in this way by alternative medicine. And where the statistics are that would provide an answer to this question.*

---

*Later I discover some of the relevant figures. Women who choose only to have alternative treatments for breast cancer are five times more likely to die during a five and a half year follow up period than those who choose conventional treatments.

39. Some Blasts Against Religion

The Theatre Of Manipulation

On the day that Pope Francis is elected, I watch television coverage of the ecstatic crowds in St Peter's Square. Mass hypnosis seems to be at work.

Perhaps both unkindly and unjustly, I think momentarily of the Nuremburg rallies. Clearly quite different events. To some extent different emotions, to some extent the same ones. But definitely the same superb talent for organising and directing The Theatre Of Manipulation.

That evening I walk into my local pub to find some friends enraptured by the same coverage that I had seen. They are not Catholics. Indeed, most of them are not even Christians. The majority of them are of a liberal agnostic disposition. Nevertheless they say to me "Isn't he wonderful!" Two of them add, only half-jokingly, "We're thinking of becoming Catholics."

I ask them to remind me which aspects of Catholic doctrine they hold to. The virgin birth? The resurrection on the third day? The bodily ascension into heaven? The miracles of the saints? The transubstantiation of the host? Their own resurrection in the flesh from their graves?

They seem to shake themselves out of a trance and everything returns to normal for a while.

But a week or two later I meet them again in the same pub. They are talking once more about how wonderful this new Pope Francis is.

Before I even know what I am thinking, my ears hear my mouth say some terrible words about the newly minted pope. These words are so awful that I cannot bring myself to write them here. There is after all a Catholic church situated less than a mile from where I live. I do not want the priest and his deacons to add to their agenda the task of making arrangements for my own personal auto-da-fe.

My pals are shocked to hear that my opinion of Pope Francis, unlike theirs, is far from complimentary. Very far. On another planet in fact. So quite naturally they demand justification from me for my extraordinary view.

Well, the fact is that by now we have the news that Pope Francis has reconfirmed The Catholic Church's interdiction against barrier contraception. In this way, he has guaranteed that AIDS, syphilis and other venereal diseases will continue to be spread unnecessarily amongst innocent babies and economically disadvantaged, poorly educated women in the Third World.*

Whereas if he chose to, he could substantially lessen the amount of misery on the planet by a simple stroke of his papal pen. One papal signature on one papal document. Interdiction lifted. And it would not have cost his Church a penny.

My friends are awash with admiration for him because he has eschewed living in the gilded luxury of the pope's apartment in The Vatican. He has chosen instead to live in the papal guest house. What a hovel that must be. What humility he manifests.

My view is that the world would be a better place if he slept in the golden splendour of his Vatican apartment but com-

---

*In addition, Pope Francis has at the same time reconfirmed Catholic belief in the literal existence of the devil. Yes, he has warned the faithful that Satan really does walk among them. Surely nothing has kept Christians, and those who come under their sway, more psychologically dwarfed for nearly two thousand years than this pernicious superstition.

About two and a half thousand years ago both the Stoics and the Buddhists, to give only two examples of alternative forms of thought, had a better understanding of the workings of the human psyche than the average Edwardian curate did in 1908

manded his Cardinals to distribute lorry loads of free condoms to the Catholic faithful. A more comfortable night's sleep for Pope Francis. Fewer dead babies and dead women in South America, Asia and Africa.

That sounds like a fair exchange to me.

****

The King Of The Jews

The following snippet of conversation genuinely takes place, although it may beggar belief. Just before Easter a friend of mine is on the phone to her mother, who is eighty-seven years old and lives on a Scottish island. Her mother is a lifelong member of The Wee Frees, aka The Free Presbyterian Church Of Scotland. It was on this same island some years earlier that a Presbyterian minister lay down on the slipway of the dock one Sunday morning. He was trying to stop lorries from boarding Caledonian MacBrayne's first ferry ever to set sail from the island on the Sabbath.

My friend's mother:- "Tell me, dear, why did they call Jesus 'The King Of The Jews'?"

My friend:- "Well Mother, he was Jewish, you know."

My friend's mother, after a pause:- "Oh no, I don't think so! He was one of us!"

This calls to my mind the saying attributed to various American politicians going back to the late nineteenth century. "If the King's English was good enough for Jesus, it's good enough for Americans." But whereas that was probably always intended as a joke, my friend's mother is speaking in all earnestness. She will after all have spent her long life looking at pictures of a Jesus who has remarkably Caucasian features. Not swarthy. Not dusky. And definitely, heaven forfend, not Semitic.

****

Scrutinising Sir Roger Scruton

I hear the philosopher Sir Roger Scruton assert in a talk on BBC Radio that Europe needs to rediscover its Christian values. Apparently Sir Roger thinks that this would be a jolly good thing and would improve European civilisation no end.

Perhaps Sir Roger has in mind Torquemada. He improved European civilization by directing the Inquisition. Many "heretics" could attest to how Christian values contributed to their wellbeing whilst dislocating their joints as they lay on the rack.

Or perhaps Sir Roger is thinking of Matthew Hopkins. The self-styled Witchfinder General improved European civilisation in England by hunting out women who had committed themselves to the service of Satan. As a result, approximately three hundred were hanged within about three years. In other parts of Europe, over a longer period of time, perhaps two hundred thousand "witches" were tortured, hanged or burned, leaving Europe a far happier and a much safer place.

Maybe Sir Roger is referring to Pope Innocent III who initiated The Albigensian Crusade, in which Christians asserted their values by massacring other Christians of a somewhat different theological persuasion. It is estimated that about one million people were killed by the Pope's armies. With each death, European civilisation no doubt flowered in more and more glorious ways.

Or Sir Roger may be considering Christianity's more contemporary gifts to our civilization, such as the protections afforded to paedophile priests by church hierarchies. As just one example of this, senior clergy of The Church Of England acted to protect a bishop who was a serial sex offender. Details of Bishop Peter Ball's offences were not passed on to the police and instead he was allowed to retire with a pension and to carry on with certain of his priestly duties. Some of these duties involved his continuing involvement with children. Meanwhile, in another European country, high-ranking officials of the Papacy expend endless energy ensuring that priests who sexually molest children are protected from the criminal sanctions of the state. Presumably Europe rejoices at this assertion of Christian values too.

You the reader may be growing weary by now of the repetition in this account so I will end it here. Sadly, on the topic of the civilising effects of Christianity on Europe, there is much to be repetitious about.

****

Why Does God Send Hurricanes?

I hear on the news that a particularly vicious hurricane has just devastated a large part of Florida. Hurricanes, we are told, are occurring more and more frequently and with greater and greater strength.

Soon some evangelical preachers will state that this hurricane, like others, has been sent by God as a punishment because America tolerates homosexuality. Probably the first of these pronouncements has already been made.

I wonder why no evangelical preacher ever supposes that increasingly violent hurricanes are sent by God as a punishment for man-made global warming. I am no logician, but I suspect that the causal chain linking hurricanes to global warming may be more direct than the causal chain linking hurricanes to sodomy.

****

The Resurrection Of The Flesh

During a discussion of faith on BBC Radio, a representative of one of the Abrahamic religions patiently explains why we must be physically resurrected from our graves. It is so that God can judge us and, if we are not worthy of salvation, cast us into hell to be tortured for all eternity. It is necessary for us to have a physical body as otherwise we could not experience this torment.

Not one of the other panelists, who all sound like quite reasonable twenty-first century men and women, thinks it worth commenting on this poisonous belief, nor on the nature of such a monstrously evil deity. No one states that this opinion sounds psychopathic. Or possibly psychotic. Everyone lets it pass, I suppose in a spirit of interfaith tolerance, as if the religious scholar had said nothing more remarkable than "The weather's looking good for tomorrow."

****

Trendy Vicar

I am sitting in a cafe with two friends after a tai chi class. It is a very good cafe so we come here regularly. As usual it is full of young mothers with toddlers, lycra clad cyclists and a few businessmen working on their laptops or holding discreet meetings. Mashed avocado, sourdough bread and healthy smoothies feature prominently on the menu.

Today, sitting opposite us, is a vicar. He is a trendy, modern vicar. He has a shaved head and he is planning his church business with an associate on his iPad. He is the very same vicar who has banned our tai chi group from using his church hall.

I do not want to engage him in conversation. I prefer to enjoy my latte. But as he gets up to leave, my friend Simon asks him "Why won't you let us use your hall for our tai chi classes?"

The vicar patiently explains. "Many people" he says "believe that tai chi is simply an innocent form of exercise. But it's not. It's a Taoist practice. Taoism is a non-Christian religion which is trying to make converts in this country. As a Christian, I believe that if I let you use God's premises for your tai chi classes, he'll be angry with me. Then when I die I'll have to explain myself to him."

To show that there are no hard feelings, he shakes hands with each of us as he leaves. At this point I cannot help being drawn in. I grip his hand tightly so that he cannot easily withdraw it, look into his eyes and say "The problem you have is that you don't really know what kind of God you're going to meet when you die. God might turn out to be Taoist. Then he might be angry with you because you didn't let our tai chi group use your church hall."

He does not say anything to this. He looks momentarily confused. Then I let his hand go.

I want to add "Do you realise how psychotic you sound to ordinary people like us?"

I want to add it but I do not.

Printed in Great Britain
by Amazon